CLASSICAL FIVE-ELEMENT ACUPUNCTURE

VOLUME III

THE FIVE ELEMENTS AND THE OFFICIALS

PROFESSOR J.R. WORSLEY

Classical Five-Element Acupuncture

Volume III

The Five Elements And The Officials

Professor J.R. Worsley

Founder President of the Worsley Institute of Classical Acupuncture, Inc. (U.S.A.)
Founder President of the College of Traditional Acupuncture, (U.K.)
Founder President of the Traditional Acupuncture Institute (U.S.A.)
Founder President of the Traditional Acupuncture Society (U.K.)
Professor of the College of Chinese Medicine (China)
Master and Doctor of Acupuncture, Honorary Professor of the Department of
Oriental Medicine, Won Kwang University, Korea
Vice-President of the World Academic Society for Acupuncture
Honorary President of the Compagnonnage d'Acuponcture Traditionelle, France

Published by J.R. & J.B. Worsley
Copyright 1998 J.R. and J.B. Worsley
All rights reserved

For further information about Classical Five-Element Acupunture, a list of qualified practitioners, teachers, and schools, or a list of related books and publications, please contact The Worsley Institute of Classical Five-Element Acupuncture, a not-for-profit educational organization, at 1-800-549-3531

Other books by the same author:

Is Acupuncture For You?

Talking About Acupuncture in New York

Traditional Chinese Acupuncture Volume I - Meridians and Points

Traditional Acupuncture Volume II - Traditional Diagnosis

CONTENTS

THE FIVE ELEMENTS AND THE OFFICIALS

Foreword: The Spirit of Nature	i-v
Acknowledgements and Author's Note	vi
Five Element Chart	vii
1. The Five Seasons: The Spirit of the Elements	1.1-13
2. The Wood Element	2.1-13
3. The Fire Element	3.1-9
4. The Earth Element	4.1-9
5. The Metal Element	5.1-9
6. The Water Element	6.1-9
7. The Relationships of the Elements	7.1-13
8. The Correspondences of the Elements	8.1-11
9. The Spirit of the Officials	9.1-11
10. The Officials of the Wood Element: Liver and Gall Bladder	10.1-17

11. The Officials of the Fire Element:
    Heart Protector and the Three Heater   11.1-13

12. The Officials of the Fire Element:
    Heart and Small Intestines   12.1-13

13. The Officials of the Earth Element:
    Spleen and Stomach   13.1-11

14. The Officials of the Metal Element:
    Lung and Colon   14.1-13

15. The Officials of the Water Element:
    Kidney and Bladder   15.1-15

16. The Relationships of the Officials   16.1-13

    Glossary

    Index

FOREWORD

THE SPIRIT OF NATURE

The five Elements, Wood, Fire, Earth, Metal and Water are not just the foundation of this wonderful system of medicine: they are the foundation and spirit of all Nature around us. We would do well to ponder on these words occasionally and to reflect on how profound a statement this is. The Elements are alive both around us and in us; they describe the movement of all life and all energy and embody all the qualities which we encounter in Nature. Through understanding the five Elements we may begin to understand both Nature and ourselves. In this book, therefore, I hope to show a little of the essential nature of the Elements, the qualities which they bring not just to our own lives but to life itself. This may sound rather all-embracing but it emphasizes from the very start the breadth and importance of a task to which no-one can ever do total justice.

Volume II of this series dealt with the Traditional Diagnosis and focused on the development of our senses for mainly diagnostic purposes. By and large we all lose to a great degree the clear faculties with which we are born. We no longer see anything, hear anything, or even touch anything with the same wisdom and understanding we had when we were babes in arms. Only when we have begun to regain those faculties can we begin to use our senses to diagnose disease, and diagnose it accurately. Then we can see the signs of an imbalance in someone's energy appear clearly in a color on the face, a sound in the voice, an odor from the body, and an inappropriate emotion which becomes predominant in someone's character and behavior. These signs point to the Causative Factor, the Element which is the principal cause of the overall loss of balance. By using our senses to identify the color, sound, odor and emotion created by imbalance and using our skills in acupuncture, we can then set about helping Nature to restore harmony and balance amongst all the Elements in the person.

By using these self-same skills which help us to see imbalances in our patients we shall then be able to begin to understand the broader patterns of energy within Nature, not just in the form of imbalances and disharmony but in the natural flow and rhythm of Qi energy as it follows the Dao. Then, when we are able to see how the Elements appear in Nature we shall begin to appreciate and understand them in people better than we can learn from any textbook. We are, after all, only a part of Nature.

Classical Five-Element Acupuncture

In order to look at Nature in this way, however, we have to set aside a habit which is dear to us, that of dividing everything up into patterns of our own making and then treating all the parts which we create as separated and unrelated. The Elements exist in Nature and their patterns are visible all around us and in us. If only we could use our God-given senses to the fullest we could observe this simple truth.

This book is about the Elements and the Officials. Many people will have heard of the five Elements, but the Officials may be a concept entirely new to them. The Officials bear the Western names of the organs of the body, but their similarity to the Western concept of an organ is only superficial. Each Official represents and controls a group of functions, attributes and abilities in body, mind and spirit. Together the Officials are a manifestation of the five Elements in us, the means by which each Element's essence is made real in the body, mind and spirit of every human being. An understanding of the Elements in us must include an understanding of the Officials in order to be complete. The same is true for an understanding of the Officials - the Elements must be included.

Not only do we need to understand the essence of each Element and the way that this spirit is manifested through the Officials; we have to understand the relationship between each of the Elements and between each of the Officials. This is where the form of a book is really inadequate for the purpose of showing the beauty and wisdom of the Elements in Nature and the Officials in ourselves. For the sake of clarity we are forced to sub-divide and separate. Even though it is the indivisible spirit of the Elements and Officials which we are trying to capture we have to deal with the parts rather than the whole. Once we have developed our senses and learned from Nature itself we may be able to move from the parts to the whole, but I would venture to suggest that very few of us, if any at all, will ever reach this stage.

The danger, of course, is that looking at the separate parts of the unity of Elements and Officials will encourage people to use the framework as an analytical tool. Many students of Classical Acupuncture would be only too happy if such a book existed, a kind of reference book in which we could take a problem in a physical faculty, or mental capability, or spiritual identity, then look at an index and identify which Element or Official was in distress. Diagnosis would become a great deal easier, as would the understanding of people at large and of life itself.

Foreword

Those who have read Volume II will already know that Traditional Diagnosis cannot be reduced to formulae, however: symptoms do not point to the Causative Factor. We shall see again in this book that the labels we apply to the Elements and Officials, like the symptoms we come across in diagnosis, may often be totally misleading and serve only to confuse if they are not understood and used properly. The Elements work together and are found in combination, as are the Officials. We need all of our faculties to be able to function properly in the world and to live and work amongst other people. We will see in the pages that follow, however, that each of our faculties depends on all the other faculties within ourselves. Within this complex web of interdependence any weakness in one Element or one Official is bound to have effects everywhere else. There are no obvious conclusions which we can deduce immediately because we recognize a malfunction in a particular Element or Official, just as there is no one simple solution in diagnosis other than that which comes from our observations, and no easy way to do this other than by recognizing our limitations and re-learning the basic skills which we have squandered for so long.

Some readers are bound to be wondering already what on earth can be achieved by running through the details of each Element and each Official if they cannot trust the information which they are given. The division of Nature into five Elements and ourselves into five Elements and twelve Officials and the simple but profound insight this gives would seem to be undermined immediately by what I have just said. What I hope to show, however, is that once we have regained our abilities to see, to hear, to smell and to feel, the Elements and Officials do appear to us in such simple and obvious ways, that as practitioners of this system of medicine we will be able to see and trust the obvious. It may not, however, be the same 'obviousness' with which we started.

The ancient Chinese and other eastern cultures were very fond of training students by taking obvious and self-evident facts and turning them inside out until the students were afraid to trust what they saw. As the students regained their trust in simple facts, however, they would find that they saw not only the same apparent simplicity as before but in every simple fact a whole host of connections and relationships with other things. Nothing stood by itself, alone and simple; everything was related to everything else.

We, too, will find that the Elements and Officials are all inter-related, and that separating them for the purpose of giving an insight into their powers and properties itself ultimately becomes a confusing abstraction. The more that we isolate individual Elements and Officials, the more we shall feel constrained and want to talk about them as they relate to each other. This is what makes the system so exciting and dynamic.

We do not live in a world of five primary colors and five primary sounds, with five primary odors and five predominant emotions. We have looked at this in learning about the Traditional Diagnosis, and have seen that there are probably five times five shades of blue that we can recognize, let alone the reds, yellows, greens and whites. We must do the same when we look at the Elements in Nature around us.

It is only our own laziness which can prevent us from seeing this enormous variety and which will, if we are not careful, hinder our understanding of the Elements and of the Officials. It may seem far easier, for instance, to go through Element by Element, Official by Official, and describe a pathology of each one to help practitioners of classical Five-Element acupuncture to diagnose and understand their patients better, but I think that this would be quite an arrogant approach. It would make it appear that we knew already how the Elements fitted together in Nature and exactly how Nature functioned in all its rich variety. This is not the case, as any natural scientist working with plants, rocks, or climate can tell you. Every day we are making new discoveries on a simple physical level, and beginning to realize just how little we know about the planet which is our home. If we know so little about the body of the planet, how much less do we know about the mind and the spirit of the planet?

It is because of this ignorance that I hope this book may encourage people to look with their physical eye, their mind's eye and their spirit eye at the world around them, and to use all their senses to gain a deeper understanding of the Elements within us and around us. This will take them to the spirit of Nature as it manifests everywhere. The bare details on the page of how the Elements and Officials relate to each other and their individual properties are as removed from this reality as an alphabet is from the most beautiful poetry.

What people will see very quickly is that there is a great deal of harmony in Nature, especially the Nature which humans have not yet totally blighted. This is one of the most important lessons for anyone treating with classical Chinese medicine, and is good reason for staying away from an entirely 'pathological' view of the Elements and Officials. Learning how to recognize and eradicate

# Foreword

the most obvious imbalances is only the first stage in a process of recognizing the power that comes from the Elements in balance working together. The blueprint for this lies in Nature, not in a book. Not only that, it exists in a positive state of balance between the Elements, not in a state of disharmony and imbalance. Looking for the spirit of the Elements in Nature is as much about what we can become as about what we are.

I have often said that children are our best teachers, and when we come to look at the Elements we would do well to follow their example. I cannot imagine little children being told about five wonderful Elements that were a part of everything and not wanting to find out what and where they were, and how each of them affected the others. They would not settle for a grid on paper and play mind-games with this five-sided dice, and nor should we. As practitioners of this system of medicine we need to explore and discover the Elements to make ourselves better instruments of healing, and as human beings we need to develop our understanding to appreciate and respect the natural process of which we are a part.

ACKNOWLEDGEMENTS

I would like to express my sincere appreciation to the Editor, John Wheeler who, through my son John Worsley, used my notes and taped material to reproduce my teachings into this text book form, and whose style has preserved the essence of the original lectures.

To my dear wife Judy who has amended and proofed the book for content and for her contribution in upholding the spirit of this system of medicine. To Dr. Mel Becker for editing the book and to Mrs Maureen Postins for its desktop publishing and layout and for her invaluable advice.

Professor J.R. Worsley

AUTHOR'S NOTE
My previous volumes have used the word 'traditional' in the titles. 'Classical' more accurately describes the fundamental roots and essence of this system of medicine. Although 'traditional' has been replaced by 'classical' in the title, I have chosen to continue using the word 'traditional' when referring to the diagnosis procedure as so many practitioners trained by me are familiar with this term.

Foreword

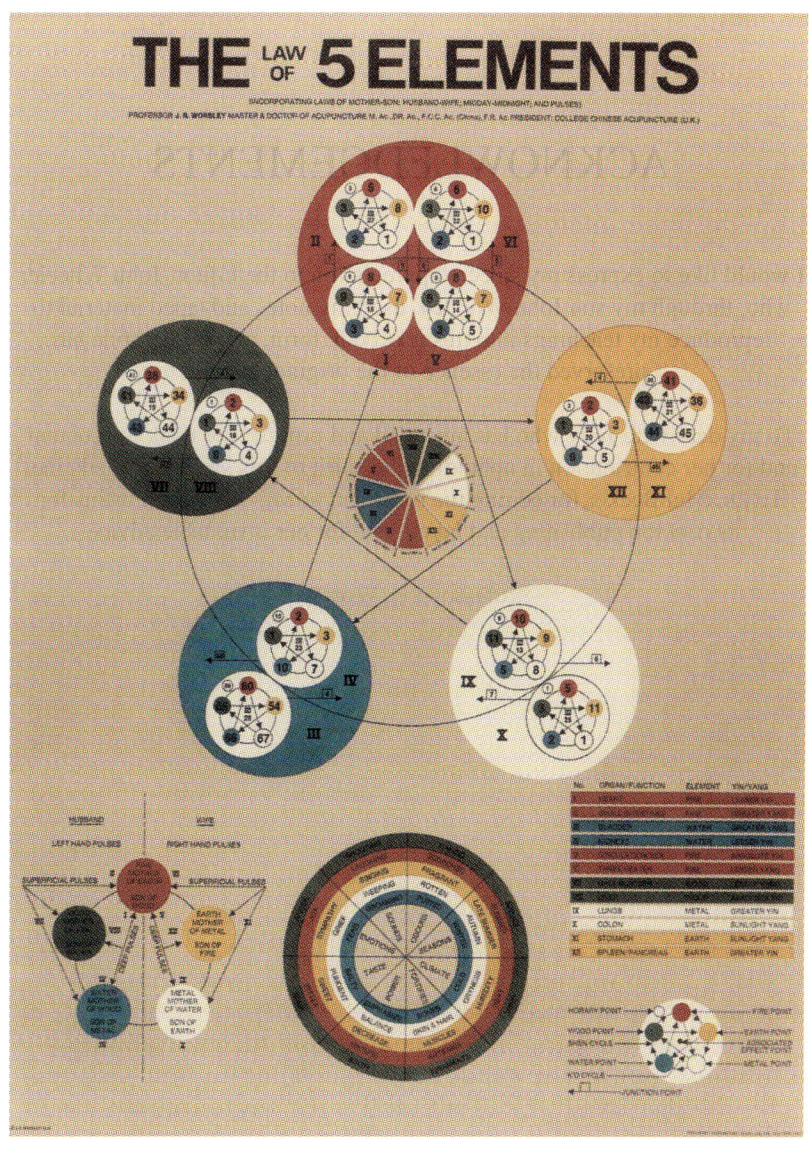

Enlarged copies of this chart are available through
The Worsley Institute of Classical Five-Element Acupuncture,
1-800-549-3531.

CHAPTER ONE

THE FIVE SEASONS: THE SPIRIT OF THE ELEMENTS

Every living thing and every person on the planet is a unique embodiment and combination of the five Elements. This is sometimes interpreted in a very literal way as though the Elements were different colored building bricks. Many readers will be familiar with both Chinese and European texts which take this view and then identify hundreds of examples of the Elements in Nature, both in their 'pure' form and in combination. The numerous tables of what are called the 'correspondences' or 'associations' of the Elements bear witness to the thoroughness with which this work has been done in almost every category of human experience and of the material world.

We must always remind ourselves, however, of a starting point which it is very easy for us to forget, that there is only the One, not the Many. Putting it this way may sound unduly mystical and alien to the western ear but it is a truth to which we shall return over and over again. The ancient Chinese never saw the Elements as five distinct 'things' or 'types of matter' because ultimately there is only one Qi energy and one Dao. Qi energy, the vital life force, constitutes and shapes everything on the face of the earth. It is in a state of constant change and transformation, and the patterns of its movement create and sustain all living things.

The five Elements express and embody the aspects of this change and movement within Qi energy. Each Element describes a particular phase of its movement and the particular qualities which belong to that part of its changing patterns. Together the Elements help us to understand the process of dynamic harmony and balance in the whole system of energy. Through this they give us the insight which allows us to promote balance by our systems of medicine. When we look at the individual Elements, therefore, we always have to keep in our minds that we are looking only at parts of a much larger picture. As practitioners of acupuncture who treat the whole person, this must be one of our most important guiding principles.

In order even to begin to look at the detail of the Elements, however, we need to look first at their essence. This may sound like the most obscure and abstract place to start but it is here that the deepest wisdom and understanding is to be found. The spirit of the Elements, the unique character of each in the cycle of change and transformation, is what sustains life and gives the whole of Nature, ourselves included, a sense of purpose, growth and fulfillment. Without an insight into the Elements at this level we shall never fully grasp and understand the wealth of detail which surrounds us.

In order to explain better the essence of each individual Element we can draw on no better example than a complete cycle which shows us the heart of the Elements and their relationships: the cycle of the seasons. The seasons are often included only within the other correspondences and associations as just one more detail, another cake to slice into five pieces, but they deserve a much more special place than this. In the character and quality of each season we can see not only how the Elements express themselves in Nature but also how the deeper patterns in Nature unfold.

The seasons are also a wonderful example because their ceaseless cycle reminds us that there is no beginning and no end to Qi energy, only change and transformation. Our calendars and diaries may show dates which fix the boundaries of months and years but we have to recognize that these matter not one iota to the vast tides of Nature which will continue to ebb and flow as they have ever since life has flourished on the earth.

SPRING - THE WOOD ELEMENT

Spring is associated with the Wood Element. Some people may wonder how exactly this reveals to us the essence of the Element. "Surely", they will say, "the idea of springtime probably evokes as many different pictures and feelings as there are people in the world". For all the variety of images unique to each of us as individuals, there are some which most of us will agree on as the essential aspects of its nature. Spring is the time of birth and regeneration. The burst of activity which surges out of the stillness of the winter has no equal elsewhere in the year; there is an energy and dynamic force abroad which brings life and vigor to everything.

We have only to think of the small miracles which happen with every spring to see this rising energy. Seeds thrust their way through the earth with astonishing strength. Even when their paths are blocked they will find a way around. Plants unfold and burst into growth in the warmer air and longer hours of daylight. The

The Five Seasons

country fields are full of young animals grazing on the new pastures and charging about, "like spring lambs", as we say. The springtime is noisy and exuberant, a total contrast to the quiet and stillness of the winter which it follows. Even the very color which returns to Nature is a relief after the stark and bleak outlines of the winter horizon.

As we describe each of the seasons in this way the very words which come to mind reveal something of the spirit of the Element associated with the season. The spirit of Wood in springtime is expressed in all the force and upward movement, the flexibility and vigor, the birth and regeneration. We can recognize in describing it just how vital such a quality is, not just in the spring and in times of growth but throughout all the year and in everything that we see and do. The quality of life without this energy is unimaginable.

This does not take us completely to the heart of the Element, however; for that we must look more carefully at the character of the growth and regeneration which we find. To describe the spring as a time of unchecked vitality is to miss the true nature of each seed which grows. The seed bears within it the blueprint of the plant, just as the fertilized egg bears within it the blueprint of the bird and of the animal. The springtime which urges both of these to develop from seed to adult sees the fulfillment of an inner purpose, the following of a predetermined plan.

The word 'blueprint' may give the impression of something fixed and static, but no plan that rigid has any hope of success. The plan is the end of the journey, not the journey itself, and the good plan allows us flexibility in meeting its goals. Some seeds are going to fall where growth is difficult and they may have to adapt to the surroundings in which they lie. Each, however, will try to become what its purpose dictates and will follow this distant aim unswervingly. There is nothing random or unchecked about this: it is purposeful and structured. Each living plant and animal has a proper size and shape, and must grow at the proper rate to be in accord with the seasons which are destined to follow.

We may then begin to see that the spirit of Wood is more than just about growth. It is about ordered growth, a sense of purpose and the flexibility to adapt in order to meet that purpose. We can look further than this. We have to remember where spring falls in the cycle of the seasons. The nature of winter is quiet and bleak. What movement there is tends to be slow and beneath the surface. The

1.3

Classical Five-Element Acupuncture

sudden outburst of activity which arrives with the spring does more than signal an end to the stillness. It brings with it a sense of the future as the barren landscape rapidly fills with an abundance of life.

Each growing seed and each new-born animal is a sign of the future. This means a future not just for them but for their species, and in the end for the earth itself. It is this sense of 'a future' which takes us beyond mechanical and literal reproduction, beyond a world where every new year and new spring brings a replacement for whatever has died away over the rest of the year. The springtime brings both increase and progress. Each plant and animal tries to grow and extend year by year. Plants spread over the ground, trees sink their roots further and their branches wider, and animal herds increase in size.

When we sense within ourselves the possibility of growth and development we often have a vision, a picture of what this future will bring us and where we will be. From this grows the hope that the vision will be realized. This sense of hope which arises with the spring is one of the Wood Element's greatest gifts to us, and the heart of its very essence. For it is only through vision and hope of this kind that we shall ever find the motivation and the sense of purpose for everything that we do.

In the next chapter we shall look at the specific ways in which the Wood Element manifests in us as human beings. However, most people will recognize from what little I have already said, something of the true essence of Wood, the qualities which it brings to Qi energy. Key words will appear time and time again, words like 'birth' and 'growth' 'hope' and 'vision', which we can see at work in our bodies, minds and spirits. If we look at our own memories and experiences of spring these are thoughts and feelings which come to mind far more readily than any others.

The image of the tree is often used to illustrate the essence of the Wood Element, an embodiment of all the qualities which we have just mentioned. We shall return to this when we look at the Elements in relation to each other. Then we shall see that the more we try to focus on the Wood alone, the more we are drawn to look at the Earth, the Water, the Fire and the Metal which sustain the Wood's growth and in turn depend on it for their own balance.

The Five Seasons

SUMMER - THE FIRE ELEMENT

When we look for the spirit of the Fire Element in the season of summer it is not difficult to see how warmth and enjoyment are likely to be our immediate associations; the word itself will already have conjured up these images. We have to go beyond the obvious, however, and ask ourselves what qualities Fire brings to the movement and character of Qi energy.

What, then, do we see in the summer? When the upsurge of the spring has passed its peak there is a subtle change as growth slows down and gives way to the flowering of plants and the ripening of crops. Plants no longer strive upwards as much as spread outwards, and flowers open and bloom rather than climb further towards the sun. The hours of the summer days are longer, and everything in Nature which has grown through the spring reaches ripeness and maturity in the summer heat, soaking up as much heat and energy from the sun as it can to prepare for a good harvest. Summer is truly the zenith of the year.

The full glory of summer shines in the colors which delight the eye wherever we look, the flowers that clothe the fields and the fruits which ripen on the branches. The greens of spring and delicate blossoms which follow the quiet shades of winter are nothing compared to the blaze of color at the height of the full summer. These colors serve their functional purpose in the cycle of regeneration of plants and trees but the pure fun and joy which they bring, far beyond their simple purpose alone, are expressions of the very essence of the Fire Element in Nature.

There is such a profusion of wonderful colors, sounds, smells and tastes that it should be impossible not to enjoy and find happiness in them. The longer hours of the summer mean that we can do our day's work and still have enough time left over to meet our friends, to socialize and to share the longer evenings. The warmth and the fullness which we feel around us spills over into our relationships with each other. We are more open and relaxed. We have time to share things with each other and to talk to each other. Our love of life and love of each other can find their fullest expressions in the hot summer months.

What lies behind these qualities of warmth, joy, fullness and maturity, the true spirit and essence of the Fire Element, is the love which Fire pours into everything. This love is given without stinting to everything and everyone. It permeates every part of our body, mind and spirit. The warmth of this love from

1.5

Classical Five-Element Acupuncture

the Fire Element helps everything to flow on all levels. The fluids which bathe all living cells flow more easily when warm. The exchange of ideas and feelings between us is greater when we are warm and relaxed and our deeper relationships flow more easily when warmth and love are present. When the Fire Element is lit within us and feeding us, our spirit is able to communicate with the spirit in other people and in Nature.

The Fire Element expresses more than this, however. The warmth and love which the season of summer gives us is not poured out at random. We have already seen that the growth in the spring does not run unchecked and unbounded. The essence of the Wood Element offers a sense of inner purpose and direction which gives growth a shape and a target. In the same way we can see that the love warmth from Fire is given in appropriate measure and within proper boundaries. If it were not controlled the same love and warmth that fuels everything could scorch and destroy life.

We have only to think of the effects of a long, hot summer where the sun burns down day after day long after we expect it to fade away. The grasses and plants turn brown and wither, the reservoirs empty, and the balance of Nature through the rest of the year is endangered. Yet even when this happens a part of us will be saying, "just one more hot day, please, don't let it grow cold again". If this is how we feel about the heat of the sun imagine how we shall feel about the great love and warmth from the Fire Element. Unless we were rationed we could take in this love without ceasing, and we need its boundaries and limits to protect us.

When we look at Elements like this, in isolation from each other, it makes our task a little more difficult. When we look at the Earth Element next, however, we shall see the importance of these limits and boundaries to the love and warmth which Nature receives. A bountiful harvest depends on everything growing according to its nature and following its inner plan. Then it needs the right amount of heat and light, neither too much nor too little, and the summer draws on this part of the spirit of Fire to guide all living things to ripeness and fullness. As we follow the seasons through we can see the broader pattern of the oneness of the Elements emerging from the cycle of growth and life.

LATE SUMMER - THE EARTH ELEMENT

Many people wonder how the five Elements and our four seasons fit together.

The Five Seasons

'Late summer' sounds like an afterthought, a short interlude before the autumn. We begin to feel this transition as the heat and warmth give way to the chills and mists of autumn mornings. The days shorten, and evenings are heavy with humid haze. The flowers which were ablaze yesterday are today drab and fading, their colors mottled and dull after the bloom of summer has left them. It is like the end of a wonderful party when everything is just losing its sparkle and the proper time has come to bring things to an end.

The flowers which garland Nature's summer party are more than just decoration, however. Their color and smell have served their purpose and, as the flower fades, so the fruit ripens. The drooping petals fall aside to reveal the swelling berries and pods, the ears of wheat grow full and firm, and the root crops under the ground bulge out of the soil. All the light, warmth and energy of the summer has been captured and stored by the flowers and leaves, and now surrounds the new seeds as a store from which they can draw their nourishment in the coming months.

Nourishment and harvest are the two words which more than any others characterize the season of the Earth Element. The Earth, like a mother, provides us with all the nourishment we need to live through the year. This is not just the nourishment for the body, but for the mind, and for the spirit. The long days and warm nights of the summer have given us time to enjoy everything around us to the fullest and to take in far more than we can appreciate at the time. The harvest time is when we not only store our physical crops but our mental and spiritual crops. When the cold sets in during the winter months we shall have all the memories and fruits of a wonderful summer on which we can draw. When we sit down in front of the fire in winter and look through our holiday photos we are feeding our minds and spirits from those memories and savoring their tastes and flavors until we can harvest again.

The harvest brings the security which we get from our physical mother. When we have a good harvest we have the certainty of surviving the winter months until growth begins again in the spring. It is sad in many ways that we can now fly our food from country to country, and therefore the harvest festival does not have the same importance in our lives. If we think back to only a century ago we can imagine how it must have felt to have set aside enough grain, fruit and vegetables for the winter. Could there be any greater sense of satisfaction and security than knowing that the storehouse is full?

1.7

Classical Five-Element Acupuncture

The Earth Element is our Mother in every way. Everything which nourishes us comes from Nature, from the moment we leave the womb of our physical mother to the day that we return to it. This truly is a gift, with nothing expected in return; just as with our own mothers there are no conditions and strings attached. We are given everything that we need to feed us in body, mind and spirit. This is the spirit of the Earth Element which manifests in the late summer.

Beyond this, however, we need to ask ourselves what other qualities of the Element, which are not so immediately obvious to us, does the season show us - and for this we need to think a little more about our mothers. What makes our mothers so special is that they have no favorites. A good mother loves all her children equally and will make sure that they are all nourished wherever they are and at whatever cost to herself. Never mind that there is not very much in the cupboard; she will make sure that each gets an equal share appropriate to their needs.

This is a quality of the Earth Element revealed in the season which tells us more about its own place within the pattern and movement of energy. The Earth ensures that there is nourishment everywhere and has the power to spread its bounty to support life wherever it tries to grow. What would be the good of a harvest being gathered and distribution limited to one small area when there was enough to feed everybody in the area at large? Would a mother pile all the food on one child's plate? Movement and distribution are all a part of the Earth Element.

This may seem at odds with how we see the Earth beneath our feet as the solid ground upon which we stand. We talk of being 'earthed' and 'grounded', and might feel that this does not fit with the idea of movement and distribution. But the Earth beneath our feet only provides a grounding in the very literal sense, and what really counts is the feeling of stability and security which the earth provides. This feeling comes not just from being in contact with the physical surface of the earth but from contact with the spirit of the earth which each year renews its guarantee of nourishment for all parts of our bodies, minds and spirits.

When we look at the Earth Element words like 'nourishment', 'stability' and 'security', together with 'distribution' and 'movement', are the key to understanding its place in the ceaseless cycle of energy.

1.8

AUTUMN - THE METAL ELEMENT

The flowers of summer fade away, and by harvest time the fruits ripen and fall from the trees. The reason for holding a harvest festival, however, was not only to celebrate the harvest but to give thanks for having gathered the harvest in time. The climate changes dramatically as the autumn sets in. The cool and damp mists beset us and anything which has not been harvested and stored soon rots away in the fields. The harvest is always a race against time to gather as much as possible before the weather turns.

The autumn, the season of the Metal Element, is a time of decline and death, yet even now the trees and plants have a final flourish of color, a special and beautiful dying fall of ochre and rust, after which they drop to the ground and begin to rot in musty piles on the woodland floor. Everything in Nature lets go in the autumn, and stops hanging on to the life and warmth of the summer and fullness of harvest time. This letting go is even reflected in the movement of the dying plants as they fall downwards to the earth. Everything becomes quieter, lower and more subdued.

The decline of autumn after the peak of the summer is a natural process. Without the death of the plant life which produced the seeds and new roots there would be no room for the vigorous new growth of spring. The old leaves fall away to make room for the new shoots. When we look at the essence of the Elements, therefore, we can easily see how the Metal Element shows an almost opposite movement to that of the Wood Element. Instead of birth we have death; instead of upward movement and vigorous activity we have downward movement and increasing stillness. With the Metal Element we begin to see the cycle turn full circle.

We also saw, however, that the Wood Element contained more than just growth; it carried within it a sense of direction and purpose. In the same way the falling leaves and fruits do not just represent dying and decomposition. The Metal Element is not to do with empty destruction, with things just rotting away to nothing. As the fruits and leaves fall to the ground all of the nutrients and goodness which they still contain make their way back into the soil and enrich it. When the remainder breaks down under the action of the molds of the forest floor it, too, becomes a valuable nutrient for the next year's growth. The new shoots and the new crop depend entirely upon this enrichment, without which next year's growth would be poor and without quality.

Classical Five-Element Acupuncture

The process of the return and replacement of quality in the soil is at the very heart of the Element Metal. The essence which is distilled from rotting and dead matter is the essence which the Metal Element itself represents, the special quality which it alone contributes to the flow of Qi energy and the pattern of life. This happens not only in the physical body but in the mind and the spirit. Wherever there is growth in body, mind, or spirit it will depend on this vital spark from the Metal Element for its inner quality and value.

There is yet more to the Metal Element than this. The rotting away of old material is just the passive aspect of the process of dying and decay. It does not just find its way back into the chain of growth without further ado, its value has to be recognized for it to be taken up again. It is the Metal Element that grants us the power to recognize this vital essence amongst the rubbish and to be able to take it in. Everywhere in Nature we see this process. As something dies it falls and leaves a space, a void which has the potential for growth but no substance. The Metal Element is the part of Nature which both creates and fills that void by bringing new substance in. Not just any substance but that whose quality makes growth special and vital.

Just as our mother, the Earth, offers us food from the soil below, the Metal Element offers us a different kind of food, the pure essence from above. For the Chinese this was very much a connection with Heaven above. As the Metal Element allows old and dying material to fall away downwards it also takes in new material from above to fill the space. It is easy to see from this how the Chinese developed the idea of a connection with the heavens as a Father, as a natural balance to the connection with the earth as the Mother. Our nourishment depends both on the food from our Mother, the Earth, below and a different kind of food from our Father, Metal, above. It is only by virtue of the energy from both that we can be fully nourished. Just as we gain security and stability from the nourishment of our Mother so we literally gain inspiration in the vital Qi we breathe in from our Father, the Heavens.

It is the single movement which embraces the dying and letting go and the power to recognize and take in the pure essence which is the key to understanding the part of the Metal Element in the pattern and movement of Qi energy.

The Five Seasons

WINTER - THE WATER ELEMENT

The winter months are a time when life seems to have stopped. The days are short and cold and the sun, low in the sky, emphasizes the stark and barren landscape. There are no leaves, just the bare stems of plants and trees standing out in silhouette. In total contrast to the heights of activity in summer, everything we see in winter is the year's low point.

When the autumn has brought the plants and leaves to the ground the winter rains wash away the last rotting remnants of waste back into the soil and the rivers. The snows and rains of winter represent a great leveling and cleansing process. This is one reason for winter's clarity and emphasis: everything is washed clean and bare. It brings to an end the growing and harvesting cycle and clears the stage for the next one to begin. In the middle of its phase everything appears still, cold, quiet and lifeless.

Appearances are deceptive, however. Life does not stop during the winter months. The seeds which have fallen to ground are still alive and waiting beneath the soil for the spring. The hibernating animals, too, slow down and sleep until they sense the first hint of the spring warmth. Life is there, but underground, hidden and slow. Even the winter landscape under snow takes on the appearance of the water of the oceans where everything is hidden beneath a silent and featureless cover which gives nothing away. This elusive and impenetrable nature is something which will always come to the fore when we look at the Water Element, but this is its outer manifestation, not its essence.

The miracle of winter is that plants and animals do grow and survive underneath this hard and barren surface, and in doing so show us the inner quality of the Water Element, the strength of reserves and endurance. The ability to create and draw on reserves is absolutely essential to all life. Without them nothing would survive, and nothing would pass down from generation to generation. Reserves are an inheritance with which everything is endowed at birth and which pass on at death to secure the future of the family. The ability to survive through the winter depends on the reserves which the Water Element represents and expresses.The Water Element is easy to associate with endurance and survival. Even with very little food and shelter we can endure for many weeks on water alone, while without water we are dead within a matter of days. The lakes and reservoirs which surround our towns, the water-holes to which the animals flock in the bush, and the streams and rivers which traverse the lands - all of

1.11

Classical Five-Element Acupuncture

these swell and fill in the winter rain to provide for every living thing for the whole year.

Reserves alone, however, are not enough to guarantee survival; endurance is not as simple as having enough to eat and drink. What underlies the survival of all living things through the rigors of the winter is a will and determination to see the season through to the next spring and renewed growth. The will to live and the will to survive are the means by which things live through the winter but are also the impetus for growth in the spring as the wheel turns full circle. It is not simply a blind will, however, a kind of rugged determination to hang on no matter what happens. The seeds which fell from the trees in the harvest time and were bathed in nutrients by the compost of the autumn have a destiny. Every living thing has a potential to grow and multiply. What carries each through the dark age of winter is the ambition and drive to see its own future take shape. Such is the key to the Water Element. Beneath its dark and impenetrable surface is a vast and unyielding force which powers the flow of season into season.

THE FIVE ELEMENTS

When we begin our look at the Elements in this way some readers are likely to feel that the descriptions seem vague and ill-defined. If I have fulfilled my purpose, however, this should be the case. It would be very tempting to say 'Metal is this' and 'Water is that', but this is not what the Elements are. They are not building blocks, or 'things'; they are not the result of a clearly defined conceptual grid with sharp edges which we fit over things and read accurately. This is always a shock to our Western minds.

The Elements are a way of describing the patterns in the movement of Qi energy, patterns which are forever changing and transforming. When we look through them again in greater detail in the next five chapters we shall see how these rather general descriptions of the essential qualities of the Elements become more concrete, especially when we look at them in small and finite human beings like ourselves.

What we must bear in mind all the time, however, when we find similarities between the spirit of an Element and the more specific details - the color or the emotion or the sound or the odor - with which it is associated, is that this is not

The Five Seasons

our creation, only our discovery. We are not taking the Elements and dividing things up according to their proportions. The pattern of movement which we see in the spirit of the Elements is the same in all the natural phenomena, in our minds, and in our spirits. We are not inventing them to fit into a pattern. The pattern already exists and we must develop our understanding of the Elements in their true essence to observe and understand that pattern.

As practitioners of this system of medicine it is ultimately through these most abstract of terms that we shall understand our patients. When we move away from the symptoms of disease, the distress signals which appear when our natural balance is lost, to the underlying cause, our understanding may well draw us to use the same terms as we have used with the spirit of the Elements. We may find people without reserves, people without purpose, people without any essence and vital spark within them, people without nourishment, and people without the warmth of joy and love. When we can understand the Elements at this level we shall be able to understand our patients at the very heart of their distress.

CHAPTER TWO

THE WOOD ELEMENT

The last chapter may have left the impression that the concept of the five Elements is far too broad to use with any precision. Like the concepts of Yin and Yang which are also fundamental in Chinese thought it may seem to the Western mind to be too vague and too open to personal interpretation. In the West we tend to assume that words should be like printed labels which we can stick on things and define once and for all. If we tried to define the Elements in this way it would produce some very poor distortions of Chinese thought.

What we have to remember is that the Chinese were principally concerned with understanding change and transformation. Their analysis of Nature and human life was dynamic rather than static. Instead of looking at the results of processes and putting a label on them they would look at the process itself and try to understand how it worked. This is how we looked at the cycle of the seasons in the last chapter in order to get a feeling for the movement of energy. It is a far richer method for understanding the pattern than merely naming the separate constituent parts.

There is a considerable gap, however, between the rather general concept of the Elements and the rich diversity of life and people on earth. The five Elements in classical acupuncture are the central foundation of a system of diagnosis that is one of the most precise and most wonderful ever devised. We need to develop our understanding of the Elements a little beyond a broad picture of the seasons in Nature. Even though the major part of our ability to diagnose will come from re-learning to use our senses as Nature ordained, we can guide our learning by looking more closely at the Elements and by drawing on our own experience of them.

We also need to remind ourselves that the Elements describe the way in which we could function in accordance with Nature; they reveal to us the true extent of our natural powers in body, mind and spirit. They are an important picture of what we have the potential to be; if we were in balance we would be able to use and enjoy all of these powers to the full. Only when our balance fails do we start to lose their measure and find ourselves using these faculties inappropriately, some far too little and others far too much. In order to make an observation like this we need to understand what would be appropriate and for this we need to have a sound understanding of how the Elements should work in us in order to recognize when they are out of balance. In this chapter, therefore, I shall try to explain in more detail the powers which the Wood Element expresses in us.

THE WOOD ELEMENT

Even when we look very briefly at the springtime, the season of the Wood Element, we shall probably find that certain key words frequently come to mind and form a pattern which we may well recognize. Words like 'birth', 'growth', 'regeneration', 'future', 'vision', 'hope', 'activity', 'vitality' and 'exuberance' are naturally and commonly associated with the spring. This process may seem a little arbitrary but the fact remains that these words form a kind of 'family' where the resemblance between the ideas is natural and easy. They are not identical, any more than the members of a family are, but together they all share a common theme. If anyone felt moved to test this they could stand on a street corner for half an hour and ask passers-by what words they associated with the springtime. Many of these particular words would be used over and over again.

This should be no great surprise. The Wood Element exists in us just as it does everywhere else in Nature, and when we describe it or call on its qualities we are touching the spirit of the Wood Element within ourselves. For many of us it will feel as though we are contacting a distinct part of ourselves; we may even automatically begin to experience many of the associated images and feelings which these key words trigger. Many of these associations and references will be our own unique pictures which give our experience of the Wood Element its personal context, but underlying them will be a core of meaning which, by and large, we all share.

There are probably going to be differences in how easily we can all find this part within ourselves. We are all unique individuals, and we are all in different states of balance within ourselves. Someone with a major imbalance in their Wood Element may not find it as easy to associate with the feelings and spirit of springtime; the power and qualities of the Wood Element may not be as alive within them and accessible to them. For someone who suffers in this way these words may not have such a clear meaning. Talking about hope, for example, to someone who has always felt hopeless and despairing may be very difficult, but it will never be totally pointless. The Element, weak as it may be, still resides

The Wood Element

within all of us and its essence is there to be reached and nourished if we can find the appropriate way.

This essence within us is very important because it is the means by which we can recognize how the Wood Element expresses itself in all parts of our body, mind and spirit. If we look at the words which we associate with the Wood Element in the spring we can see that the majority are words of 'activity', and activity of a particular kind. They mostly refer to movement which has structure and purpose, especially the upward and forward movement of new and vital growth which goes beyond existing boundaries. Many even echo the noise and exuberance which we associate with the spring as everything bustles and bursts out. When we examine these qualities we may begin to recognize where the Wood Element is alive within Nature and within us.

If, for example, we were to consider which of all our emotions most closely shared the characteristics of the Wood Element the answer which comes straight to mind is anger, or an abnormal lack of anger. We talk about anger rising within ourselves and of letting our anger out and of wanting to scream and shout with anger. The movement which we associate with anger is of a feeling welling its way upwards in ourselves and bursting to be let out. We expect it to be vigorous and forceful, and we expect to shout with rage. We also know the feeling of frustration and resentment which can arise when this growth is blocked.

Anger seems on the surface to fit very well with many of the ideas which we associate with the Wood Element and is, indeed, the emotion which for the Chinese corresponded with the Wood Element. It is important in diagnosing when Wood is out of balance. 'Anger' is not by itself a very useful label, however, if we want to understand the Wood Element. The meaning of the word can seem so 'obvious' that we no longer observe carefully what is happening when we say that someone is angry. There are many reasons why people can be angry. Anger can arise from a burning sense of outrage and injustice, from being vulnerable and hurt, from not being given any attention, from not being accorded the proper respect, and from sheer terror at the prospect of being forced to face the unknown. Each of these expressions of anger has a different root, and because of this each has a very different quality.

Someone might argue that even with their different roots all types of anger share a similarity, but we know from our own experience that this is not so.

There are some people whose anger manifests itself in a very cold, precise and cutting way. To be on the receiving end is to feel like meeting the blade of a sharp knife. There is no noise or exuberance in what they do, nor even any vitality, and yet we can tell from the context that they are angry. Equally when people are terrified they can become angry. When we come across someone frozen with panic and we have to talk them out of danger, they may react with a great deal of hostility to any suggestion about moving even one millimeter from where they stand. This hostility, however, even though it is full of the challenge and confrontation which we might identify with anger, may not be the vital, active and forceful expression of the Wood Element. It is something entirely different, something wrenched from the person out of sheer terror of taking any more risks.

The word 'anger', then, is not enough. The emotion which arises from the Wood Element has its own unique quality. It is noisy, vigorous and forceful. When its expression is blocked we may see all the resentment, the hostility and the frustration which arise from containing this force. It is these qualities which make us aware of its real source. They are what determine the association with Wood more than the label 'angry'.

This shows the real value of looking at the Element before looking at correspondences. There are a multiplicity of emotions, and many draw on and exhibit the life and vitality of the Wood Element in our emotional make-up. We all need the power to express ourselves forcefully and to give vent to emotions which rise up in us, not only in anger but in other loud and exuberant outpourings of our feelings. These qualities express the true essence of the Wood Element as a part of our overall balance and help us to understand it more fully than by a label which we may apply to one emotion.

This takes us immediately far beyond a simplistic view of the associations of the Elements. If someone is angry in sheer terror, for example, we might want to call this a 'fear-anger' or 'Water-anger' because its qualities have more to do with the essence of the Water Element to which 'fear' belongs than to the Wood Element with which 'anger' is associated. The fear is the true key to understanding what is happening, not the anger or the hostility. Once we have understood this we shall find that the Traditional Diagnosis takes on an entirely richer character than we first suspected.

This is an important matter and we shall return to it later. A serious problem

The Wood Element

with the correspondences lies in the simple pictures of the Elements which we make for ourselves. It would be better if we thought of the five emotions which correspond to the Elements not as five points of a compass but as five segments of a circle. With this we could perhaps develop a better picture of how each Element creates a predominant tone which is to do with its essence inside which other emotions could still find their own expression. With a 'five points' picture we end up with a very one-dimensional approach which cannot do justice to the richness of life.

This is easier to explain by looking at the seasons. Spring is the season of birth and growth, but not only and exclusively these. It, too, has its share of death and decay, fullness and harvest, but these appear within the overall character and feeling of spring. In its own season each of these would have its own added poignancy as an embodiment of the prevailing spirit of its time. In the spring, however, the grief, or fear, or joy is overtaken and colored by the sheer force of optimism and vitality which the season inspires.

Just as we described situations of outrage, injustice, or indignation where a certain degree of rage, hostility or anger would be expected in a situation of imbalance within Wood, this anger may exceed the normal range of appropriateness so we may have a situation where the response from the person is so lacking in force or appropriate outrage we recognize an abnormal lack or absence of anger. The person may be so defeated, resigned, or unable to assert him or herself that vigorous growth and vitality has dangerously dwindled.

The seed of life has burst open the shell of the seed. There is a tiny speck of life. However, the growth and strength needed to force the spurt of life into the new shoot is just not available. The vitality of this element is therefore weakened by the absence of this expressive, dynamic quality.

We have to be constantly careful in this way not to be lazy in accepting labels without using our senses. The sound of voice associated with the Wood Element provides another clear example of this. For the purposes of the Traditional Diagnosis, where we look for the inappropriate color, sound, odor and emotion in the patient, the inappropriate sound of voice which arises from the Causative Factor being an imbalance in the Wood Element is 'shouting' or 'lack of shouting'. The words 'shouting' or 'lack of shouting', however, are in themselves no better than the words 'anger' or 'lack of anger' in helping us to recognize the Wood imbalance.

There are dozens of 'shouting' voices. Many draw on the qualities which belong to the Wood Element without automatically pointing to a Wood imbalance. A voice can be exuberant, or lively, or loud without being what we could properly call in Five-Element diagnostic terms a 'shout'. The qualities of the Wood Element contribute, after all, to the whole range of sounds which we want to make just as much as the five colors combine to produce every other color. If someone wants love or attention or respect and is being ignored they may well express their need with a great deal of volume and vigor without this being 'shouting' in terms of Five-Element diagnosis.

By contrast someone in a voice no louder than that used in normal conversation can use all the emphasis, assertion and vigor that characterize a true 'shout'. There may also be an over-structuring of the words and a 'telling' quality. The diagnostic key to this is the fact that the qualities from the Wood Element appear predominantly in everything that the person does, be it whispering, or shouting, or laughing.

Lack of appropriate shouting is an equally distressing signal of imbalance as excess shouting. There is a certain degree of force and power that a reasonably healthy person should manifest in appropriate situations. When this force is absent or significantly diminished it signals imbalance

The point which I must stress time and time again is that although the correspondences seem to offer a short cut to understanding the Elements the reverse is true. The apparent simplicity of the five tastes, five sounds, five emotions and five of everything else is an illusion. It is only when we begin to understand the essence of the Elements, individually and together, that we can begin to develop a real understanding of the correspondences. If we then concentrate on the qualities of the Wood Element, abstract as they seem, and ask ourselves how the Wood Element is going to manifest in each of us in body, mind and spirit, we shall find that it is not quite as impossible as some may have begun to expect.

If we look first at the Wood Element in the physical body and use the tables of correspondences we find that the Chinese regarded the tendons and sinews as a physical manifestation of Wood. We may see an 'obvious' connection with the movement and flexibility which we associate with the Wood Element, but there is more to this than just having the requisite parts of the body able to move. An understanding of the Wood Element itself may show us that the movement

The Wood Element

which it controls will have a particular kind of energy and assertion. It will be movement that has purpose and forward direction, that can adapt and be flexible in the different situations in which it is placed. When we recall how fast plants grow in the spring we will also realize that the movement associated with Wood is relatively rapid. All of the Elements provide movement in their own way but there is a vast difference between the quiet descent of autumn, the ponderous crawl of winter, and the bursting speed of spring activity.

When we look at it in this way we can see the obvious association of the Wood element with sinews and tendons. Our picture of the movement associated with the Wood Element will be dynamic, involving strength and flexibility. In order to make our way around obstacles at speed our movements have to be carefully planned and controlled. We can all draw on our own experiences for examples of people performing complicated tasks in a whirl of coordinated movement, and we can see in our mind's eye just how vital the sinews and tendons are to these tasks.

This does not mean that every movement which we make calls on these particular qualities, only that when they are called on they can be made available to us. There are dozens of circumstances in every hour when we need to move in a way which has a purpose and a goal, and when we do so we are embodying the Wood Element's powers. The importance of the sinews and tendons is that they enable this movement, and if for any reason the Wood Element in someone is weak we may find that both their movements and the means by which they move are affected.

The Chinese very often used the metaphor of the tree to describe man and woman because they saw both representing an upright connection between heaven and earth. When we come to look at the Wood Element in imbalance this metaphor of the tree can be very illuminating. The flexibility of the branches as they first grow, for example, is often likened to the sinews and tendons of the body: they provide strength and suppleness for the tree's movement. As the sap ceases to flow and the tree ages the branches become more rigid and fixed, and are in greater danger of breaking. Their movement is not so free and they are not so adaptable. This is often how an imbalance in Wood can appear in the physical body, not only through age but through disease. We may sometimes see in our patients the creaking and stiff movement of an aged tree.

The Wood Element is not only about movement; it is also about vision. When we look at how the Elements manifest in the physical body, we should not be surprised that the most simple and obvious connections hold good. There is a very strong connection between the Wood Element and eyes, the faculty of vision. This has not only to do with the physical eye, but also the mental eye and the spirit eye. There is also the importance of regeneration and birth in the Spring as an embodiment of the essence of Wood and by the same logic we might also expect that there is a connection between the Wood Element and the reproductive organs. This does, in fact, exist, both in terms of function and particularly in the pathways of the meridians associated with the Element which traverse the genital area in both sexes.

The important point in all of this is that there are no dramatic or complex deductions in these correspondences and connections. The associations themselves are simple and natural once we begin to understand the Element. The complications only start when we let our heads get to work. The Elements themselves are only a description of the ceaseless flow within the One, a graphic illustration of the continuous rise and fall of the cycle of energy. There is nothing arbitrary about the relationship between Wood and tendons, or Wood and sight, or Wood and reproduction. They are natural expressions in us of the essential qualities of Wood, the part of our own system and cycle of energy which mirror that of the Wood Element in Nature itself.

When we look at how the Wood Element expresses itself in our minds and mental processes it is easy to see how in the powers of reasoning and the development of ideas we demonstrate these same essential qualities. What we have touched on so far talks of birth and growth, and of structure, order and purpose. When we look at our own mental functioning in this light we cannot fail to see the connection with the Wood Element in the creation and development of new ideas, the powers of reason and the structure of chains of argument which build purposefully to deductions and conclusions. All of the complexity and orderliness of our modern rationality seems to stem directly from the qualities of Wood. Not only that, these qualities of the Wood Element remind us that thinking is an activity rather than a form of passive contemplation.

These attributes are not some special quality which only the gifted few have. We tend to forget just how complex life has become in our modern world, and we all exhibit a high degree of mental coordination and activity to perform even the most basic tasks. The simplest journey across a large city like London

The Wood Element

involves an enormous amount of thought and preparation. Being in the right place at the right time calls on mental powers like planning, decision-making, foresight and setting goals, which all derive from the Wood Element within us. In this respect we are no different from the trees and plants around us which each year have to follow their own plans to grow and ripen in the right place and at the right time.

When we try to describe how the Wood Element expresses itself in our spirit we are going to find this more difficult, however, as we shall with all the Elements at this level. Our age is not given to much care and consideration of the spirit, and we do not readily have the words or experience to touch this level of our being. As a consequence there is much disease starting here through neglect, illness and misuse which we do not even have the capacity to recognize and understand.

When we look at the Wood Element in the spring we can see how beyond the simple material changes there is a profound feeling abroad of optimism and hope for the future. When the first shoots fight through the soil and start to force their way skyward there is the promise of a crop and the hope that the promise will be fulfilled. These little shoots represent a future and a sense of purpose. Words like 'hope', 'vision' and 'purpose', however, are not as common a part of our vocabulary as their opposites like 'despair', 'futility' and 'hopelessness'.

This is a tragedy. There is no more wonderful a feeling than to be at one with the spirit of the natural world around us and to share in this pattern of growth and purpose which we feel most vibrantly in the spring. We are not talking about spirit in any abstract sense here, but spirit as the vital force within Nature which pervades everything and gives to all things a sense of purpose and the power to move towards their goals.

The one word which captures the essence of Wood on all levels is **vision**. We have the physical capacity of sight in a world where movement and color feed us for all of our waking hours. We have the ability to use our mind's eye to think, plan, decide, judge and imagine, and we employ this faculty throughout every minute of our day in everything which we do. Then there is the vision which we do not recognize as clearly, our spirit eye, and yet of the three this is the most important. We are fed by hopes and dreams of the future, the next hour, the next day and the next year. Everything we do is aimed towards a goal in the future, whether it be a simple material goal like the new car or the new house, or

Classical Five-Element Acupuncture

something much less tangible like the goals that determine the quality of our living such as peace, harmony and balance. It is visions like these, especially the more intangible ones, which keep us alive. For however materialistic we may be as a race in modern times, there are very few people who do not feel the need for goals beyond the immediate gratification of their physical or mental needs. Without them the other goals would be pointless and life would have no purpose.

The spirit is like any other part of us. It needs warmth, nourishment, quality and reserves, and each of the Elements provides these. The Wood Element gives our spirit hope, vision and the potential of growth. It is through the Wood Element that our spirit has the power to grow and rise to new levels. In Chinese thought this upward movement was understood very literally. The part of the spirit which they associated with the Wood Element was thought to survive the material body at death and rise upwards to join a different plane of non-substantial existence. For them this was a logical extension of the sense of purpose and direction which they saw coming to the spirit from the Wood Element.

When we look at the qualities which the Wood Element represents in our lives it is difficult to imagine a worthwhile life without them all working at their best. Yet this is the lot of all of us to a greater or lesser degree. None of us are in perfect balance, and where any of the Elements are in distress then all will be affected.

If the flow of energy within us is disturbed and the Wood Element is affected the disturbance will be felt in the functions which it governs. On a physical level this may well result in a change in the quality of the sinews and tendons. Where they were once flexible enough to give the power of free movement they can become stiff and unyielding. Where movement once used to be easy and graceful now it is jerky and rigid. Instead of giving way and bending, tendons sprain or snap. Sometimes the tone and control of the tendons go and all movement becomes lank and gangling, as though people were shambling purposelessly along.

The analogy with the tree is very apt, both for this physical problem and for others. When the sap does not travel to the branches they lose their flexibility and suppleness. When the sap does not rise in us our eyes may also be affected. Our physical vision may deteriorate, and the eyes themselves may become sore and painful, as the Wood Element no longer spreads its energy and moisture upwards. We may also see people like trees in which the sap rises too freely. They may suffer from a feeling of pressure as the sap builds up and cannot find an escape. All manner of headaches and pressure in the eyes can arise from this kind of movement.

Disease never falls on one level alone; we must always remember this when we encounter what seem to be simple problems. If we come across people who cannot see with their physical eyes we should ask ourselves whether they can see with their mental and spirit eye as well. Equally when we see patients who have lost their ability to see any future for themselves this may also manifest as a literal failure and loss of physical vision.

If the Wood Element is out of balance this can manifest in qualities which the Element represents in our whole being. Spring is a time of rapid movement, and we may come across people who act as though they are always chasing after a distant goal or target, never slowing down to enjoy the fruits of their labors. We can see the likeness between them and plants which grow out of control, always twisting and turning to keep on with their desperate race forward. We sometimes see the opposite, someone utterly rooted to the spot, solid and dependable, but totally incapable of any real movement.

We may see the same qualities of disturbance on the mental level as well as the physical level when the Wood Element is out of balance. Instead of having the power to be flexible and to try out different angles the mind becomes fixed and cannot bend and yield. Rather than taking things to their proper limit the mind rambles on and on, growing without check and aimlessly expanding for no apparent purpose. The Wood Element is all about clarity and vision, and when this is weak in someone the power of their thought also lacks clarity. We cannot see what they are talking about, and we may suspect that they have lost sight of what they are trying to say. The simple directness that comes from a clear purpose has been lost.

This is often a striking feature of the Traditional Diagnosis in which a patient has a great many thoughts and words to organize. When the Wood Element is out of balance in someone the consultation can sometimes turn into a rambling and chaotic monologue. At the other extreme the mental functions can become so rigid and orderly, so fixed and unyielding that dialogue is impossible. The Traditional Diagnosis can become like a military briefing under these conditions: concise, impersonal and over forceful. "This, this, and this are the problems:

now, you do something about them."

We have to be careful, however, when we start to use generalizations like these. There are many different reasons why a single mental faculty may not function as Nature intended. A weakness in one Element will lead to a loss of balance in all of the Elements, with its consequent effect on the faculties which spring from them. The same reservations apply to the imbalances which manifest in the spirit of the person. When any one Element is out of balance at the level of the spirit it will cause resignation, chaos or unrest everywhere in the person.

It is very clear from what we have seen already, however, that the Wood Element is what gives the spirit its sense of hope and purpose, its vision in the most important sense. When this fails we may well be confronted by someone who sees no future for themselves and who is plunged into the most abject despair. It is difficult for those of us that have a sense of the future to imagine the terrible extent of this darkness and depression. What must it feel like to have no spring in the year, no birth or growth in their spirit, and nothing to plan for? If people have lost their sense of purpose at this level they will also manifest a great many other problems at the mental and physical level. If the spirit has no sense of purpose what sense of purpose can there be for anything else in the economy of the body, mind and spirit? The utter resignation and despair can be the worst which we ever encounter.

When we come across someone with an imbalance in their Wood Element we should look and listen carefully for the messages coming from their spirit. For all the physical aches and mental anguish there will be a sad and lost voice within this chaos saying ,"help me to find a direction, help me to see where to go from here, give me hope". What the person will seek more than anything else is a plan, a structure, and a vision for all levels of their being in order to feel the strength and flexibility of the Wood Element inside them again.

CHAPTER THREE

THE FIRE ELEMENT

The Fire Element follows the Wood Element on the Sheng cycle, the cycle of creation, just as the summer naturally follows the spring. The spirit of Wood has to do with direction, with setting aims and goals for ourselves, and with feeding our own spirits with hope and a vision of the future. The Fire Element which follows in the cycle of creation is that future becoming real, the stage of the cycle which sees our hopes and dreams fulfilled.

The Fire Element is about the present. Time stands still in the heat of summer. The sun rises high in the sky and everything reaches its peak of bloom and brilliance. When the spring has been successful we can see the crops in the soil and fruits ripening on the branch ready for the harvest time, and there is nothing more to be done than to relax and enjoy the warmth. After the hard work of the spring we feel a lightness of the spirit and a sense of freedom. Now we have the time to enjoy this wonderful feeling and share it with our friends.

The love and joy which are an expression of the Fire Element in us are two of the greatest gifts it is possible to receive. Both are a manifestation in us of the highest point which Qi energy reaches in its ceaseless cycle. Each Element has a peak in the year when we re-charge our own batteries with its pure essence. The gifts of the Fire Element are the high point of the year's own peak; the energy which we take from here will warm us for the whole of the year to come. Without this essence of Fire in the summer the rest of the year would be dark and spiritless.

The love which we receive from the Fire Element bathes every part of our lives. It fires our spirit and gives us an inner communion with God's love, allowing us to share in the spirit which pervades everything in the universe. It flows through our relationships with our partners, our families and our friends, and it is the power by which we transform ourselves and one another. It feeds our relationships and enables us to feel at one with people we happen to meet, even with people whom we pass in the street. There is no greater joy to be had than to be able to walk down the street and feel warmth and love for all the people who pass by. It enables us to set aside the petty jealousies and prejudices which blight our lives and to reach the very heart of everyone.

Classical Five-Element Acupuncture

For practitioners of this system of medicine it is vital to reach inside for this love, the essence of the Fire Element, and to find a connection with it when we work with patients. For however unlovable some of them seem, and however unpleasant some of them will actually be, this essence exists within them too at some deep level. It is the certain knowledge that this is so which should hearten and inspire us to seek to reach that level within ourselves and within them.

When we are in touch with the essence of the Fire Element it is a source of great joy in us. Through this joy we have the heart to involve ourselves fully in everything which we do. It makes us energetic and enthusiastic, and lightens our tasks. It is impossible to imagine what life would be like if there were to be no fun at all in our work, duty and play. When we have the strength of the Fire Element within us there is fun to be had in all that we do, even in the most trivial tasks.

This love and joy are also what feed all the best aspects of the community which we share with other people. Our feelings flow outwards from us and spread to our friends and acquaintances in the same way that the blooms of the summer unfold and spread. When love and joy are alive in us we reach out naturally to other people to share warmth and friendship with them. We make contact with people, we communicate with people, and we form friendships by the grace of the feelings which the Fire Element nourishes in us. It represents the very best in our relationships with other people.

The best image of the way the Fire Element manifests itself in the body, mind and spirit is that of the fire of the sun. We have to remember that we are looking at the movement of energy and the different qualities which that movement has. Just as the tree embodies the spirit of the Wood Element in the rising and growing phase of energy, so the sun symbolizes the zenith of the cycle of energy within us. The energy of the Fire Element is the fullest and warmest, just as the summer sees the sun at its highest in the sky for the longest time.

The 'inner sun' of the Fire Element in our physical being provides us with our physical warmth. We need and depend on heat to survive. Without heat we cannot function at all; we grow cold and die from the extremities inwards and all of the physical processes within us slow down and ultimately stop. In good health, heat helps everything to move and flow. The blood in our veins moves

The Fire Element

more quickly, our digestion and assimilation of food speed up, and all the chemical processes which maintain our life are more efficient. Even our growth is enhanced by the warmth which the Fire Element gives us. When there is enough heat our Qi energy can be transformed and transported to fulfill all our needs in body, mind and spirit and bring us to maturity.

It is easy to see from this how the Fire Element comes to be associated with the blood and blood vessels since these are the means by which heat is channeled from our core, our vital organs, to the whole body. When the sun beats down on the plants it is the circulating fluids which pass the heat around to every cell and ensure that there is enough energy for life and growth to take place. We are no different. Without warmth spread evenly throughout our body we cannot function in harmony and balance.

When there are disturbances in the Fire Element we should expect to see problems in how the body is heated inside and maintained in equilibrium with the outside world. When the 'inner sun' is weak there will not be enough energy to go around. This may affect everything by making the whole body cooler, or just parts of it like cold hands and feet. If the inner fire is blazing out of control the opposite will be true; there will be far too much heat in the system. A person may feel hot to the touch, and there will probably be a great deal of red on their face and body as the color of fire literally breaks out on their skin from the excess heat trapped inside.

When there are imbalances in any of the Elements we should ask ourselves what we might expect to happen by drawing on our experience of Nature to help our understanding. When somebody's Fire is out of control we should picture what happens when the summer keeps on burning long past the month when it should fade into harvest time. The excess of heat produces a drought, and the crops which were bursting through the earth in the spring start to wither and die in the fields, taking with them any hope of a good harvest and making the reserves for the winter fall to a dangerous low.

When we look at the physical body of someone with a serious Fire imbalance there may be similar signs and patterns. The excess of heat may show in a red face and red skin. There may well be a thirst, and all the secretions which keep the body moist may dry up. Without moisture many of the bodily processes are going to be badly disrupted, and reserves will burn up and vanish. The excess in the whole body will be like having a heating system on top setting in midsummer, its boiler and pumps hammering away without any restraint. The system itself may start to show signs of stress; conditions like high blood pressure, palpitations and swellings will abound. Everywhere that the excess heat builds up tissue will either start to wither and die or burst out in inflammations.

By contrast the weak and sickly inner sun of an unhealthy Fire Element will barely have enough heat to share and to bring anything to maturity. There may be only a poor and lukewarm flow which does nothing to encourage the bodily systems to work at their best. Everything inside will be dark and cold, and with no heat to disperse the dampness of the winter and spring everything may stay waterlogged and sodden. When someone has a Fire imbalance the physical symptoms often show evidence of this dark and wet coldness. When the blood is slow and cold this is often reflected in the face. We describe people with a drab pallor as bloodless, and the Chinese themselves judged the quality of the spirit of Fire by the complexion. A good flow of warm blood gives us the same bloom that the summer flowers have at their peak; we radiate our good health.

The association of Fire with the blood and blood vessels also shows the simple and direct wisdom embodied in the Chinese understanding of natural processes long before the development of modern biochemistry. The Fire Element has a great deal to do with communication and contact, and we principally apply these concepts to the emotional and mental levels. With the bloodstream, however, we see the same process on a physical level, for this is the means by which everything is channeled and communicated around our physical bodies: heat from our central organs, food from our stomach, air from our lungs, and even the chemical messengers of our own internal organs, the hormones.

The power to communicate emotions and thoughts also depends in large measure on the physical power of speech and the tongue which the Chinese considered to be under the control of the Fire Element. The connection between Fire, the power of speech, and the tongue is similar to that between Wood, the power of sight, and the eyes. Every detail like this can give us wonderful diagnostic information. When the Fire Element is out of balance or is put under severe stress we often see a disturbance in the physical, mental and even spiritual ability to speak and communicate. An inability to control the tongue can make people stutter, stammer and slur; it may even cause people to lose the power of speech entirely. It is a stock cliché in films to see people speechless with shock and panic, then talking utter gibberish for a few moments. When the

The Fire Element

Fire Element takes a heavy blow the power to speak and communicate is threatened on all levels. Everything which flows to make speech possible stops at source, and with no energy to drive it the tongue weakens, the voice falters, and the mind and spirit seize up.

The Fire Element in good balance lights up and fires the mind with enthusiasm. It represents the peak of life and achievement, and at the mental level this expresses in lively and keen intelligence and in the ability to have clear thought and memory. The way in which we use the word 'bright' appropriately captures the essence of this idea, just as the word 'dull' captures its opposite. When the Fire in us is strong our thoughts have life and energy.

This energy can get out of hand, however, and a similar problem may manifest on a mental level as besets the physical body when there is too much heat. Excitement makes most people talk and think a little more quickly. We often hear this when a party starts to take off: voices suddenly become higher, faster and more excited. When someone's Fire is out of balance this is a sound that may begin to appear in every context. Everything overheats and moves a great deal too quickly. The words tumble out of control and race away. When the Fire burns too brightly the talkativeness can border on the hysterical.

At the other end of the spectrum weak Fire energy may leave the mind lackluster and weary, the voice without life and spark, and the person very flat and uninspiring. Thei words and ideas come slowly and they can make even the most exciting news sound really boring. For someone whose Fire is ailing in this way there really is not very much to get excited about, and it does not take long for someone to feel lifeless and apathetic.

These pictures help us to understand the association of the sound of the voice that arises with a Fire imbalance. The correspondences themselves are labeled 'laugh' and 'lack of laugh', but like any labels these are not as helpful as the context in which we can see and hear what is actually happening. If we think of the Fire Element providing the spark which gives joy and excitement to the voice we can get a much clearer idea of what happens when the Fire is out of balance. A voice that bubbles with excitement all of the time and in the wrong contexts will sound as odd as a voice whose flatness and lack of spirit cannot rise to the times when the person tries to join in with warmth and joy. The same is true of the quality of the emotion associated with a Fire imbalance, which we label 'joy' or 'lack of joy'.

3.5

The true value of this liveliness in our ideas and thoughts is that it fuels our ability to share and to express what we have been thinking about. When our Fire Element is in good balance we take pleasure in letting people know our thoughts and feelings, and in hearing their views as well. This is the essence of good communication: we give and receive in equal measure. When people share ideas and the flow is good they can produce things as a group which none could do individually. The sense of common purpose and achievement is a source of real fulfillment.

If one word characterizes the gift of the Fire Element it is 'understanding'. With the giving and receiving of ideas, of thoughts and of feelings, the sharing and the exchange, we become as one in our conversation and communication. We can really understand what other people feel and are trying to tell us, and we have the power to explain to them what we feel and think. We are open and honest, and our exchanges are among the most mature which we can ever manage. From this spirit are born kindness and generosity, and many of the feelings which are the best we ever display.

It is feelings such as these which prompt us to take the time to listen to people properly and to find common ground with them. More often than not, however, we do not allow ourselves the few extra minutes to try to understand or even listen to what people are trying to tell us. As practitioners of this system of medicine we should be keenly aware of this. It is quite a temptation to become a symptom fixer, remote from our patients and in a desperate hurry to get their physical body better, when all that they are crying out is, "For God's sake please understand me, the pains will hurt far less if only someone will take the trouble to understand how I feel inside." People in hospitals will tell you that for hours after visiting time their pains are less, such is the power of understanding and sharing the sufferer's feelings and pain.

Sharing involves a proper balance of giving and receiving. If our communication is good we each have our say and we can reach understanding. When this balance is disrupted we are not able to give and receive in equal measure. Someone whose Fire is out of balance may be desperate to be understood, so desperate that he or she may begin to appear selfish and attention-seeking in his or her search to find someone who knows exactly how they feel. Sometimes our natural inclination is to give someone like this a wide berth, but we have to think just how terrible it must feel inside this person. Perhaps they cannot find the love in themselves to unlock other people's trust and giving, or, worse still, cannot accept the love which comes with other people's compassion. The easy flow of warmth which comes from the Fire Element is not alive within him or her.

Describing Fire imbalances in these terms naturally draws us to images of doors and gates under the control of the Fire Element. When energy flows as it should the barriers can open and close as we need them to, but when imbalance takes root the gates can jam open or shut. So much of what we describe as the positive aspect of Fire speaks of openness between people and implies trust and safety. If that openness is jeopardized then we shall see people who are over-defensive or defenseless, over-trusting or suspicious, and unable to communicate with ease any longer.

These problems surface most clearly in close relationships where we share our feelings with each other. It is not just that the Fire Element makes our relationships closer or better. Without them we do not have physical, mental, or spiritual relationships of any value. When we think of the openness and sharing that we associate with the summer time we can see how we depend on this in order to break down the foolish barriers which spring up between people and to quell the fears which people have of exposing themselves. When we are warm, relaxed and open we no longer worry about what harm can come to us and we share our inner thoughts and feelings without fear.

People who lack this ability suffer the most terrible distress. Someone whose Fire is out of control cannot help but open up all the time, not just when it is relatively safe but at times when it is dangerous and exposed. He or she has no protection for himself or herself or for others, and he or she may radiate an emotional heat which is so intense that it scorches everything it touches but has no barrier or gate to save a little for his or her own protection.

At the other end of the scale there are people whose fires barely spark, with so little reserve and so little security in themselves that they dare not expose themselves outside their inner sanctuary lest what little fire they have will be extinguished. Without the true warmth of the Fire Element within them they have to spend their whole life covered up and protected. An imbalance such as this will leave someone feeling vulnerable and frail. The life of someone who cannot share love with trust and confidence is going to be dominated by the fear of losing love or the fear of losing himself.

When we talk to patients in the Traditional Diagnosis we can find out much about the Fire Element in them by asking about their relationships, both social and sexual. Where the Fire Element is out of balance and suffering this is likely to manifest in the way they live their whole lives. We have to ask ourselves what it must be like to go through life with the sun always behind the clouds, or just as bad, with the sun of the desert burning down without shade for year after year. Fulfillment in relationships, the maturity which comes from the Fire Element, is always beyond their grasp.

The real essence of understanding this approach is to be able to draw on Nature and on our own experience to recognize the particular qualities which underlie any behavior and patterns which we observe. Everyone, for example, wants to be understood. The real question is what feeds this desire and how is it expressed, and what happens to the person if we fail to understand them. Someone's response will guide us to the Element which is calling for help if we learn to recognize how the Elements function within people.

We are most likely to be led astray with the Fire Element as it manifests at the level of our spirit, for in many ways it is by virtue of the Fire Element, the 'inner sun', that we have a spirit at all. In times such as we now live through, this light has dimmed in many people, but we cannot straight away conclude from this that everyone has a major imbalance in their Fire Element. The spirit, like the other parts of us, needs to grow, to be nourished, to be inspired, and to have time to rest and build up its reserves. If it is deprived of any of these we shall see weakness and suffering instead of strength and resolve. When it is the spirit of the Fire Element that weakens, however, the suffering will go to the very heart of our being.

When we are lacking food or sleep, or when we are run down and missing out on things of quality in our lives, it is our contacts with our friends and our ability to share our pain and struggle with other people which may keep us going. When we have the love and understanding of friends around us we can hold on. When our spirit can find communion with the spirit of God or in the Dao, then too we know that we are safe. In the Nei Jing it is said that "when the spirit is strong then suffering is minute". This spirit, the soul's Fire, is what sustains our lives.

If, however, we have no friends, or are cut off from their love, our problems may magnify until we really cannot see a way forward. If we can imagine this we

The Fire Element

can just about begin to understand how someone feels when their own spirit is so weak as a result of Fire imbalance within that it cannot share or communicate with anyone else at this level, or with the universal spirit. No amount of nourishment or reserves are going to be of any use when this is lacking. There is no joy, no warmth and no love. Everything is cold and dark, with no 'inner sun' to light the way. Without warmth, love and happiness their lives are going to be flat and monotonous. Without the light of Fire in their spirit they are going to be disheartened, defeated and resigned. In the end they may even become bitter and resentful.

Somewhere inside them, however, there will always be a frail and weak Fire sending out its distress signals in the hope of finding help and succor. Some people may crave physical warmth, love the summer, follow the sun, and grab every second of heat. Others may seek emotional warmth, and look for an intense love and warmth beyond the capacity of their lovers and friends to give. Underlying both of these may be a desperate desire for warmth and heat in the spirit, for a love that can kindle their weak Fire to the maturity and fulfillment which they so badly miss.

The Fire Element, therefore, represents many of the things which we think of as most human and which engage our deepest feelings of love and sharing. When the Qi energy is at its peak and at its most expansive it allows us a fullness in our lives which has no equal in the ceaseless flow of the seasons.

CHAPTER FOUR

THE EARTH ELEMENT

In the late summer, the season of the Earth Element, the sharing of joy and laughter gives way to a different kind of love, the love of a mother for her children. The Earth Element is usually described more prosaically in books as a provider of nourishment and stores, a giver of harvests and a distributor of Nature's bounty. There is nothing wrong with this description; it is an integral part of understanding the Earth and the way that we take in our physical nourishment. It is, however, only a small part of the overall picture.

The proverb which says that man does not live by food alone, means that we need to be nourished in our body, mind and spirit if we are to live a full and happy life. In modern times there are higher standards of physical care and comfort than ever before, but there is just as much disease. Where previous generations fed their minds and especially their spirits, we mainly feed our bodies and pay relatively little attention to the spirit. While we escape the disease which arises from poor nourishment we suffer from a much deeper and more terrible malnutrition from which physical food alone cannot protect us.

This is the reason why we need the total nourishment which we get from this part of the cycle of energy and why it is akin to the love of a mother. For not only do we get physical food from our mothers, but also food for the mind and spirit. It is the mother who feeds from the breast until it is time to wean the baby onto solid foods. It is the mother who first provides the little child with the mental stimulus to learn and teaches the child its first words. It is, above all, the mother who gives her love unconditionally to the child, something which the child depends and counts on until becoming an adult and even beyond. This maternal love is the foundation of a secure and nourished spirit. When we have a good mother we shall always have a home around us and within us.

The Earth on which we live, the embodiment of the Element Earth, is our mother in just that same way. Our physical food comes to us from the harvests which we reap every year. Our minds, too, are fed by all the sights, sounds and smells which form the root and basis of all our knowledge, and fed equally by the security and stability which the certainty of our physical nourishment gives us. We draw comfort and support from the earth, whether we recognize it or not.

Classical Five-Element Acupuncture

In many ways it is a shame that the supermarket shelf exists, because it deprives us of the experience of growing and harvesting our own food and the wonderful sense of satisfaction and security which this gives.

Most importantly, however, is the way that the Earth as our mother feeds the spirit. It is not only that we see, hear and feel around us all the manifestations of the spirit in Nature. We also get from Nature what our own mothers give us, a sense of belonging and a sense of home. When we have the power of the Earth Element within us we can feel at peace within ourselves because we are grounded and balanced. We talk of having our feet on the ground, and at the level of the spirit this is one of the most vital qualities which we can acquire. Our spirit needs a home just as much as our physical body and our emotions.

The Earth Element, associated as it is with nourishment, is responsible for the physical functions of taking in, digesting and assimilating food. The two Officials of the Earth Element, the Stomach and the Spleen, have exactly this function at a physical level. The Stomach churns up the food which we ingest and mixes it with our digestive juices. The Spleen takes the extracted nourishment in the food and distributes it to all parts of the body to keep us warm and active and to power all our bodily functions.

If we are well fed and getting the correct nutrients from our food we are going to have a good covering of healthy flesh. The Chinese spoke of the flesh as the physical manifestation of the Earth Element and it is easy to see why. It is both a food store and a protective cover. By flesh we should remember that what is meant is muscle bulk, not fat. This is more the substance and reserve power of muscle. The tensile strength and use of the muscle itself is more usually seen as under the control of the Wood Element.

The Chinese were not advocating that people should regard excessive flesh as an advantage, but that people should have adequate reserves to keep them warm and protected. When our muscles and flesh are in good shape we have all these things. We have energy to move, energy to warm ourselves by shivering if we need to, a layer of insulation to keep out the cold, and reserves of energy as an emergency resource. The Earth Element is like an internal harvest within us which takes the goodness which we derive from food and lays it in store to meet our future needs.

We have to remember, however, that when we feed ourselves we do so on all

The Earth Element

three levels, body, mind and spirit together. There is no such thing as 'just eating', as though the physical body could look after itself whether or not the mind and spirit were involved. For our physical food to taste good it has to appeal to our minds and our spirits, and when it does appeal to them it provides them with nourishment at their own level. We shall never be truly satisfied by physical nourishment alone.

I have often illustrated this in my lectures by referring to the renowned English cream cakes. I talk about them, draw them, describe their taste, texture and smell, and generally try to stir up such an enthusiasm in the class that the students are utterly ravenous on every level. Then to emphasize the fact I contrast this with the picture of a person who tells themselves that they have to eat nothing but brown rice, and although their mind and spirit may scream out for something different they endure this strict and perhaps, for them, unappetizing routine.

It is stretching the point to absurd extremes, but it is a simple point worth making. There is no such thing as physical food alone, and although the brown rice may be chemically and nutritionally healthier it is of little value if the mind and spirit derive nothing from it. Being nourished has to take place on all levels or we really do not derive the maximum benefit from the food which we eat. If food bores us we do not digest it at all well and it sits like stone in our stomachs. If the cream cake, on the other hand, excites us on all levels we shall extract every tiny atom of benefit which our bodies, minds and spirits can find. Only when we are fed like this can we feel really satisfied and extract the maximum goodness from it. And, I hasten to add, I urge moderation as the key to all eating habits.

The way in which we take in our mental nourishment is no different. Indeed, many of the words we use to talk about learning new facts and taking in information borrow the words of physical nourishment. We digest facts, chew over details, swallow stories, get our teeth into books, and generally make a meal of what we learn. If we want to understand how the Earth Element feeds our minds we need do no more than draw on the parallels with our physical food. A good rich store of information and knowledge makes us feel secure and able to cope with all manner of situations. We file things away mentally for future use just as we store our excess fats and sugars for the future.

Everything we feel about our physical food applies to our mental food. If it is to our taste we take it in with relish. If it is not, it is much harder to digest and far less satisfying. Everyone will remember studying for the childhood exam in a detested subject and finding that no matter how hard they tried it would not go in any better than the green vegetables they were forced to eat when they were little. Yet when adults take up studies again in later life out of real pleasure and excitement they often discover abilities to digest information which they have never experienced before.

When the Earth Element is not in particularly good balance this whole process starts to come unstuck, and we use almost identical words to describe both the physical and mental effects of this. On a straightforward physical level we see abdominal distention, discomfort in the epigastric region, flatulence and the retention of food in the stomach. We can get the food inside us but from there it does not go any further. All that happens is the formation of an unpleasant brew which ferments in the stomach and causes pain and discomfort.

If the food is not being digested there is nothing to distribute and as a consequence there is very little energy in the system. Without stores of energy people cannot manage to live a full life and will always feel weak and lethargic. Sometimes this will involve the whole body, sometimes just the limbs. This is often the case, since the Official responsible for transporting food is himself too weak to distribute energy to the extremities. Without energy there is not only no movement but no heat. Some Earth imbalances manifest in cold feet and hands as there simply is not enough energy to reach and feed all the body.

When people talk about their indigestion they use words which apply as much to the mind as to the body. We find things churning around and not able to go down. We lose our appetite for things, and we feel too full and stuffed to take in anything else. Once our digestion starts to suffer we feel a sense of unease and discomfort on all levels of our body, mind and spirit. What is more, we often find that if we cannot digest food we cannot digest ideas, and the other way about. Someone whose mind is troubled by problems which they cannot solve is no more able to eat than someone with stomach pains is able to concentrate on their studies.

It is dangerous to associate specific body language and behavior with imbalances in Elements because many imbalances can create the same patterns of behavior. One pattern which we may come across frequently from an imbalanced Earth Element, however, is a rather blank and puzzled stare on the patient's face and a need to repeat information several times. When this happens it may be a very literal demonstration that nothing is going in because there is no flow of digestion. The patient cannot process anything, and in some cases is so full of undigested material nothing can get in at all, hence the blank stare. If it does go in it may not get much further, but sits heavily in the mind and churns around exactly as the food churns around the stomach without being digested. Patients suffering from worry and anxiety, which have their roots in an Earth imbalance, will often use these very words to describe what it feels like inside themselves.

In no other Element is the relationship between body, mind and spirit so clearly seen. When the Earth Element is out of balance we often see the extremes of physical size, the obese and the anorexic, as the process of harvesting goes badly awry. Some people harvest and harvest away until their stores overflow, and instead of muscle reserves they develop layer upon layer of fat. Others deny themselves a harvest. They leave the fruit ripening on the branch to fall and rot and instead start to use up what little reserve is left. In some cases this is a physical problem, but more often a problem of the emotions and the spirit.

A good harvest leaves us feeling secure and stable; we have the power to survive whatever is thrown at us, and we have no reason to worry or be anxious. If we cannot trust that harvest then we have every reason to worry. There can be no safety, no center like the home and hearth when we feel that we cannot draw on the support and abundance from the harvest. When this unrest starts people become obsessed with worry and anxiety about their security. There are enough harrowing images in the world's media today of people whose harvests are uncertain and we see in their eyes the worry and fear which arise from this.

Faced with this problem inside themselves some people eat to excess. We say that people eat for comfort and there is more truth in this than we sometimes realize. It is not the physical comfort which they seek but the emotional and spiritual comfort. There is no harvest in their emotions and spirit, and they desperately try to replace it with a harvest of the physical kind which they can find more easily. Other people have this barrenness within them to such a terrible extent that nothing excites their interest or appetite. Without an appetite for nourishment in their spirits or their emotions, there is no way that they can derive any pleasure from the thought of physical food alone. It will seem utterly futile to feed the body when they cannot feed the mind.

In order to understand fully the way that the Earth Element expresses itself in the body, mind and spirit we can do no better than return to the image of the mother. The essence of motherhood is to take care of the child, to feed, love and support it as it grows. This takes place on all levels and when the Earth Element is strong within the person, a good mother within, we should expect to see her well nourished on all levels. She takes in and stores food and distributes it to all parts of her body. In the same way she handles ideas. She also has the ability to take in nourishment for her spirit and her emotions. We describe people as well rounded, and this would fit well with our picture of someone in whom the Earth Element is in good balance.

Equally we should see from this person the quality of caring which comes from the mother. She should be able to feed others on every level as well as herself. When her friends need comfort and support she should be able to give it. Sympathy and compassion should come easily to her. We see this very often in little children. When the child has a good mother it knows that it can go to her when it is in distress. When one of its little friends is hurt or upset it naturally plays the role of mother and gives comfort and support.

When the child does not have a good mother, however, the situation is very different. When it does not get the attention it needs it becomes desperate. It craves just a little of the soothing touch and warmth that a mother gives. If it does not get anything it screams all the louder until it forces the mother to pay attention. Can we imagine how this will turn out if the mother never responds? The child will go through life screaming for attention, always looking for the support and nourishment that it never had from its mother. It will never be able to look after anyone else's needs if all its attention is focused on its own.

This is not always how matters turn out. The child may become barren inside. When it realizes that it will not get its mother's attention it may become bitter and hateful. "If nobody cares for me, I shall just take care of myself and the rest of you can leave me alone." It may not even care for itself either and carry around with it a terrible resentment for being deserted by its mother in this way. The beauty of these images is that in essence they are no different from the picture which we could put together about the lack of a physical harvest. What we gain from them, however, is a direct and simple picture of the kinds of behavior which are going to turn up when someone's Earth Element is badly out of balance.

To begin with there is the needy person who craves the missing harvest. This

The Earth Element

may manifest as obsessive eating, or in attention-seeking behavior. More often it shows in a desperate craving for sympathy. There are some people to whom we shall never be able to give too much sympathy. There comes a point for most people where enough is enough, but some have so little of the mother in them that they seek it at every turn. Every cut, sprain, ache and bruise is another opportunity for someone to sympathize, and if sympathy is not forthcoming they will find something else more deserving of our sympathy, something which we cannot ignore. Every gesture and every word says, "Please support and nourish me, make up for the missing harvest in me".

At the other extreme of imbalance we find people who really want nothing to do with sympathy of any kind. They function perfectly well in many ways and take extremely good care of themselves, but in the odd moments when they do run into trouble not only will they not call on any help and support from their mother, but they may brush it aside and reject it. Most people are only too glad to receive sympathy when the situation demands it, and we are all usually happy to give it. When someone rejects the sympathy we offer it can feel like a slap in the face.

An unhealthy Earth Element can also lose the appropriate balance of caring for self and caring for others which it controls. There are people who spend their whole time looking after others, to their own detriment. These are the nurse-figures who will go to any lengths to look after someone else's needs in spite of the harm it may be doing to their own health. The harvest is a wonderful time of year but Nature does not give us a harvest all the time. There has to be time to rest and recuperate and for the new crops to be planted and grown. When someone offers a harvest from themselves whatever the season, the crop will become weaker and weaker and the stores depleted. The person may literally fade away an exhausted martyr.

Another frequent manifestation of imbalance is for people to go to extremes in looking after themselves. This can range from an almost obsessive pandering to the details of physical appearance and clothing, to the other extreme of not caring how they look. Most of us will remember the fuss our mothers made when we were children to make sure that we were always clean and tidy when we went out. The same instinct lies in us as a part of this Element, and its strength or weakness can often be seen in the way in which people look after themselves.

4.7

In the previous volume of this series I talked about sympathy, the emotion associated with the Earth Element, as a balance of care and concern for self and others, and we can see that just by exaggerating the balance to either side, or by exaggerating one part of it, that all manner of recognizable behavior patterns can arise. Each will show that something is out of balance in the harvest that everyone needs to feed every other part of the system.

When we try to apply some of these ideas to how the Earth Element expresses itself in our spirit we are looking not so much at the nourishment and the harvest which the spirit needs as at the feelings which arise from the certainty of the harvest in us. This is not because the spirit does not need to be fed; the spirit needs to be fed more than any other part of us. When we touch the spirit of someone whose harvest has been good, however, what strikes us most of all is the security and stability which they radiate. Someone who is strong and certain in their spirit feels grounded and solid, as though their connection with mother Earth was more than just physical. This sense of equilibrium and centerdness is the essence of the Earth in our spirit. Through this we are in touch with the abundance and riches of the greater spirit of the One.

When we have this security from the Earth Element in our spirit it grounds the aspects of our spirit which come from the other Elements. We can even see that in the literal picture of the Earth itself. Our hopes and vision have a solid medium in which to grow, and our love and warmth are absorbed and retained by the soil. The vital essence and quality which come from the Metal Element and the reserves of the Water Element are gathered up in this base. In some parts of the Chinese tradition the Earth Element was placed in the center of the other four Elements rather than being an equal, and it is easy to understand how this version developed.

When the spirit of the Earth Element in us is harmed it is devastating to the spirit as a whole. Without a strong Earth Element the spirit is uprooted, unbalanced and unprotected. The love and protection which it gives to the other Elements is missing, and like any other family which loses its mother, everything is in distress. We lose our foundations and feel as though our spirits are not grounded. Someone who comes to us with an imbalanced Earth Element will show at all levels the agitation we see in the little child who has lost its mother. A greater distress is difficult to imagine.

The Earth Element

I shall discuss a little later the relationship of Element to Element, and the earth beneath our feet will be important in understanding how all the Elements belong together. When we look at people around us, however, be they patient, friend, or passer-by, we should remember that the earth is as diverse as the people on it. We talk sometimes of the particular relationship of the Wood and Earth as of that between a tree and the soil, but whereas we allow for the possibility of hundreds of different types of tree, we tend to think of only one type of soil.

The narrowness of our awareness is due to the dullness of our senses. When we look closely at Nature we shall see soil that grows one crop but is useless for another, soil that is rich and loamy, soil that is dry and sandy, and all of the other kinds which abound in Nature. When we try to understand the spirit of someone we have to begin to understand the Earth Element in them in terms of the kind of soil which they represent, just as the farmer has to appreciate the different soils to have any hope of raising successful crops. Only then will we have a clear idea of the foundation upon which and in which all of the other aspects of the spirit thrive and prosper.

CHAPTER FIVE

THE METAL ELEMENT

The Metal Element, like the season of autumn with which it is associated, shows the cycle of energy turning full circle as it begins to decline and fall. After the seasons of growth, maturity and harvest, the leaves on the trees and plants fall and die. The air becomes heavy with mist and rain and the withered foliage rots on the ground. This process has not one, but two aspects, however; the rotting and decomposition not only makes way for the new growth in the following spring but pours essential nutrients back into the soil. The decomposing leaves serve as a rich basis for the new plant life of the next year.

At a superficial level we often tend to contrast the dying of plants in autumn with their growth in spring and see nothing else in the autumnal part of the cycle. The lesson of Nature, however, is that death and dying is of no value if the essence distilled from the remains of the plants does not find its way back into the soil. The earth is only fertile to a degree and cannot by itself support life indefinitely. Before long it becomes barren and sterile unless it recovers the trace elements and minerals which were taken up by last year's growth and now fall back to earth as the plants decompose. The rain which cleanses and purifies the trees and plants by washing away the dead growth of last year carries these precious minerals back into the soil, and together they form the foundation of vigorous growth in the following spring.

When we look at how the Metal Element expresses itself in man and woman we see the same process at work, letting go of the old and taking in the new. The two Officials of the Metal Element, the Lungs and the Large Intestine, are responsible for this natural flow within us. The Large Intestine disposes of and casts away all the waste and rubbish within us. This is not just the physical rubbish, the waste products of our food and body functions, but also our mental and spiritual waste. Once we have enjoyed the harvest in body, mind and spirit, we let go of the remains to make room for new growth. The Lungs, on the other hand, are responsible for taking in new things. On a physical level this is simply the air that we breathe, but we need this function just as much on other levels: to take in new ideas for the mind and new life for the spirit. The word 'inspiration' captures this wider sense of the Lung's function.

The vital aspect of this natural flow, then, is the essence and quality which is brought into our lives by the Metal Element. On a simple physical level we can see this in our breathing. The lungs are described in the Nei Jing as the 'receivers of pure Qi energy from the heavens', and it is from the air that we breathe that we take in the pure Qi energy without which we cannot live. Just as plants need nourishment from the trace elements as well as nourishment from the earth itself, so we need the Qi energy from the air to mix with the Qi from our stomachs in order to nourish ourselves fully. Without the air that we breathe our other food would be useless.

The Metal Element adds the same vital quality to the food for our minds and spirits. Many forms of meditation in China and elsewhere in the Far East understand and use the principles of breathing exercises to enhance the mind and spirit directly. This is captured in the imagery which the Chinese associated with the Metal Element. For just as they saw the Earth Element as the Mother, both for us and within us, they saw in the role of the Metal Element a natural association with the Father, the giver of pure essence in body, mind and spirit from the heavens above.

We do not, however, have to conjure up an image of God the Father, the Lord Buddha or another deity any more than we need summon up an image of female goddesses when we describe the earth as our mother. The heart of the association is the connection between heaven and earth, the fusion of the different forms of Qi out of which the dynamic unity of life arises and is sustained. In man and woman the Chinese saw a literal manifestation of the connection between heaven and earth. The pictures of the Father and Mother serve to help us to understand the depth of this connection in the Nature of which we are a part.

This relationship of Father and Mother, Heaven and Earth, is one which we touched on earlier when we looked at the core and essence of each Element, not just its surface appearance but its inner qualities. The Metal Element represents the special core, the divine spark which fires the whole process and whose pure and refined essence enhances the body, mind and spirit. Indeed, the word 'quality' itself, not as an abstract noun but as the adjective by which we describe things being 'of real quality', is one which we could easily use to describe the part which the Metal Element plays in all of the processes and functions of body, mind and spirit. Every Element is qualitatively enriched in its own Nature by the Metal Element. This divine fire is with us at all times, and is the fire which lights the spirit even when we are in the darkest times. If we need to have a picture of this, then it is like the molten core of the earth, the metals and minerals whose incandescent fires lie beneath and within the earth.

The idea at the center of an understanding of the Element, therefore, is the connection with the Heavens and the Heavenly Father. Someone who has this connection, whatever they may call their God or gods, will be strong in spirit because they will both receive and display the qualities which are embodied in the idea of the Father, whether this be a natural father or the father of our intellect, faith, or calling. We look upon the father as a figure of authority, as a source of wisdom and, most importantly, as a guide. A father is someone whom we trust and whose advice we gladly follow. Someone in whom the Metal Element is strong will manifest all of these qualities.

A word which we associate with these attributes and which attaches naturally to the Metal Element is respect. Respect is one of the most important notions attached to the idea of the father in almost every culture. 'Honor thy father' comes from Christianity but is echoed in every other religion. A person who has this connection with the Father will be both respectful themselves and able to command respect. If we each look to our own experience I have no doubt that many of us will be able to recall meeting spiritual teachers in whom this connection was strong. Not only have they projected a powerful sense of respect for people and Nature around them, but through this they have been deserving in return of an equal respect.

'Respect' is a word which we should apply just as readily to our attitude about ourselves as to others. When we consider the inestimable value of the divine spark which arises from a balanced Metal Element within us, we can see that it too should command our own respect. When we can feel this spark alive and vital in our spirit we know that we have a value and a worth in ourselves, and from this our sense of self-esteem and self-respect will be strong. The Metal Element gives to our lives a sense of quality. It may not change what we do or who we are, but it gives it a special significance by virtue of the ability we then have to see and feel the connections with the universe around us and our own place within it. It helps us to develop our ability to be true to our own essence by showing us what that essence is.

What applies at the level of the spirit applies equally to the expression of the Metal Element in our minds and bodies. When we are able to make judgments of value and worth, to recognize the quality of our decisions and plans, we can respect and honor what we take into our mind and body and how we maintain it. Our self-esteem resides not just in taking care of ourselves and nourishing ourselves but in making ourselves become the best we possibly can. When talking about it in this way words like 'best' and 'special' crop up again and again.

It is fascinating to see how many of the qualities and words which we use to describe the Metal Element are intrinsically linked to the value we place on the precious metals which we find within the earth. We even use precious stones and metals to confirm our feelings of someone's value by giving them as medals and as tokens of respect. This connection is as old an idea as the earliest Chinese texts, and should again remind us that we are not inventing the ideas, only allowing ourselves to see what has been there all along.

As well as talking about respect and value, however, we must not forget that the other aspect of the Metal Element is just as significant. The autumn is as important for letting go the dying remains of the year as it is for recycling the quality and essence of the minerals which have made growth possible. We have to be able to let go once the harvest has been gathered or we shall never be able to have a spring and harvest next year. Our ideas, our emotions, our food, even the stages in the growth of our spirit, all have their hour and then have no more to offer. Once they are finished we have to be able to let go and move on.

When the Metal Element within us is weak, however, we are sometimes not able to let go at the appropriate time. This can affect us on every level: our physical digestion, our ideas and our spirit. We may either begin to throw things out too soon or hang on to them long after we should have thrown them away. The diarrhea and constipation which afflict our physical bodies have their counterparts in the mind and spirit. We sometimes cast aside things of value before their time or we become blocked by poisons which we cannot release.

Where we can see this most clearly is in the emotion of grief which corresponds to the Metal Element. Again, knowing the word is less important than understanding the process, the letting go of what is past. When someone or something is lost we have every right to grieve, to feel sad and to miss them. This may be very intense for weeks or even months but as time passes the loss wears off and we can begin to reconstruct our lives. The season of autumn often instills in us a sense of melancholy, but by letting go of the past each year Nature signals the start of a new growing cycle and we naturally cast aside our sense of loss in order to move on towards the future.

When someone loses the ability to accept loss in an appropriate way because of an imbalance in the Metal Element they may well show a total disregard for loss and death. More often, however, they may feel such an overwhelming sense of regret that it drags on for years. It is not uncommon to meet people whose lives are still blighted by the death of someone close to them many, many years ago. It may not even need to be a death which triggers this response. If someone really cannot let go then the loss of anything will be a body blow, however unimportant it may seem to us. Instead of meeting life face on such people may be heading through life facing backwards, always full of regret and wishing that things were still as they had been, or thinking that things might have turned out better, "if only this or that had happened instead".

Looking at grief in this way will show us many concrete examples of not letting go or letting go too quickly. To see the real essence of grief, however, we do not need to look at lives which are affected by fortuitous loss, or the chance and circumstance which shape our daily existence. Even were someone never to lose anything close to him or her, be it a person or a possession, he or she could still be racked with a grief so powerful that their spirit was dying inside. All we have to do to understand this is to imagine what it would be like to be cut off from the connection with the Heavenly Father, and to have none of that divine spark within ourselves. This is a source of a grief far worse than any chance event which life can bring us. When someone dies it leaves an empty space in our lives, but this is nothing compared to the emptiness inside which comes from the absence of this spark. Here lies the root of a real coldness, not just a lack of warmth but an empty, cold void, a chasm which there is no hope of filling. Without this connection there is no guidance and direction from the Father, and nothing of any quality in anything that he or she does.

Faced with such an emptiness many people turn to desperate searches to fill the void. It is not unusual to see someone with an imbalanced Metal Element chasing from guru to guru, following spiritual trails which take them around the world and back, always searching for the essence that is missing inside them.

Each new trail will produce a new guide and a new authority, but none of these can make good what is lacking inside. People can become quite fanatical or even obsessive about some of these quests in their attempts to be filled by what they seek, but the void in their spirit will never be totally satisfied by what they find. It is never a surprise to find that with these imbalances many may shortly afterwards become just as fanatical about something or someone else.

To some the futility of this quest becomes apparent, but then they are confronted with the emptiness inside. Can anyone who does not know from the inside imagine what depths of resignation this causes, the feeling of being irrevocably cut off from any guidance and direction from above? The feeling of utter desolation and of being lost is at the heart of the grief which comes from the Metal Element, a terrible anguish over an emptiness that they feel will always exist within and will never be filled.

The connection with the divine spark within us also feeds our own self-respect and self-esteem. Without it we cannot have a real sense of value, either of ourselves or of the people around us. Without self-respect we may lose all sense of care for ourselves because nothing really matters. There are people who devalue everything that they do, and are forever negative about themselves. Without a sense of self-respect and self-esteem they conclude that they are no good and useless, and no amount of trying to convince them will change their minds because they are only too aware of the void inside themselves which they think we cannot see. A loss of self-respect can even appear at a very basic level. Some of the people in whom the Metal Element is out of balance rank as the scruffiest and most unwashed people we shall ever see.

At the other extreme, however, a Metal imbalance can produce some of the most scrupulously tidy and precisely neat people. We always have to remember that imbalance may lead to exaggeration on either side of the appropriate level. Inside some people there may be terrible emptiness, or worse still the squalor of uncleared rubbish, yet they may try to compensate for this with the most immaculate facade. This cover-up, the thin veneer which conceals the feelings of worthlessness or self-disgust inside, often extends into the material trappings of their lives. They may seek material wealth, even the ostentatious display of gold, silver and precious stones, to bolster up the sense of self-esteem on the outside and conceal the void inside.

The same attention to precision and purity can manifest in the mind and the spirit as well as in the physical appearance. When someone cannot find the real source of perfection within they may try to absorb it from the mental and spiritual clothing they wear. A meticulous and fastidious attention to detail

The Metal Element

may attach to everything that they do, almost as though they were trying to recreate the purity of the essence which they lack within by the subtle brilliance of outward appearances. Again we have in our language an enormous number of metaphors for this kind of precision which draw on the properties of the physical metals, pictures of untarnished, sharp and clinical instruments whose glint and shine reflect the purity and precision of their purpose.

The language which we associate with the physical metals describes just as well the qualities which come from the Metal Element in people. To understand this we need only think of the way that we describe the reaction of metals to heat. The right amount of heat renders it workable, able to be shaped and used. It has strength and yet can bend if that is what is needed. If we apply too much heat it melts and loses its form, and eventually burns and oxidizes to ash. If it does not contain enough heat, however, it remains cold, inert and unyielding. When we try to work it we find it hard but brittle, too rigid and inflexible for our needs. Under pressure it no longer bends but shatters into fragments. In this day and age it is the absence of the divine spark which is most frequent, and the patient in whom this inner fire does not glow often appears exactly the same as the physical Element, cold, rigid, inert and brittle.

With the other Elements I have mentioned some of the physical problems which commonly arise from their imbalance. In the case of the Metal Element a great many of these relate directly to the functions of the Officials, the Lung and Large Intestine. As well as reflecting the weakness in their own functions it often shows how the failure to remove poisons or the failure to take in goodness from the air directly affects other physical processes. I will cover these in greater detail in a later chapter.

Imbalances in the Element often affect the skin. The skin was seen as a part of the Metal Element, partly because it shared with the Lung the body's only direct contact with the outside air and partly because it shares the same functions as the other two officials by eliminating toxins in the sweat and in some senses 'breathing'. It is often referred to as the 'third lung' for this similarity. In the broader tradition of Oriental medicine the Lung and the skin are also seen as a combined unit of defensive protection for the body.

When the Metal Element is not in balance we very often find a history of skin trouble, ranging from dermatitis, acne, eczema and psoriasis, to rashes, spots and boils. The importance of this is not in the precise etiology of each complaint as much as in the fact that each represents a loss of quality in the skin. We even remark on whether someone has good skin or bad skin without referring to any particular diseases or infections. What strikes our attention is the fact that the skin may be physically unremarkable but is lacking that essential quality which gives it a healthy bloom.

This is a difficult idea to explain clearly at this level of generality, but the same will apply in diagnostic terms to many of the parts and functions of the body when the Metal Element is out of balance. Everything may function adequately, but lack that special quality which enables it to reach its own potential for optimum health. The word 'lackluster', when applied to physical metals, captures this sense of a dull presence which shows no sign of the fire within. In a much more sad way this often applies to the person at the level of the spirit. The feeling of emptiness inside is one that we may often recognize in people. On the surface we see perfectly competent human beings, but in some ways they look rather like a shell, as though they were mechanically performing tasks without being fully engaged in what they do. This is very often how we see people when they are first stricken by grief. They cling to a routine in order to get by and we see them do normal, everyday things as efficiently as they could wish, but they are not really present in what they do.

The real evidence of this often lies in the eyes. Someone with a Metal imbalance may have the same hollow and empty eyes as the person whose grief is overwhelming. The eyes also tell us about the devastation that this imbalance causes by where they are focused. Many times we shall see the eyes always cast down to the floor in the way that we sometimes see tramps and derelicts gazing down as they shuffle along the pavement, and at other times we see eyes that are fixed and staring slightly upwards, forever looking heavenwards for the connection to some greater purpose and with their focus beyond or through the things and people immediately around them.

We have already seen in the Wood, Fire and Earth Elements the gifts of growth, love and nourishment and how these are affected by imbalance. The Metal Element gives us the spark of quality, the essence which comes from a connection with the Heavenly Father, and when it is in imbalance we shall find at this very deep level a call from some patients for all those special qualities which we associate with the father, especially for guidance and for respect. We may get a sense that they want to be taken in hand and shown the way, exactly as the child puts its hand into the hand of its father and allows itself to be led.

They need direction and a connection with the wisdom of the Father. This may not be immediately evident from how they present themselves, for they may be as cut off from us as they are from the essence in themselves, but if we can reach them in their emptiness and grief this is what we shall find.

CHAPTER SIX

THE WATER ELEMENT

The Water Element is the most elusive and impenetrable of the Elements within us. This quality is apparent if we consider the season of winter associated with the Water Element. Winter is a time of rest, a time to protect the reserves gathered in the harvest and, at the same time, to draw on those reserves to prepare for the growth of the following spring. On the surface, however, there is no sign of all this patient and stealthy work. The trees and plants stripped bare of their leaves stand stark and still in the winter landscape, and under the thick falls of rain and snow the gradual and inexorable movement of this process lies hidden from view.

Water itself is naturally elusive and resists definition. It can hold any shape, and yet cannot itself be grasped and held once and for all. It appears to have boundaries, and yet will find a passage around any dam or obstruction wherever it can. Despite this, however, it forms the greater proportion of the solid structure of all living things on the surface of the earth, and without water nothing could live or grow. There would be no movement and flow, no change and transformation.

We tend to underestimate the importance of the Water Element, exactly as we in the West tend to take for granted the physical substance water which is all around us. In Great Britain, for example, water has always been plentiful. We have always had adequate reserves and stores. In recent years, however, the climate has been far less predictable. There have been two or three unusually hot, dry spells, and people have been on the verge of being deprived of their water supply. Suddenly that certainty, that absolute assurance that we can have water literally on tap, has been taken away, and people have become apprehensive and fearful. For some people it is almost too enormous a prospect to take in, the unthinkable prospect that they cannot do something as simple as drinking, preparing food, or washing.

Those who have been affected by recent droughts, or have been in droughts before, will understand better than by reading a million words how vital the Water Element is to our body, mind and spirit. The lakes and reservoirs which we maintain today are no different from the pools and ponds which farmers have kept for millennia, and all for the same reason. Unless we build up and maintain our stores and reserves in the winter there can be no growth in the spring and summer, and then no harvest. This brings anxiety not just over whether we have a good harvest or a poor harvest. This is the worst prospect of all, no harvest of any kind.

When we experience feelings like this we may begin to understand the emotion of fear which is associated with the Water Element in the tables of correspondences. People can be frightened of many things and for many reasons, but there are some situations which we might describe as 'everyone's worst fear', things such as drought, war, earthquake, or, in this modern age, global warming. These are all things that are so enormous in their consequences that it is impossible to imagine what they could or would be like, and even more difficult to imagine what kind of future would emerge from them. These fears, the terrors of an unknown future, are characteristic of the fear which arises from an imbalanced Water Element for their 'unthinkable' quality, and each of us has our own inner equivalents of the droughts and wars, things which we dare not even imagine.

In order to understand better how this fear gains such power we have to look more closely at how the Water Element manifests in the body, mind and spirit. The image of the farmer with his reservoirs and irrigation systems is more typically Eastern than Western, but it is not a difficult picture to comprehend. In the rainy season there is abundant water and the prudent farmer saves and stores what he can. As the year unfolds this water becomes a lifeline for his family and his crops. It is used to nourish and to cleanse both farm and family, and if the supply is adequate it will do so for all the year, even under the greatest heat of the sun.

If the rainy season is poor, however, or the farmer does not bother to gather and conserve enough water, the dry season will bring disaster. There is not enough to fulfill all his needs, and some crops will have to perish in the heat since he cannot get more water until the rains come again. Once his ditches and irrigation system fall out of use the channels fill with rubbish, and without a flow of water this pollution and filth stays where it falls. Unless he attends to this, his next year will be just as bad, for even with a good supply and reserve he will not prosper. Either it will not get through, or worse still, it will bring all the rubbish and filth with it to pollute his drinking supply and kill his crops.

The Water Element

The point of this extended analogy is that the Water Element plays just as important a role within the body, mind spirit. We are in many ways nothing but a water store, a large skin-covered container three quarters full of fluid. Our cells are full of fluid, and our whole blood system is largely water. The fluid within us, especially the blood and lymphatic systems, carries nutrients, oxygen and hormones, everything which we need to fuel our growth and provide us with protection in all parts of our bodies. It also carries away all the waste products, and through the work of its two Officials, the Bladder and the Kidney, filters out and removes impurities for us. More than just feeding and cleaning us, however, it keeps us flexible and fluid. We depend on the secretions and fluids throughout our bodies to be able to move with ease. Every joint of our physical structure, every moving part and every process, can only function when it is lubricated by the secretions within us.

When the Element is out of balance, therefore, it affects every single cell in the body. If there is physical excess of water, which may arise from both a state of excess or deficiency in the Water Element in the body, we become swollen and edematous. When there is insufficient water the Fire within us, our body heat, may run out of control and produce dryness and withering. Water also oils the body and keeps its movement smooth and flowing with the synovial fluids and joint capsules. Without this lubrication our joints seize up, and we develop arthritic conditions and stiffness of movement, especially in the back and the limbs where we need to be most flexible.

The strength of the Water Element resides as much in the force of its flow as in its quantity. If the flow is too weak it cannot cleanse us, nor does it have the power to cleanse itself. If it cannot pass through the body tissue it will not carry away the impurities which are spread throughout the whole system. Most of us will be familiar with images of suffering kidney patients hooked up for hours at a time to the massive dialysis machines performing the function which the Water Element can no longer carry out in them. A poor flow like this may allow impurities to gather which may also give us a legacy of gout, stones in the kidney and gall bladder, and a general silting up of all our inner channels.

These physical problems find their parallel within the mind and spirit where we need the cleansing flow of fluid as much as in the body. The rainy months of winter are a time of true cleansing within nature as the abundant flow washes away the debris of last year to prepare for the new year. The same process happens within us. There is a great deal to be left behind each year, and if the flow within us is weak we become stuck and fixed, unable to clean out and dispose of old ideas and dreams. Like the brackish streams which we see around us in Nature the mind becomes stagnant and sluggish.

The spirit, too, falters with the rubbish that begins to clog and stifle it. There has never been a time in history when the purity and strength of the spirit has not been under threat and challenge from the darker sides of human nature. Even though we ourselves might try to lead blameless lives we can easily be harmed by the very presence of the baser spirits in our midst. We need the power of the Water Element's flow of water within our spirit to wash away the pollution which can affect the very core of our being. Many religions use the physical act of baptism with holy water as a token of this cleansing of the spirit of any impurity and filth, often performing it in sacred rivers which unite the spirit of the individual with the spirit of Nature.

The reserves which come from the Water Element, the strength to survive through each year and from year to year, are just as important. Without reserves our spirit goes the way of our physical body, shrivelling up and dying away with no will to survive. A person in whom the Water Element has long been out of balance at the level of the spirit may be literally burnt out, their reserves so depleted that they can not recover without resurrecting the spirit.

These three aspects of Water, the reserves, the flow, and the cleansing power of Water's movement, underlie any understanding of the correspondences of the Element. When the Water within us is threatened or out of balance, the natural and steady flow of secretions goes to pieces and we see some of the physical problems which we have come to associate with fear, the emotion of Water. The mouth begins to dry up as the secretions stop, and immediately someone cannot speak. He or she may break out into a cold sweat as the water breaks free of the body, or he or she may even lose control of his or her bladder as the water flows away in fright. These are extreme examples of disturbance in the Water Element, but there are many similar and less dramatic degrees of the same problem. The steady rhythm and flow of perspiration and urination are often affected.

The mind can suffer similar problems when we experience fear. If someone's mental flow is also disrupted, he or she may either babble with nerves or become frozen and rigid in mind, unable to think just as he or she may be unable to talk. The whole system stops dead. When we remember that the fluid in us

The Water Element

is in every single cell and vital to every single function it is not surprising that the fear which an imbalance in our own water provokes is so total. The feeling that this may dry up or run away is overwhelming and unthinkable, a sign of the end of life itself.

When someone with a Water imbalance is ruled by fears as great as these, he or she will have to hold on as tightly as he or she can to keep the fear in check in order just to get on with everyday life. The constant flow of adrenaline which tenses everything up to be ready for action will cause some to dash about in a panic trying to avoid what they fear. Others will do what many of us do when we are terrified, distracting themselves as best they can from having to confront the terrifying visions of the future which they have.

We may well find that these reactions are unconsciously reflected in the look in the eyes of people with imbalances in the Water Element. Some have eyes which dart this way and that, like animals looking desperately for a way out of danger. Others have a blank and unfathomable gaze coming from deeply within themselves, so much are they hiding on the inside where they try to stay safe and ignore the danger because the enormity of the situation is too huge to encompass. This is just as real a show of fear as the wide-eyed stare with enlarged pupils, or the darting glances, which we normally associate with fear when our 'fight or flight' reactions are at their peak. On a conscious level people may literally tell us, "I can't bring myself to think about the future, can't even get my mind to picture it".

Sometimes people can become so adept at hiding from these unthinkable fears that they become in turn immune to the ordinary dangers which the world offers, what we call 'lack of fear', and as important as the 'fear' which we associate with the Element. If someone can hold his or her inner terrors in check by not confronting them and has done so for years, what possible danger can hang-gliding or parachuting pose? They merely rank as one more thing to keep at bay and are no better or worse than any other terror. Foolishly dangerous sports and pastimes may be the only way to find any real exhilaration and generate the kind of adrenaline flow which we all seek from time to time.

There is, however, a deeper aspect of the Water Element within us. The winter season is a struggle for survival for the plants and animals living through the resting period of the year. To exist through the cold, dark months on the reserves gathered in the autumn takes will and determination, a powerful resolve to carry on through hardship. The essence of Water is embodied in this indomitable strength, and if our images of water itself do conjure up this quality we should perhaps remember the relentless force of the oceans pounding away at the cliffs, eating them away inch by inch for thousands of years, patiently wearing down any resistance.

We often tax our reserves, for fun in sporting events, of what we call endurance and stamina, but beneath their apparent frivolity is an important aspect of our own survival. Without this power to draw on our reserves of strength we would not have survived from generation to generation, and would not sow the seeds of future generations to come. Even after the worst disasters which Nature can sometimes throw at us, the earthquakes, the hurricanes and the droughts, people still find the inner stamina and endurance to pick up the pieces and re-build their lives.

Physical strength alone is not enough, however, and there is often evidence of this in the pictures we see of disasters. There will be strong men and women reduced to immobile statues in the face of the terror, their features stony and their eyes blank with fear and shock, while around them struggle the young and the weak, who are driven by the inner reserves of their spirit to carry on when their stronger relatives have given up. The body, mind and spirit are a unity, and without the reserves of the spirit the bodily reserves are only of limited use.

This will and determination of the spirit is one of the most wonderful expressions of the Element within us. The path to enlightenment and truth in our spirits, to understanding and knowledge in our minds, and to health and well-being in our bodies, will not always be easy and straightforward. If we were not blessed with this inner reserve we might capitulate at the first sign of hardship and lose all hope of achieving our own potential.

Like all gifts which we take for granted we can easily abuse them. Some people use their reserves without regard for the future in the same way that people will always waste water during a drought. If we are in good health we can afford to tax our reserves a little. Young people, for example, are blessed with energy enough to stay up all night if need be, and business people can sometimes take work home for a short while and work into the early hours to clinch that important deal. Nature, too, has its long summer days and brief warm nights when everything is coming to maturity. There comes a time, however, when the shortage has to be made good. If the pressure on our reserves carries on and on we begin to suffer.

There used to be a certain foolish mystique in the idea of 'living fast and dying young', but few people who used these silly words realized their literal truth. Small wonder that the results of abuse like this appear in later life as total and utter exhaustion on all levels. Like every other blessing which we are given we have to use the power of will and endurance to its appropriate extent, and will pay the penalty if we do not allow ourselves an inner winter to rest and to rebuild our reserves.

When this terrible depletion occurs, whether it be from our own foolishness or from weakness and imbalance in the Water Element, it is going to be the source of the worst fear imaginable. Without reserves there can be no future and the end may come at any moment and without warning. Our hearts always go out to those poor souls who walk around with a cardiac problem for which there is no cure and who might die at any moment, yet there are millions more whose life is just as badly blighted and do not have a medical name for what has happened. Once the spirit is so run down that it is as good as dead, it does not matter that the physical body and the mind carry on. The person is as good as dead already, and once a part of the body, mind, spirit has fallen, the other two cannot be far behind.

When we were children and our dreams frightened us our moms and dads gave us reassurance, not just by holding us but by turning on the lights and telling us, "See, there is nothing behind the cupboard door". When we grow up we still seek the same reassurance, for someone to tell us that it will be all right and that there is nothing to worry about. When we are afraid we may need to have all the facts and the pictures, to be literally shown the evidence, whether this be X-rays, or records, or textbooks. It becomes vitally important to know that there is an answer which we can see.

When we treat patients with Water imbalances they are likely to be the ones who constantly seek reassurance that they will get better, that we have seen other people with the same problems get over them. However often we do this, they will carry on asking every time they come to see us. We have to remember what it was like as little children, for sometimes, even after we were told there was nothing behind the door, we still kept on believing this for night after night until the dream lost its power. For someone in whom fear is a constant presence there is never reassurance enough to dispel the power of their imaginings, especially if the fear is within the spirit. The reassurance of words alone will not reach this far.

When we look at the Water Element, therefore, the miracle of survival through the winter months, and all the qualities which this needs, should be foremost in our minds. When we recognize these we shall be able to see in our patients how well their reserves have been tended.

THE FIVE ELEMENTS

Now that we have looked at the five Elements in what may seem a fairly abstract way, some readers may be tempted to contrast this approach with the more academic and analytical systems favored by many students of Oriental medicine. We must never lose sight of the fact, however, that every single one of us alive on the earth needs the powers of growth, love, nourishment, guidance and reserves. These qualities, broad as they seem and difficult as they are to grasp in abstract form, underlie all the manifestations of the Elements in the body, mind and spirit in us, and are the ultimate key to understanding Nature around us.

Every single patient whom we treat with this system of medicine will have a major weakness in one of the Elements which will stand out above all else. This will be just as obvious and just as destructive as a missing season in the annual cycle. If there were no summer, for example, we would all long for the heat of the sun and take any and every opportunity to gather its warmth. A person missing the inner sun of the Fire Element will be just the same, looking for the missing warmth and love. Nature is a process, however, and where one is weak all are affected. We now need to deepen our understanding by looking at the relationship of the Elements in order to understand how the vast complexity of our individual lives is formed by their subtle interplay.

CHAPTER SEVEN

THE RELATIONSHIP OF THE ELEMENTS

The previous chapters have dealt with the meaning of the Elements and the beauty and the wisdom which we can uncover within Nature by observing its inner essence. In order to make matters easier, however, I have talked about the Elements as separate and distinct phases without addressing the vital relationships between them. It is to these relationships that we must now turn because in reality Qi energy and the Dao are nothing but the unity of all the Elements.

There are two very important aspects of this unity. The first is to be seen in the sequence of the seasons, the peaks and troughs of energy throughout the year which mirror the qualities of movement within the Elements and Qi energy itself. If any one of the seasons is either too dominant or too weak, the whole annual cycle will be affected as a result. The Elements are interdependent. Where one is too weak, others may run out of control or be weakened in turn. Where one is too strong, others may be weakened.

The second important aspect of the unity of the Elements is that of the infinite variations which are possible even within each single Element. We often speak of the Earth Element, for example, as our mother or as the ground beneath our feet, and the qualities which we associate with both can be just the same as those that are found in the Earth Element in people. There are, however, a thousand types of earth and a thousand types of mothers. The essential qualities which they share are close enough and bear enough of a 'family resemblance' for us to recognize the spirit of the Earth Element in each one, but there are also a vast number of subtle differences. This diversity is both one of the most wonderful gifts of Nature and at the same time a challenge for our understanding.

We talk, for example, about the Earth but are we remembering the rich, dark and loamy soil of the lush arable belt, or the dry, sandy and sparse topsoil of the desert fringes? Is the Fire which we see in our mind's eye the dry, crackling blaze of dead timber or the damp glow of the smoldering peat? Is the Water which we hear the silvery trickle of an upland stream or the pounding rage of an ocean tide? Each of the Elements expresses itself in a vast array of possible forms which vary not only in scale but also in quality.

Classical Five-Element Acupuncture

When we examine these qualities we begin to see how they arise not just from the external relationship of interdependence between the Elements but from an internal relationship between Element and Element. Each Element is said to 'contain' the five Elements within it. This idea, that there are 'Elements within Elements', is sometimes difficult to make sense of as an abstract theoretical notion, but we shall find that it is one which follows our common sense observations and judgments with ease.

These relationships, between Element and Element and of Element within Element, are both essential when we apply an understanding of the five Elements to Traditional Diagnosis. The Causative Factor, the Element that is the true cause of the overall imbalance, may produce utter chaos in the whole system of energy, so much so that without our ability to use and rely on our senses we would never be able to discover the source or cause of the overall chaos and distress. Once our natural faculties have played their part in identifying the Causative Factor, we may then begin to understand the pattern which exists in this apparent chaos, by tracing how the Causative Factor has affected every other part of the system through the relationship of Element to Element.

We then have to look at the Elements within the Causative Factor to understand how one person with an Earth Causative Factor is so very different from another person with an Earth Causative Factor. This is not just a question of the scale or degree of imbalance; it concerns the quality of imbalance. If the problem were only one of scale we should see the same effects from this imbalance in everyone else to a greater or lesser extent, or be able to trace external factors in their environment and relationships which clearly made the difference in quantity. Once we acknowledge that there is a real qualitative difference, however, we need to find the patterns in Nature which reveal to us how the unique quality of each imbalance can arise.

THE SHENG CYCLE

This cycle, the cycle of creation and nourishment, is fundamental in the relationship of Element to Element. When this cycle is represented in diagrammatic form the Elements are shown in the shape of equal sized circles, one for each Element, with the circles themselves arranged at equal intervals in the pattern of a larger circle. The line which forms the circumference of the

The Relationship of the Elements

larger circle joins Element to Element, and very often the line has little arrows on it to indicate clockwise movement.

I have described the diagram here because to write out what we normally see may remind us of the wealth of 'obvious' information which the diagram contains. None of the Elements is shown larger than the rest, since no Element is more or less important than any other. They also occupy the same 'amount' or 'slice' of the circle, which in turn should remind us that each has an equal share and space in the cycle of energy flow. Thus a simple diagram can dispel straight away any illusion that one may be more important than the others.

The diagram also shows something of equal importance, that there is a natural order and progression of energy flow as it is represented in the Elements, and that this flow has no beginning and no end. It is exactly as we have described the seasons following on from each other. Spring always naturally follows winter, and the reverse can never be true. It would be an offense against Nature for this to happen, and for this very reason we often refer to some of these simple descriptions as 'Laws of Nature'.

The Sheng Cycle is not just a description of flow and movement; it is a cycle of creation and nourishment. The Elements do not just appear as if by magic, any more than each season automatically bursts into life no matter what has just happened. In this special relationship between succeeding Elements each one not only follows but depends for its very existence on its predecessor for its birth and its nourishment.

We may take as an example of this the relationship between Wood and Fire. I could use the simplest picture of all and say that without Wood, the physical wood which we see around us, we could not have Fire. Either we burn the fresh timber which falls to the ground or which we have cut, or we burn the remains of timber in deposits of oil, gas and coal which have been compressed for millions of years. Wood is our most plentiful source of Fire, and in this literal sense Wood nourishes Fire. Once we have started a blaze we pile on more wood, coal, oil, or gas, and we feed the flames.

Wood, however, not only nourishes the Fire but also creates it. When the word 'creates' is used here it does not mean 'creates from nothing' as we might expect from our popular understanding. Without an initial spark of Fire there would be no blaze, no matter how much wood we piled on the grate. In just the same way spring does not create summer from nothing, but without a spring the dormant spark of the potential Fire of summer can never be realized and grow.

This has to be so if we reflect on the nature of the Elements. There cannot be a single Element which creates another from nothing, or we would have a hierarchy, and a whole pattern of causality which has no place in this pattern of Oriental thought. If the spring is weak and poor, it does not mean that the summer can altogether be missing, just that the summer is never really born and welcomed into life, 're-created' by the spring. We recognize this naturally when we speak of a nondescript season having 'never really happened.'

People may wonder how this is of diagnostic value, but in the simplicity of the picture lies one of the most profound laws of Oriental medicine. If we do not have enough Wood, then the Fire cannot be created or nourished. The two Elements stand in relation to each other as does a mother to her child. Without the mother the child cannot be born or nourished and kept alive. If the mother is weak then the child will immediately fall sick because it does not get the proper attention and nourishment which it needs.

If we look at the seasons we can see how this simple truth is realized. If the spring brings no growth and development there cannot be a good crop maturing in the summer months. If the heat of summer is not enough to ripen the crops the harvest of late summer will be weak and poor. If the harvest is poor, the autumn is barren and empty, with no rich leaf-fall underfoot. Without this autumn fall enriching the seeds and the soil there will be no gathering of reserves to endure the winter, and a poor winter with no inner reserves cannot nourish the seeds of spring.

If any one of the seasons is out of balance the Law of Mother/Child (as we describe this Sheng Cycle relationship) shows us that we can expect that all of the seasons, especially the following one, will be affected in turn. When we apply this wisdom to our patients we shall find that the same law applies. If there is an imbalance in the Wood Element within someone the Fire Element within him or her must also be affected. The Qi energy flows through the cycle of Elements in them just as clearly as it flows through the cycle of the seasons in Nature. If through this Wood imbalance the Fire Element is affected then the Earth Element which follows it will be affected in turn, and each Element to a lesser degree.

The Relationship of the Elements

The importance of this relationship is so great that I cannot overemphasize it. For every Element that is affected every function of body, mind and spirit which is controlled or given by that Element will not function as it should. If, for example, there is no love and joy in someone, or if they seem to be humorless and vague, or if they manifest problems with the heart or the circulation, we can see that these may well point to distress in the Fire Element, but we really have no immediate idea what is causing that distress. It may be that the Fire Element itself is where the true cause of disease lies, or it may be that Fire is distressed and malnourished because its mother, Wood, is suffering. It might be a problem in the Water Element that feeds the Wood Element, or the Metal Element which feeds that. When we understand this we can begin to appreciate much better how useless symptoms are as a basis for proper diagnosis. They are only a manifestation of disease and distress, not a reliable sign of its true cause.

The picture of mother and child which illustrates this relationship reveals the profound wisdom of Oriental thought. The child which suffers from neglect and which is starved of its mother's love when she is ill often screams and howls in its suffering, and yet for all its noise and shouting for attention this is not where the distress lies. The mother may bear her ills quietly, but until they are sorted out the child will never be quiet. If we sought out the noise and thought that the louder the complaint the more important the problem we would be entirely wrong.

The seasons teach us the same lesson. When we have a poor summer we may grumble a little and complain about the weak and sporadic sunshine, but it may not cause us any major upset or problem. It is only when we miss the fruits of the harvest that the true extent and cause of our loss begins to emerge. In Nature this can result from too strong as well as too weak a season; the mother can overwhelm the child. If the rains of winter drive down for months on end and flood the soil the growth of spring will be harmed as badly as if there were no water at all. The Water Element, the mother, may overwhelm and drown her own child, the Wood Element.

Other relationships on the Sheng Cycle show the same pattern. The wisdom of modern science has helped us to understand how minerals are formed by the intense pressures and heat operating on the earth itself, but it is not a literal creation of Metal from Earth which we need to find, however, any more than Fire is the literal creation of Wood. We have to think more in terms of the minerals contained within the earth, and the earth giving them up almost as if it gave birth to them. This is not as far-fetched as it may sound; there were many ancient cultures who mined for precious minerals and revered Mother Earth as the creator and benefactor of their bounty.

The relationship of Metal with Water has the same depth. We could point to the way that the minerals and rocks channel the small streams of water into the rivers or how the minerals enrich the water with the power of life. The Chinese had other subtle and beautiful images of the nature of the Metal Element in autumn. The association of dryness with Metal arises from the process by which the air is cleansed of moisture as the droplets of water condense and fall downwards, following the natural movement of the autumn. The same condensation which leaves the air dry and crisp 'creates' the water which pools on the ground.

The relationship between Water and Wood also provides a wonderful illustration of the creation of Element by Element. Perhaps the school curriculum has changed in recent years, but most people reading this will remember the experiments with the germinating seeds from their school days. A little water soaked onto blotting paper was enough to trigger the seeds into life and before long the shoots sprout and grow. The seeds could be kept for months or even years, but nothing happened until that precious drop of water signaled the start of growth and life. Water does not create the seed, but activates the life within the seed, and a no more important act of creation can exist than this.

The Sheng cycle, therefore, describes how the Elements create and nourish one another. Growth and change do not run unchecked in Nature, however, and it is another relationship between the Elements, the Ke Cycle, which ensures that each season remains within its allotted span and does not run out of control.

THE KE CYCLE

It is important to look again at a diagram of the 5 Elements to see how this cycle is represented. The lines drawn between alternate Elements, arrowed to indicate a clockwise movement, reproduce diagrammatically exactly what the Ke Cycle represents, a strengthening bond which holds the Elements in their place and maintains their equal separation.

In talking of the Ke Cycle the Chinese were fond of drawing on natural

The Relationship of the Elements

examples to illustrate the relationships, and it may help our understanding to do the same. Fire controls Metal, and most of us in our mind's eye can already see the flame melting the mineral and rock and the lava streams pouring down the hillsides. Earth controls Water, and immediately we can visualize the banks of the river which channel and contain the flow. Metal controls Wood, and in Nature the harsh and jagged edges of the mineral formations cut their way through the vegetation. Water controls Fire, tempering its heat and ensuring that it does not blaze out of control. Wood controls Earth, and what better picture is there of this than the trees and plants whose roots keep the topsoil in place and prevent the movement of Earth in the wind and rain.

If we look in the same way to the seasons for our examples, we have only to look at the relationship of winter and summer, the Water and Fire of the natural cycle. When Water controls Fire as it should, the winter is cold and wet and reserves of water build up to stave off the worst of the summer heat. If the control is too great the winter brings floods and we sometimes find that even the best of summers cannot bring the ground back to its normal fertility. It may take another year of the growing cycle to recover. If, on the other hand, Water does not control Fire because the winter is mild and dry, the heat of the summer soon burns off the reserves and the grasses scorch and crops wither under the relentless heat.

The Ke Cycle relationship adds another dimension to what we uncover in the Traditional Diagnosis. Someone with a Wood Causative Factor may have a deficiency in Wood but be showing symptoms in Fire because Fire as the child of Wood is not being properly nourished. There may be signs of distress in Earth because this in turn is not fed by Fire. When we consider the additional effects of a weak Wood within the Ke Cycle, the complexities of the imbalance increase. Without any control the Earth Element may start to stray from its proper boundaries, and may begin to exert an unexpected power over Water. The Metal Element which controls Wood meets no resistance to its force and it, too, may start to oppress the very Water which is trying to feed Wood.

We can illustrate this with a thousand examples, and each will only repeat the simple truth that one Element in imbalance will cause imbalances throughout the entire system of energy. When a weakness exists in one place we will find that symptoms can arise literally anywhere, emphasizing once again how futile it is to chase and treat symptoms, for there can only be a cure if the true cause is treated.

THE ELEMENT WITHIN

Imbalances in the same Element can differ very greatly in their quality from person to person. Two people with an imbalance in the Earth Element as their Causative Factor may share a basic need for nourishment and for the love of the mother. One, however, may seem to express this need with considerable joy, while the other may reveal the same underlying need but with a complete lack of structure and purpose in how they go about meeting it.

These differences will be very obvious when we do the Traditional Diagnosis if we make effective use of our God-given skills. The predominant character of the imbalance, the need for the love and nourishment of the mother, the desire for sympathy, and the love of attention, will all be very clear. In one case, however, we may find this tremendous need expressed often with a great deal of inappropriate laughter and joy, and in the other through a great deal of anger and frustration.

If we only make rapport on a very superficial level, it is easy to be side-tracked by the other qualities along with which the need is expressed, as if we were to recognize the clothes rather than the person inside them. The apparent joy or the apparent anger that accompanies the underlying inappropriate and excessive need for attention can easily appear on the surface to be in itself the more fundamental imbalance, and we can easily mis-diagnose what is really happening. We must go right to the core of the person to see the real need. If we give warmth or instill a sense of purpose in someone whose real need is for sympathy and attention we may get a temporary change in them but not one that endures. When we feed the real need, however, we shall receive from someone the recognition, revealed to us in subtle changes in color, sound, odor and emotion, that we have understood exactly who they are and what their problem is, and with that recognition begins real transformation.

In order to understand how the unique quality of an imbalance is created we need to look again at aspects of the Elements which we covered in an earlier chapter. In discussing 'anger' as a part of the essence of the Wood Element, the point was made that all of the Elements have the potential for feeling and expressing anger in a way that is unique to them. If someone's main imbalance is, let us say, in Water and they are mainly predisposed towards inappropriate fear or lack of fear, this does not mean that this is the only emotion which they ever experience. Their fear, or their lack of it, may be the most evident and it will be clearly inappropriate in many of the situations in which they show it. The other emotions will exist in them, however, and have their right and proper place. Someone with Water imbalance will still be angry, fearful, grieving and in need of love or attention. Their over-riding fear or lack of fear may, however, set a prevailing tone and context for the rest of their emotions.

This is the same as in Nature itself. The winter is a quiet period of rest and recovery when we prepare for the growth of the spring which follows. It does not mean that for this time of the year nothing else happens in the pervading stillness. There is birth, death, maturity and harvest even in winter time. It will always have first and foremost, however, the character of the winter. We already recognize this in our everyday language when we talk about 'winter crops' and 'winter flowers' which have their special quality of growth and ripeness within the cold season. The 'winter sun', too, describes a kind of pale warmth which most of us can easily picture.

It is important to stress this possibility to avoid any tendency to believe that a particular imbalance reduces a person's reactions to only one type or one set. A Water imbalance in someone does not mean that he or she only responds with fear and the other associations of Water in any set of circumstances. This predominant imbalance may color their responses but all of the Elements are alive within him or her and are each capable of making their contributions when they are needed. The best illustration of this comes from Nature in the trees around us.

The tree itself, as a whole, stands in and is nourished by the earth, is sustained by the water, heated by the fire of the sun, and enriched by the minerals and by the air from the heavens. Although it embodies the essence of growth and regeneration of one Element in relation to the other Elements, within the tree itself these same Elements are at work. The tree must have the power of growth and the upward movement to force its sap to the growing tips of the leaves. There must be warmth and flow within the tree, and there must be stores of nourishment and water along with the precious minerals which give every living cell within it its quality of sustaining life.

This is to take a very literal and biological view of the Elements at work within the wood of the tree. The tree, as any other living creature, needs to grow, to mature, to be fed, to cast away dead growth, and to gather and prepare its

Classical Five-Element Acupuncture

reserves for regeneration. It, too, has its cycles and rhythms which depend on the balance of the Elements within it. If any of these qualities is weak or deficient, then the tree will not be able to fulfill its purpose and destiny and will be out of balance within itself.

The same applies when we look at the Elements within each person. Each governs or represents a number of functions within us, and for each of these functions to work appropriately there needs to be a balance of the Elements within the function itself. Growth, for example, the essence of the spring, itself needs to rise, mature, deliver its riches, and then fall away to subside and recover for its next cycle. Each of these Elements has to be balanced within growth itself for it to be effective.

If there is little warmth within the growing part of the cycle, a weak Fire Element within the Wood Element, the quality of the growth may be stiff and inflexible. The person with this imbalance may be warm enough inside themselves, because the Fire Element as a whole is in reasonable balance, but the Fire Element within the Wood Element is not properly functioning, and this becomes the cause of the particular type of Wood imbalance which we see on the surface. If we were to treat the Element Fire because of a Fire imbalance within the Wood we might create disharmony and imbalance and have no real effect at all where it is needed. It is the Wood we must treat, and our knowledge of the Element within may help us to choose points whose effect on the Wood is to set right the imbalance at its very heart.

Lest anyone get carried away with the notion that in spite of what I have said this wisdom is simple to apply, they would do well to reflect on the fact that each 'Element within' has its own 'Element within' which can clearly be the cause of the imbalance of this element within the causative factor. This must be so if we have understood the basis of this system of medicine. There are no 'first causes' or 'fixed points'. Everything describes movement, change and transformation, and our labels are a very poor approximation to what we actually observe.

Someone may well ask how this level of imbalance can be obvious to us, and the answer is the one I have already given in a previous volume. The color 'green' which appears on the face with a Wood Causative Factor is never 'just green'. It is either a green-green, blue-green, yellow-green, white-green, or red-green. In fact, it may even be a yellow-white-green, and so on. The color, the

The Relationship of the Elements

shade which we can distinguish among the millions of shades, is directly related to the nature of the imbalance of the Element within the Element, and the Element within that. The only limitation on the ability to observe this is the poverty of our own senses from the years of misuse and neglect.

The same applies to the sound, the odor and the emotion which appear with imbalance in the Causative Factor. There is shouting-laughter, weeping-aughter, singing laughter, groaning-laughter and, surprising as it may sound, laughing-laughter. There is no reason that stops an Element from being out of balance within itself. Indeed, this imbalance may be one of the most profound, if the Element does not even have the essence of its own being within itself. Can we imagine how hard it must be to be deprived of the essence of nourishment and love because this part of the cycle is itself malnourished within, like an underfed mother trying to feed her own child? In this example we would have an Earth Causative Factor with the Earth within Earth the imbalanced Element within.

Odors appear in the same kinds of variety. We shall find five different 'putrids', five different 'rancids', five different 'scorcheds', five different 'fragrants', and five different 'rottens'. When we have learned how to smell these we shall find a further five within each of these, each level taking us nearer to an understanding of the true and inner nature of the imbalances in the person before us.

The emotions associated with Elements within Elements can be a source of the greatest confusion. With colors, sounds, and odors we need primarily to develop our senses, and to observe what is before us. With the emotions, however, we need to elicit responses from a patient and judge how appropriate they are. This involves not only a clear intention and detachment within ourselves of what we are attempting to elicit and a clear execution, but also clear observations of how the patient is responding.

This takes us full circle to where we began with the example of the Water Element. Someone with an imbalance in Water will experience all of the other emotions, but their underlying imbalance may affect the quality of their responses. The anger of someone with a Water imbalance may be very different in quality from the anger of someone with a Fire imbalance. If we are able to observe the patient carefully enough, however, we shall see that one of the Elements within Water is itself out of balance by the fact that one of the emotions within the fear is inappropriate. The anger, or sadness, or grief, or worry, or even fear within their over-riding fear may also stand out as inappropriate and point to the cause within Water of the imbalance. At this level of diagnosis we shall start to make terrible mistakes unless we use all of our senses and remind ourselves that we need four diagnostic signs to reach a sound conclusion, not just the one.

This discussion, however, takes us into an area of diagnosis and treatment planning which is far beyond the immediate purpose of this volume. It is also taking us further into an area where words are almost redundant in helping people to understand this level of sophistication, and where only supervised clinical practice will suffice. What I have hoped to show with this short summary is that the apparent simplicity of Five-Element Acupuncture becomes less so when we develop our senses and observe with greater care what is happening.

To some readers the five Elements may still seem to operate at a level of generality which makes it difficult to understand how we can diagnose with such accuracy. The Elements, however, are expressed within man and woman as the Officials, and when we turn to these in following chapters we shall see how they relate very directly to the kinds of physical systems which most people connect with Western or allopathic medicine. We shall also see how they relate to functions of the mind and spirit which show their deeper purpose and essence.

Firstly, however, we must complete our survey of the Elements by considering the aspect of them with which many readers are already familiar, the 'associations' or 'correspondences' as they are known, the classification of manifestations of the Elements in all aspects of our daily life.

CHAPTER EIGHT

THE CORRESPONDENCES OF THE ELEMENTS

In the Introduction I emphasized the fact that the Elements are neither simply a way of looking at things nor a collection of building blocks. The five Elements describe the ceaseless cycle of movement of Qi energy embodied in the process of Nature and expressed in our body, mind and spirit as a part of Nature. In order to understand a process, however, there have to be some relatively fixed points through which we can observe and measure change and transformation. The correspondences represent this very visible and concrete aspect of the Elements. As long as we are not tempted into thinking of them as building blocks, their relative fixed quality can help us to see the patterns in Nature.

The interweaving of these aspects, the Elements, as building blocks, or as patterns imposed on reality, or as both, was not such a problem for the ancient Chinese as for us. Their deep understanding of the inter-relationship of yin and yang aspects within Nature entirely sidestepped the fruitless arguments which have bedevilled western thought over whether form or matter comes first and which creates the other. For they both are essential aspects of an overall unity.

'Wood', for example, embodies and reveals qualities of regeneration, growth, and upward movement in the pattern of flow of Qi energy. At the same time 'Wood' has obvious associations with the plants and trees as a natural manifestation of that growth. We can say "Wood is ..." as easily and with as much truth as "Wood represents ...", and draw on the real, physical qualities which Wood has in Nature. It is not chance or coincidence which gives this part of the cycle and these trees and plants the same name. Fire, Earth, Metal and Water are all equally 'real things' which we find in our everyday lives as much as they are the embodiment of qualities which the Elements represent in their more abstract sense.

This identity between the abstract and the natural is of greatest value when we use the five Elements for the purposes of diagnosis. I have tried to show how the various processes which the Elements describe create certain expressions of need in people who have predominant imbalances in a particular Element.

Classical Five-Element Acupuncture

When someone's cycle of energy is blocked, weakened, or over-active this will become obvious from the basic diagnostic signs of color, sound, odor and emotion which we can observe, but will also be reflected in their behavior and in the kind of help and support which they seek.

We talk of people who above all need the love, support, structure, guidance, or resolve which they are lacking. It would be equally possible, however, to diagnose by asking literally what kind of Fire, or what kind of Wood, Metal, Water, or Earth the patient is. The qualities and variations which are present in the material properties of wood, fire, earth, metal and water are just as descriptive of the state of harmony or imbalance within the person as the more abstract terms when we talk of the spirit. A tree growing in barren soil can be as good and useful a description of a person whose inner balance is disturbed as knowing that someone has a Wood Causative Factor with Earth problems 'within' the Wood and Metal problems 'within' the Earth. One simple picture gives us the same information.

This is often difficult for the Western mind to grasp, but it has to be understood to make sense of the correspondences. For the Chinese it did not matter whether we look inside ourselves and apply what we find there in order to understand Nature, or vice versa. The same principles underlie both because it is the same Qi energy with the same laws and patterns. The correspondences should be looked at in the same way. They may seem at face value to be an arbitrary selection of objects and qualities, but only if we look at them without reminding ourselves that they make sense within the overall process.

Although I have talked about diagnosis here, we are not always looking at disharmony and imbalance when we look at the Elements. The color green which we associate with Wood, for example, is the color which appears on the face of a person with a Wood Causative Factor, and used in this way it has diagnostic value. This is only a narrow part of the understanding of the Element, however. The same green appears everywhere in Nature, not as a sign of imbalance but as an essential quality of the growth cycle which peaks in the spring and is present in all of the seasons. The sounds, odors, emotions and other correspondences are similarly not just diagnostic tools. They only become so when imbalances in their associated Elements cause them to become predominant or inappropriate in time or place. In every other respect they show us the wealth and diversity of the Elements in Nature.

The Correspondences of the Elements

The elemental correspondences are:

1*	Colour		2*	Sound
3*	Odor		4*	Emotion
5	Season		6	Climate
7	Taste		8	Power
9	Direction	10		Parts of Body
11	Sense Organ	12		External Physical Manifestation

* These first four are the main elemental correspondences used for establishing the causative factor of an individual's imbalance.

There are literally hundreds of others, from types of meat and grain associated with each Element to musical notes and numbers, and still many others more esoteric. In looking briefly at the major ones we should try to resist definitive statements which try to capture their meaning once and for all. The strength and vitality of the correspondences comes from the unique way in which each of us experiences them and the connections which they have for us as individuals.

THE WOOD ELEMENT

The correspondences of the Wood Element, some of which have already been covered, are:

COLOR	Green		SOUND	Shouting
ODOR	Rancid		EMOTION	Anger
SEASON	Spring		CLIMATE	Wind
TASTE	Sour		POWER	Birth
DIRECTION	East		SENSE ORGAN	Eyes
PARTS OF BODY				Tendons and Ligaments
EXTERNAL PHYSICAL MANIFESTATION				Nails

The key to understanding these lies in remembering that the Wood Element is associated with energy that is rising, spreading and fast moving. **Shouting** and **anger**, for example, are the obvious associations which most of us make with 'sound of voice' and 'emotion' when we look for the manifestations of Wood energy in our own behavior. This upsurge of energy is what most of us feel when we express our anger forcefully.

8.3

The character of the **spring**, the season of the Wood Element, is of a time of growth before things become fully mature. The color **green** and the **sour** taste both reflect this state of unripeness. There is probably no better example of this than the sight and taste of the unripe apple beginning to form on the branch. This idea is picked up in our everyday language over and over again. We use the term 'green' to describe anyone who lacks experience and who is still in the process of learning, and a glance at the dictionary will reveal dozens of different words in combination with 'green' which draw on this connotation of the Wood Element.

The odor **rancid** is the smell of fat or oil that has gone off. The association with Wood here is through the officials of the Wood Element, the Liver and Gall Bladder. These two are important in the metabolism of fats in the body, and if the officials do not function well within the body, the incomplete breakdown of fats leaves its characteristic odor on the person.

The correspondence between the **wind** and Wood is an important one in Oriental medicine. Wind is very changeable and volatile, its unpredictable and rapid movement true to the essence of the Wood Element. Oriental medicine often refers to diseases arising from an imbalance in the Wood Element in terms of wind because of the quality which Wood imparts to the disease process. **Wind** can also have diagnostic value; some people may report that wind can make them more short-tempered or deeply invigorated than any other climate.

The other correspondences can also be useful secondary feedback. An imbalance in Wood may lead someone to develop a craving for the sour taste and love acidic pickles and green fruit, or to develop a strong like, or dislike, of the color green in clothing or room decoration. The parts of the body associated with the Element also give some indication of areas which may show the signs of distress. On a physical level a Wood imbalance may, for example, leave someone with nails of very poor quality. The healthy Wood Element ensures that the nails are in good condition. When the Element is weakened the nails often become brittle and striated, or soft and ridged. The eyes can also be affected, either by external problems such as dry eyes or 'red eye', or internal problems with vision like glaucoma and 'floaters' in the eye.

There is, however, a danger in taking this kind of information and using it in diagnosis without further ado, tempting as this may be on occasion. As we saw in the last chapter, the Elements not only depend on one another but also

The Correspondences of the Elements

'contain' one another, and there are any number of possible reasons why an aspect of body, mind, or spirit controlled by the Wood Element might be diseased. A problem in the Water Element, for example, may deplete every Element of fluids and this might lead within the Wood Element to dryness of the eyes or nails. These correspondences, therefore, are better thought of as 'second-grade' information, reinforcement of a diagnosis rather than its basis.

Where one can talk with absolute certainty, however, is in the four main correspondences which are used in diagnosis: color, sound, odor and emotion. When the Wood Element itself is the primary Element out of balance, the Causative Factor, we see a whole phase of the cycle of energy occupying a much greater or much smaller place in the cycle than it should. This may be either a literal excess or deficiency of energy, or a qualitative excess or deficiency. The qualities which come from the Wood Element in color, sound, odor and emotion will appear in inappropriate measure, be this too little or too much. Both extremes are like having a spring season which as well as being itself too long or too short has effects which persist right throughout the year. Not only is the spring affected, but the quality of growth in the whole of the annual cycle suffers as a consequence. The correspondences show the physical evidence of this disharmony.

THE FIRE ELEMENT

COLOR	Red	SOUND	Laughing
ODOR	Scorched	EMOTION	Joy
SEASON	Summer	CLIMATE	Heat
TASTE	Bitter	POWER	Mature
DIRECTION	South	SENSE ORGAN	Tongue
PARTS OF BODY			Blood Vessels
EXTERNAL PHYSICAL MANIFESTATION			Complexion

The correspondences of the Fire Element show even more clearly than those of Wood the 'family resemblance' between the various categories. The correspondences of joy and laughing which help to establish the Causative Factor are allied to **red** and **scorched**, whose connection with the Element is self-evident in the nature of Fire itself.

Care needs to be taken with the color, however, for although the Fire Element

Classical Five-Element Acupuncture

gives us the reds of Nature the color very often appears as **lack of red** or **greyness** when there is a Fire imbalance in the person. Many years ago this would have been more difficult to describe, but the advent of popular color photography made people very much more aware of what we mean by 'lack of red'. In a faulty print the reds are very muted and dull and everything else appears washed out and grubby. This is very much how the lack of color appears as a diagnostic sign on the person's face, an absence of warmth and vitality which comes from the Fire Element.

People looking at the odor 'rancid' associated with Wood no doubt think that **scorched** sounds a far better proposition. Both, of course, can smell appetizing in due measure; the scorched smell of roasted coffee beans and barbecues can be very enticing. When the Element is out of balance, however, the odor becomes as excessive and inappropriate as the emotion and the sound of voice, and is anything but pleasant. If something overheats or burns the chances are that it will smell very unappetizing.

I have included directions for reference purposes, and there is an obvious connection in each association with the movement of the sun through the heavens which gives us a day starting in the East, peaking in the South, and declining in the West. These are not very commonly used in the practice of Western medicine but were taken very seriously in ancient China, to the extent that some emperors moved from east to south wings of the palace at the change of season, and so on around the cycle.

Occasionally the directions can be important in diagnostic terms when people work outdoors and are exposed to winds from the four quarters. These naturally tend to bring the conditions which are related to the Element, like a hot wind from the south or a cold wind from the north, and may exacerbate disease, but these are increasingly unlikely to have a great effect in modern Western society where we are largely insulated from the climate.

The Correspondences of the Elements

THE EARTH ELEMENT

COLOR	**Yellow**	SOUND	**Singing**
ODOR	**Fragrant**	EMOTION	**Sympathy**
SEASON	**Late Summer**	CLIMATE	**Humidity**
TASTE	**Sweet**	POWER	**Decrease**
DIRECTION	**Center**	SENSE ORGAN	**Mouth**
PARTS OF BODY			**Muscles**
EXTERNAL PHYSICAL MANIFESTATION			**Flesh**

All of the correspondences of the Earth Element flow naturally from the different aspects of its essence. The association with the mother is seen in the sound of the voice. People often tend to think of a **singing** voice as akin to a regional accent like Welsh, or to what we call a 'sing-song' delivery. Neither of these is necessarily 'singing' in the sense in which it is intended in the correspondences. One way to describe it is as the voice of a mother soothing the child, a sound which generally coos and falls away within each word and each sentence and which often comes from deep within the body. This is what gives it its rather musical sound. It can also have a very appealing quality; it is always asking for sympathy and drawing us towards the person.

The color **yellow** is often likened to the harvest color of the corn in the field. Despite the resonance this has for us in the West, anyone with a passing knowledge of China will know that the Chinese immediately associate yellow with the earth of Northern China which forms the rich and fertile silt flowing down the Yellow river, for the Chinese the color yellow naturally represents the qualities of the Earth as our physical mother, as the basis of our nourishment and survival.

The other three correspondences of importance which we have not already covered are the climate **humid**, the odor **fragrant**, and the **sweet** taste. When we teach students we have to remind them over and over again that 'fragrant' is not a pleasant odor. The nearest association which helps people to understand this is a greenhouse in late summer when the smell of the over-ripe blooms slightly past their best hangs in the air, an overpowering, cloying and extremely sickly odor. In fact, since greenhouses in late summer are extremely **humid** they do represent a fairly extreme version of the kind of climate which we associate with Earth when the sun is weaker but the cloud cover makes the days sultry and overcast.

8.7

Classical Five-Element Acupuncture

The **sweet** taste can be very valuable as a diagnostic tool. As a gift from Nature the 'sweet' bears no similarity to the sugary chocolates and candies which litter the shelves in the West. The sweetness which comes with the harvest is the sweetness of ripe fruit and fresh vegetables like peas and corn and, before all of these, the sweetness of the milk from the breast. When people are out of balance, however, they often exhibit a craving for the tastes which support and nourish the Elements out of balance within us. An Earth imbalance very often leads people to become addicted to candies and cakes, extremes of sweetness far beyond the natural sweetness in Nature. This in turn may produce the obesity which can often afflict people who have problems in finding nourishment of the right kind for themselves. There are also those who have an aversion to sweet things and whose under-nourishment and emaciation is just as unbalanced a condition as obesity.

The notion of proper nourishment also reflects the association of the earth Element with the **muscles** and the **flesh**, the stores and reserves of food energy in the body. When we are overstocked, it is the flesh which shows the signs of the surplus. When the Earth Element within us is weak the poor quality of our flesh and absence of stores may be the outward sign of this.

THE METAL ELEMENT

COLOR	**White**	SOUND	**Weeping**
ODOR	**Rotte**	EMOTION	**Grief**
SEASON	**Autumn**	CLIMATE	**Dryness**
TASTE	**Pungent**	POWER	**Balance**
DIRECTION	**West**	SENSE ORGAN	**Nose**
PARTS OF BODY			**Body Hair**
EXTERNAL PHYSICAL MANIFESTATION			**Skin**

The Metal Element is the connection with the heavenly father and the giver of pure quality and essence to Qi energy. Another part of its essential meaning, however, is the declining aspect of energy, the autumn of the year when the foliage falls to the ground and rots away into the soil. When we look at the correspondences of Metal they are more closely connected with this aspect of the Element.

8.8

The Correspondences of the Elements

The idea of loss, death and dying is clear in the association with **grief** and with **weeping**. So too is **white**, for although in the west we have in the main taken the wearing of black for mourning in many middle and far eastern countries white is the color worn by the mourners at funerals. The correspondences often pervade our ordinary language, even the directions. We often associate death in the **west** with expressions like 'gone west', which draw their power from the evocative image of the setting sun and the passing of the day.

The Metal Element, like the season of autumn in the annual cycle, is essential to our balance. Without autumn pouring the riches of decay into the earth and returning everything of quality to the soil there would be no growth the following spring. When the autumn carries on and on, however, death and loss take up more than their appropriate share of time. The grief and the weeping voice start to become predominant in the person, a token of the fact that the person cannot or will not let go. The weeping voice itself is a very clear representation of this. Because the person hangs on to things that are best left behind the real tears cannot flow but are frequently checked. When someone clings to their grief, the voice too will falter and break on the verge of tears without giving full release to the emotion within.

The underlying quality of death and decline is also present in the odor associated with the Metal Element. **Rotten** is used to describe anything which is rotting, whether this be the meat which hangs on the butcher's hook or the compost heaps which steam at the bottom of the garden. Most people are familiar with the smell of the dust carts which collect rubbish from street to street, and this is often the clearest and most familiar example of 'rotten' for most people.

Although these correspondences reflect the decline and fall which we associate with the Metal phase in the cycle, many of the others are closely connected with breathing, the means by which we literally inspire the Qi from the heavens which supports and nourishes us. The **nose**, both as an orifice and as a sense organ is related to Metal, and Metal imbalances often bring about respiratory problems which involve the nose and the nasal passages. The **skin**, too, often described as 'the third lung', also reflects the state of the Metal Element. Many serious skin conditions frequently arise from a Metal imbalance and there is often a progression of disease, from skin problems to breathing problems, infantile eczema to hay fever, to asthma, to bronchitis and pleurisy, when the Element is weakened from birth.

Classical Five-Element Acupuncture

Other correspondences are the **pungent** taste and the climate **dryness**. In terms of effect there is little doubt where we experience the pungent taste of garlic and onions, as our sinuses will probably bear witness. We even use pungent herbs and chemicals as smelling salts to unblock the airways and to restore consciousness. Someone with a Metal imbalance may well be drawn to food which contains hot spices and aromatic vegetables, both of which encourage the elimination of waste by opening the pores of the skin and allowing us to sweat and by stimulating the bowel.

The association with dryness is sometimes explained by the Chinese as the state of the air in the autumn when all the moisture has condensed from it and moved downwards. This condensation and drying effect of the season is not such an odd idea when we remember that the crackling of dry leaves underfoot in the autumn months before the rain of winter.

THE WATER ELEMENT

COLOR	Blue	SOUND	Groaning
ODOR	**Putrid**	EMOTION	Fear
SEASON	**Winter**	CLIMATE	Cold
TASTE	**Salty**	POWER	Emphasis
DIRECTION	**North**	SENSE ORGAN	Ears
PARTS OF BODY			Bones
EXTERNAL PHYSICAL MANIFESTATION			Head Hair

The correspondences of Water fall into two main groups which reflect the qualities of water itself and the season winter which the Element represents. There is no need to spell out in detail how **cold**, **north**, **blue** and **salty** are associated with the Water Element. The odor **putrid** is also straightforward. The essence of Water within Nature and within the person is to flow, and when a water flow is obstructed or too weak the water becomes stagnant and brackish, generating a smell which we know as 'putrid'.

The sound of Water is **groaning**, an association which at first sight is not so obvious until we reflect on the quality of water and of the winter. Winter, as we have seen, has a tendency to 'sameness' and lack of variation. Above the snows and waters of winter there is little sign of life and movement, and day after day

The Correspondences of the Elements

can pass by with no variation. Flows of water often have the same quality of the true monotone, without variety of volume or pitch. When someone has an imbalance in their Water Element the same characteristic appears in the voice, an unchanging and constant groan. Heard dimly from the other side of a wall, the voice may sound a little like a meditative drone.

As I mentioned at the beginning of the chapter, I do not want to define the correspondences too closely because, as with every other part of this system of medicine, these need to be learned through observation and feeling, not from words in a book. Thinking about the qualities which characterize the season, however, helps us to understand how the groaning sound fits in so well with the essence of Water. The groaning sound gives nothing away, not a trace of any interest or emotion to the listening ear, and we can only guess at what is happening inside. When people are rigid with fear the same stillness may manifest on the surface despite the inner panic and distress. Each of the correspondences has the same depth if we observe carefully what is happening around us.

The **bones** are related to the Bladder and Kidney official and the poor healing of fractures is often related to the state of the Bladder and Kidney. 'Bones' include bone marrow and the brain, which was considered to be an extension of the same marrow material. Many developmental and growth problems, especially hereditary ones, may be attributable to Water imbalances. These will be covered in more detail when we consider the Kidney and Bladder Officials.

SUMMARY

The correspondences, therefore, help us to understand the pattern and flow of energy in nature. They reveal to us something of the character and quality of the flow and movement itself by 'freezing', in tangible and visible form, some of the aspects of the change and transformation. The main correspondences of color, sound, odor and emotion are the basis of the traditional diagnosis, and the others can provide useful and occasionally conclusive evidence of the diagnosis.

The detail of the correspondences, however, still falls short of the detail which we need to understand fully the Elements as they appear in man and woman. For this we need to look at the Officials and by doing so reach the very essence of the Elements within us.

CHAPTER NINE

THE SPIRIT OF THE OFFICIALS

There is, both in Nature and in ourselves, an indissoluble unity of body, mind and spirit. Within this unity, however, there is always the ceaseless interplay of Yin and Yang and the constant flow of the five Elements in everything that we find around us. Both patterns exist together in Nature and are there for us to observe, and each has its own particular value and importance. There is no mystery in this. When we watch the evening tide come in, we sometimes look at the shimmering brilliance of wave after wave tumbling in to the shore, and at other times we are hypnotized by the gradual rise of the swell. Both aspects are there together within the one moment, and a thousand other aspects if we could really see the full beauty of Nature's rhythms.

Since our powers of observation are in the main very limited, however, we might say that sometimes the five Elements give us an easier picture for our standard of perception than that of Yin and Yang, and have made it that much easier for our understanding to grasp the patterns of Nature. The same logic applies again when we move on to look at the Officials. Where the Elements give us a broad picture of ourselves as human beings, a picture which may still present us with difficulties when we try to interpret and understand what we see, the Officials take us straight to the heart of the reality within us.

I can remember as a child having a wonderful book at home which showed how the body worked in all its intricacy and complexity. This book was for children, and the picture which I remember best is of the lungs. For instead of two bags of air the picture showed two little men operating a set of bellows. Silly as this may sound that picture helped me to understand how the lungs worked far better than any literal description or diagram would have done. When I thought of the two little men about their labors I could begin to grasp why and how the lungs could function and malfunction far better than all the technical words which came later could tell me.

The Chinese view of the Elements at work inside the body as the Officials, Ministers of an Imperial court, has the same simple wisdom that children find so easy to take in and which we as adults sometimes ignore to our great cost. As we have seen in the last few chapters, the Elements give us a profound view of the change and transformation within us as a part of the great flow of the Dao in Nature. The slow ebb and flow of the tide, however, is sometimes beyond our power to perceive, and we need to narrow our focus and observe the individual waves. The Officials bring us this level of detail when they show us the essence of the Elements within our own body, mind and spirit in a way that we can grasp much more easily.

When we come across familiar names, however, we must not be tempted to think that because the Officials are associated with the names of organs which we recognize in Western medicine we already know something of their meaning, and can perhaps even hope to translate between the two systems. We are looking at two distinct and separate systems in which, at the level of physical reality, some parts bear superficial resemblances. The concept of the Officials, however, is far richer in its layers of meaning and far removed from any simplistic view of organs of the physical body.

The key to understanding the Officials in Eastern medicine lies in the fact that the Officials of the Chinese court were functionaries. This is the most vital word to help us to understand the Officials as they manifest within the body - **functions**. Each Official has to be understood for what it does, not for what it is. That is far more important than the mere physical organ within the body which bears the same name.

The spleen, for example, as we understand it in western medicine, plays an important role in the storage, cleansing and production of blood. These functions are loosely linked to some of the functions of the Spleen Official in Chinese medicine, but are nowhere near as important as the functions of transforming and transporting the Qi energy from food. These two are the major roles played by the Spleen in the physical body, and these in turn are only a small part in its overall role in body, mind and spirit.

The clearest example we have of the difference between what we might understand by an organ in the West and what the Chinese saw in an Official comes from cases where the physical organ is removed. The Gall Bladder Official continues to function even when the gall bladder itself is cut away. When the spleen is removed it does not leave all the functions of the Spleen Official without root and source. If there were a simple equivalence between

East and West, then we should see a total collapse of the Official. What we find on every occasion when this is done, however, is that while the Official may need extra help because of the shock to its physical organ it can still function on all levels, including even the physical level.

This is a fact which even students of acupuncture find difficult to grasp at first. The physical organ is largely to do with carrying out the Official's function on the physical level itself. The Official, however, is limited neither to this level alone nor to the physical organ alone. Just as the Element operates in body, mind and spirit, so too does the Official. This is at the heart of any understanding of the Officials, for they embody the spirit of the Elements just as clearly as the Elements themselves. The Officials are nothing other than the life and essence of the Elements within us.

This is easier to understand if we look at the way in which the Chinese described the Officials. The following passage from the Nei Jing gives us a much better idea of just how broad the Chinese picture was.

'The heart is like the minister of the monarch who excels through insight and understanding; the lungs are the symbol of the interpretation and conduct of the Official jurisdiction and regulation; the liver has the functions of a military leader who excels in his strategic planning; the gall bladder occupies the position of an important and upright Official who excels through his decisions and judgment; the middle of the thorax (the part between the breasts) is like the Official of the center who guides the subjects in their joys and pleasures; the stomach acts as the Official of the public granaries and grants the five tastes; the lower intestines are like the Officials who propagate the Right Way of Living, and they generate evolution and change; the small intestines are like the Officials who are trusted with riches and they create changes of physical substance; the kidneys are like the Officials who do energetic work, and they excel through their ability and cleverness; the burning spaces are like the Officials who plan the construction of ditches and sluices, and they create the waterways; the groins and the bladder are like the magistrates of a region or district, they store the overflow and the fluid secretions which serve to regulate vaporization. These twelve Officials should not fail to assist one another.'

These descriptions, which present a view of the person as a small kingdom, are very common in early Chinese medical texts and diagrams. Anyone visiting exhibitions of early Chinese painting will see many beautiful anatomical

Classical Five-Element Acupuncture

illustrations which represent the body as a landscape of ditches, streams and valleys, sometimes with small figures seated in the different areas. Each feature of the landscape lies where the physical organ of each Official resides, and the flow and movement between the separate parts reflect the relationship between the Officials and the movement of energy throughout body, mind and spirit. Very often the descriptions of the Officials' functions draw on these pictures to enhance their meaning.

Although I mentioned the little men with the bellows a little earlier, however, we must not make the mistake of assuming that the beauty and the depth of the descriptions of the Officials are just an older version of the same method, a fairy tale to help practitioners of Oriental medicine to remember the processes and functions which are found within us. This may seem so at first when we come across characters like the Colon Official, the Drainer of Dregs, or the Stomach Official, the Rotter and Ripener of food. What these names preserve, however, is a simple but true basis from which we can begin to explain the real beauty of their mind and their spirit: they retain the idea of characters within us who share our human qualities. As we shall see in the following chapters this is of vital importance in looking at the relationship of Official with Official within us.

We can best begin to understand the spirit and meaning of the Officials by looking at one of them in slightly greater depth. The Colon Official, for example, is the Official whose work belongs to the Metal Element in us. When we say that the Official 'belongs' to the Element, we mean that in the same sense that the waves belong to the tide, or the flames belong to the fire. In many respects they are the same thing, but the nature of the Official is unique to us as human beings and by virtue of its specific functions, easier for us to understand.

The Metal Element is responsible for bringing quality into our lives. In order to do this, however, it has to make room for new essence by clearing away the rubbish. In the autumn, the season of the Element, the old leaves and dead branches fall to the ground to make way for the new growth of the next cycle. The death and decay which comes with the autumn is vital to the possibility of new growth. It not only clears room for new shoots but in releasing the trace elements and minerals vital for growth back into the soil it renews the quality which can sustain new life.

The Spirit of the Officials

The duties of the Colon Official as the embodiment of the Metal Element are reflected in the physical function of the colon itself. The elimination of waste from the body as faeces is vital to our lives. It is sometimes said jokingly that we are nothing but a long tube surrounded by our organs, into which we pour food and water and out of which comes waste. At this level the job of maintaining a clear passage through us is one of the most important in the whole body. The Colon Official daily maintains and preserves our lives by unblocking the pathway by which we survive.

The physical function of the colon also embodies the other aspect of the Metal Element in which valuable residues are reclaimed. The large intestine is one of the key places in the body where water and some vital minerals and vitamins are extracted or recycled into our system. The water gathering function is often forgotten, but without it we could not survive for more than a few days. The thousands of deaths from dehydration in the Far East after outbreaks of dysentery and diarrhea show us just how essential this function is.

We all know how unpleasant it can be when this Official is not performing its physical function as needed. When the waste inside us is not thrown out we become constipated and our whole system starts to clog up. We lose our appetites because there is no room inside us for anything new and we begin to feel stagnant. Worse follows, because without the elimination of waste through our faeces we have to find other ways to get rid of the toxins and poisons which accumulate inside us. This illustrates an important truth which we shall see in the following chapters; none of the other Officials can perform **exactly** the same function as any other. When the Colon malfunctions, the other Officials will each do what they can to shed the poisons inside us. We break out in spots and rashes as our other Officials struggle to cleanse us by throwing out their own rubbish in whatever way they can, but never as effectively as the specialist whose job it is.

Far more significant than the effect on our bodies, however, is the effect on our feelings and our minds, and on our spirits, too, if we could only recognize it. When we are constipated we talk of feeling blocked and stuck, of not being able to take anything in, and of feeling really sluggish inside. On deeper levels we find it very difficult to feel inspired and uplifted and to share in any deeper purpose because we are totally full of rubbish. There is just no room on any level for anything new of value or inspiration to find its way in, and what space we have is full of poison. If anything finds its way in it is immediately contaminated, and despair and resignation, such as, "What's the point?" are easy to understand.

The effect is just as disastrous when we suffer to the other extreme. With diarrhea we lose everything, not just the waste but also the food which we need and the liquid on which we depend. We cannot hold on to anything of value because it all slips away too quickly. Our minds and our spirits are just as badly affected when we are physically ill in this way. The terrible urgency and haste which afflict our bowel movements do exactly the same to our thoughts and feelings. We are unable to hold on to anything at all, and the nourishment in the thoughts, feelings and beliefs we try to take in, tumble out of us as undigested as the food from which we have gained no benefit.

In describing constipation or diarrhea in these terms, as a malfunction in the work of the Colon Official, it is natural for most of us to think first in terms of the physical malfunction, and to dwell on the colon as a physical organ rather than the Colon Official as a minister of court with a broader function. Perhaps as an afterthought we then remember to consider the effects which this kind of physical problem has on the way we feel at other levels, but the force of habit of our western background to concentrate on the physical level alone is considerable.

When we begin to understand the work of this Official and of all the other Officials, however, we shall find from experience and observation that the process is more often than not the other way around. The mind and the spirit more often cause the body to be sick. How else can we explain cases of people whose diets are exemplary and whose general health is good, and yet their bowels function so erratically they are in and out of hospital time and time again for tests? All the high fiber diets in the world will not matter one iota if the Official in charge of the ridding of waste and toxins is sick in mind and spirit and who, when this happens, cannot cleanse anything at all.

There is nothing unique or novel about this way of looking at the work of the Officials inside us. Anyone reading this book without the benefit of training in Oriental Medicine will know perfectly well that when our feelings and our thoughts are polluted or are stuck inside, or worse still, when we find ourselves afflicted by a pollution and stagnation of the spirit, we may become physically constipated. There is no need to check our diets or look for physical reasons, because we know where the real problem lies.

The Spirit of the Officials

The same applies when we feel that we want to be rid of filth and pollution from our minds and spirits as fast as we can, or decide to let go of thoughts and beliefs that we have hung on to for too long. Often this release will be accompanied by bouts of diarrhea or excessive bowel movements for which there is no obvious bacterial or viral cause. It is a sign for us of the letting go which is happening on the other levels.

The function of the Official, then, lies on all levels. There is no such thing as just a physical function, or a mental function, or a spiritual function. We are full of rubbish on all levels, and the Official is charged with the responsibility of disposing of all the rubbish in the body, mind and spirit. This is why we cannot reduce the Officials to the same level as the physical organs, not even the physical organs as they were understood and interpreted by the ancient Chinese. Our own experience will show us hundreds of times every day that if our Officials are not working properly this failure of function will affect every level within us.

Looking at the Official in this way makes it quite difficult to see what difference there is between the spirit of the Official and the spirit of the Element. After all, is not the spirit of the Colon Official the same thing as the spirit of the Metal Element, or at least a part of it, that which deals with the natural process of death and decay? Perhaps we should ask ourselves what we gain from adding a further picture of ministers of court?

The answer is that even at this level of generality we have a new and different image in the concept of the Officials, that of a team working together in co-operation and harmony. This is a different picture of harmony, for seen in this light the Officials are not bound by the same relationships as the Elements. In one sense the Kidney as a part of Water is the mother of Liver as a part of Wood, but there are many important relationships between the Officials which are more to do with the relationship of their functions than with their relationships as part of the five Elements or of Yin and Yang.

This is very important when we look at the patterns of disharmony which can arise amongst the Officials. We begin to add to the relationships of nourishment and control, from the Sheng and Ke Cycles which bind the Elements together, a range of relationships based on functions.

I mentioned in an earlier chapter that the Liver, as the planner for the body, has as important a role within the team as it has in planning for the team. When we look at this in detail we shall see not only how the whole court of the Officials needs to have an 'outer' plan, which gives the whole court aim and purpose, but also how each individual Official needs an 'inner' plan, by which it can achieve its own role in this common purpose. If the Liver Official is weak and cannot perform its function this failure to plan hits all the Officials, not only because the body, mind and spirit as a whole lose their vision and goal but because the blueprint by which each Official works goes awry.

The work of the Colon Official has the same duality of purpose and is responsible for removing the waste which it has gathered from the whole body, mind and spirit, and removing the waste which arises from the work of the other Officials. When this Official becomes sick not only does the gathered waste already stand rotting within it but the other Officials become clogged with their own particular waste which the Colon Official normally removes. When the Colon Official malfunctions, therefore, the signs can appear not only in the functions which we associate with the Colon but also in the distress of other Officials as they slowly choke with their own pollution.

The Chinese pictured a court as a place of peaceful co-operation as well as a place of clashing personalities and varying temperaments. This adds a dimension to the understanding of the energy within the body, mind and spirit which we cannot get so easily from the five Elements, a notion of something slightly more willful and less easily explained by the simple laws of Nature. Were we to look at ourselves only as a manifestation of the Elements we might be forced to ask how we manage to fail to heal ourselves and neglect our own health and well-being contrary to most other living things on the planet. The concept of the Officials who sometimes act against our own and each other's interests adds other ways to describe what is really happening within us.

The idea of clashes of personality within our body, mind and spirit is not as strange as it sounds. In our everyday world we often hear people talk about wanting to do something but, "A part of me wouldn't let me do it", and when they say this they do not attract the immediate suspicion of their friends and colleagues. No-one is committed to psychiatric care because they have little internal battles between the head and the heart over who is really in charge when their emotions and their common sense give them contradictory messages. Indeed, the fields of modern psychotherapy and hypnotherapy are now full of models of the mind and spirit which talk about trying to get agreement between

The Spirit of the Officials

the different parts of a person and negotiating between different aspects of someone's personality.

This may sound as though a picture of balance has been replaced by one of petty squabbles and jealousy, and the reader may be tempted to ask how this can be when we are supposed to be looking at a system of medicine which is derived from a view of the world which emphasizes the harmony of flow and transformation. In an ideal world the picture of the Officials at work would equally be one of peace and co-operation. There are times when any team suddenly comes together as one and at this point no-one tries to outdo anyone else or to take the limelight. Each is content to perform his or her own function, and savor the fact that everything on which he or she depends and everything which depends on him or her is going according to its nature and its internal plan.

This world is not an ideal one, however, and the relative states of imbalance which exist within us from birth lead to internal disharmony and disease. When this happens we see the signs of it in the Elemental imbalance, the color, sound, odor and emotion which reveal the Causative Factor to us. Using the Elements to describe the fine detail of our lives can sometimes be beyond our powers, however. It is the Officials which show us how the Element's specific functions exist and take place within the person and exactly how the imbalances affect and change all of our behavior. With the help of this picture we can go directly to the part which is crying out most of all for help.

In the next few chapters, therefore, I shall explain the spirit which belongs to each of the Officials, and then describe how this contributes to all of our functions on all levels. There is of necessity a great deal of quite specific detail about the physical function, mental function and spiritual function of each Official. In my experience this is likely to tempt some people to use the book and the information as a diagnostic aid, working backwards from a particular symptom to an individual Official. All that I can do is to counsel people against doing so, because the following chapters will show how the relationship between the Officials is every bit as complicated as that between the Elements.

It may be easy, for example, to conclude from a cursory examination that the Liver Official is not performing its functions very well. What we must ask ourselves, however, is whether the Liver itself is ill or whether it cannot function because it is perhaps full of rubbish, blocked with impurity, dry and

9.9

parched, starved of energy, overheating, hamstrung by indecision and timidity, or deprived of the help of any of the other Officials. The answer to this makes a vast difference to our understanding of a person and their subsequent treatment.

Our aim, therefore, must be to learn to recognize the members of this team from the spirit which they bring to the task of keeping us balanced and alive, and to learn how their various functions fit together and support each other. This is perhaps the most important aspect, and the one which is easiest to forget as we become more immersed in the more 'concrete' detail of physical and mental faculties and symptoms.

CHAPTER TEN

THE OFFICIALS OF THE WOOD ELEMENT - LIVER AND GALL BLADDER

The Officials which express the Wood element within us are the Liver, responsible for planning, and the Gall Bladder, responsible for judgment and decision making. The Wood element is associated with vision, purpose and the growth and regeneration of the spring. Plans and decisions are so central to each of these processes that it is not surprising that these are the principal functions of the two Officials of Wood. When we look at these Officials in man and woman to see how they affect every aspect of the human being, we may begin to understand the true breadth and scope of the Element within us. Through this I hope to help those who practise acupuncture to understand how they can see both the life and the disease of these Officials in our body, mind and spirit.

Before looking at them in detail, however, we must consider an important relationship between the two Officials in each Element of which the Officials of the Wood Element are perhaps the clearest example. The planner and the decision maker are like the architect and site foreman building a house. Without a plan the foreman has nowhere to start and nothing to do. There is no point in scheduling work and organizing deliveries because all that lies in front of him is a bare plot and the idea of a house. Improvising without a plan would be a very risky proposition; the last thing anyone would want are doors instead of windows, walls instead of doors, and ceilings that cave in.

The architect alone is no better. Having a plan is wonderful but houses were never built from armchairs. Deciding in what order to do things and where to start is an art in itself, and the last thing that anyone wants is the plastering done before the wiring is complete, and the site crew collecting timber when five tons of rapidly drying cement arrives. The foreman has the skills of taking the plans and bringing into life the vision which the architect has had. Having been told where to go he has to decide how to get there. Architect and builder have to work together in harmony to succeed in their common purpose, and if one cannot function neither can the other.

Illustrations like this never trivialize what we are learning, but instead bring home the full force of the relationship by the power of simple and natural allusion in which the ancient Chinese were masters. These two Officials are interdependent, and tied to each other like blood brothers from birth. They are of the same stock, and whatever affects one is inevitably going to affect the other just as badly. If the planner is sick, it is probably the decision maker who will panic most, just as the planner is likely to feel frustrated and hopeless if there is no-one to make the necessary decisions to carry out its work.

A final word needs to be said about the names of the Officials. I have headed the chapter as 'Liver and Gall Bladder', and throughout this and the following chapters I shall use the names 'Liver', 'Gall Bladder', 'Kidney', 'Bladder', and so on. When we teach students, however, we emphasize time and time again that using the names of the organs with which we are already familiar in the West must not draw them back automatically to the idea of a physical organ. I would like to think that if we have been successful we shall have people in practice who are asking themselves not, "How is the Liver in this patient?", but, "How is the Planner's work being done?". This is far closer to the essence of the element and the Official than the physical organ which bears the same name.

THE OFFICIAL OF PLANNING - THE LIVER

As an illustration I have likened the Liver Official to an architect, and in many ways we really could call this master of planning the architect of the individual. What makes this analogy so compelling is that at one time or another we are all likely to have seen the intricate plans which architects draw up, the blueprints from which the whole structure will be assembled. These blueprints are more than mere marks on a page; they enshrine the vision and hope of the architect and give everyone involved in the project an aim, a goal and a purpose. Without such a plan there can be no structure and order in what everyone else does.

This is exactly the function which the Liver Official has within the body, mind and spirit. If we are able to live according to an inner plan every part of us knows where it is supposed to be going and what it is supposed to be doing. Not only that, the essence of the good planner is to have made arrangements for the unforeseen, the contingency plans which offer alternatives when we run up against obstacles and difficulties. When we have this potential we can be flexible and relaxed, secure in the knowledge that we can take care of ourselves whatever arises. This gives us the same sense of confidence which we see in the

The Relationships of the Elements

farmers who lay down seeds each year in the spring and, having prepared the land to fulfill its purpose, know that the seeds will germinate and that they can adjust the water and nutrients to grow a healthy and successful crop.

When we think of the words and ideas which we associate with the Official of planning it is not difficult to find the areas within the body, mind and spirit which depend on that Official's continued health and well-being. On a simple physical level there are thousands of rhythms within the body which depend in their entirety on the plans which have been laid down for them, from the smallest intra-cellular exchanges to some of the rhythms which we follow in our daily lives.

Many of the systems for hormone release, for example, are the result of very complex and marvelous plans. Each has its own delicate and intricate order and logic. If the levels of a hormone such as ACTH decrease then the body's plan automatically provides for more production and the release of reserves. When the target has been achieved production stops again. When we cut ourselves and bleed a truly remarkable cascade of emergency plans are put into action to clot our blood, each one set up and planned with complex fail-safe mechanisms to ensure that we rarely find blood clotting in our veins without proper cause.

Our lives have much more obvious routines which also rely on the Liver Official's ability to function at its best. We eat and digest food according to a plan, breathe and assimilate air according to a plan, move according to a plan, and follow most paths in our lives according to plans which help us to achieve our aims. Each conscious and unconscious process bears within it a blueprint which arises from the work of the Liver Official. Each plan is so natural in its execution that we have long since ceased to marvel at how we survive and grow with each new day.

One very important bodily plan in women, and one which in diagnosis can tell us an enormous amount about the Official's health, is the menstrual cycle, the basis of the plan by which we are able to regenerate and reproduce. In classical Chinese physiology the Liver is regarded as the storer of blood, and its importance in the rhythm of the menstrual cycle has additional significance for this very reason. It governs both the plan which makes the cycle repeat every twenty eight days and the release of the menstrual blood itself. The better the condition of the Liver Official, the more regular and more smooth the periods are likely to be. 'Smooth' is a word which we would do well to remember when we think of the Liver Official at work. In someone with a healthy Liver everything works smoothly because stage follows stage in every plan like clockwork. It should remind us of the feeling of satisfaction which we get when everything 'goes according to plan'.

This is particularly evident when we look at the Liver Official at work in our minds. We are forever planning our time, both for the hour, the day and the year, and when a healthy Liver Official organizes our lives we are able to achieve our ends with ease. The Liver also gives us the power to re-arrange our plans when circumstances subvert our initial ideas. The ability to form contingency plans is the same flexibility which we see in the Wood element in Nature when the growing shoots find their way past obstacles to the light. Equally important on a mental level is the growth and regeneration of the Wood Element realized in the Liver Official's function. Once we have completed what we set out to do it is the Liver Official which makes us able to give birth to new objectives, and to carry ourselves with hope and drive into our new futures.

A healthy Liver Official is, in fact, responsible for many of the powers which we tend to describe as our powers of reason, and the structure and processes of logical argument draw their strength from this Official. When we have this power within us our rational thought has the kind of clarity which lets ourselves and other people see exactly what we are trying to get across. The simplicity and accuracy of our mind's eye pictures come from the work of the Liver Official.

Nowhere is the inner plan more important, however, than in the spirit of each person. To have a sense of purpose and to be able to grow and develop in this part of our lives is the foundation of some of our most cherished ideals. When we have spiritual goals we are able to see a future for ourselves. We have hope and vision, and we are able to set aside some of the short-term distractions around us and aim for the ends which are the most fulfilling for our inner essence and being. There is no greater joy to be had than to aspire to the vision of a distant future and to see it realized.

The comparison of these functions with what we understand by the liver as an organ in Western physiology shows straight away how futile it is to try to equate one with the other. There are, however, echoes of the functions of the Liver Official in what the physical liver does. It is an important site for the storage of blood, proteins, fats and iron, and it forms part of a feedback system, an internal contingency plan, to ensure that enough energy is reaching the tissues in the form of glycogen. Many of its other physiological functions, like the release of bile and the production of blood clotting factors, echo this sense of an inner organizational flow, with the right amounts of body chemicals being in the right place at the right time.

One aspect of the liver in Western physiology which does have great clinical significance for the acupuncturist is the detoxification of the blood, the removal of drugs and alcohol which pollute the system. The filtering of toxic chemicals is one of the most important physiological tasks of the liver, and it is the liver which bears the brunt of excessive drug use, medical and otherwise, in modern times. Points on the Liver meridian have been found empirically to have a great effect in helping people to cleanse their systems of these toxins.

As I mentioned earlier, however, the physical organ is not the home of the Liver Official, nor is the physical organ and its function the only indicator of the health of the Official. The meridian (energy channel) of the Liver is the Official's residence in the body, and its influence extends on the physical level to the whole pathway. The superficial channel (i.e. that which lies closer to the surface of the body and on which the acupuncture points lie) starts at the lateral nail point of the big toe, rises up the medial side of the leg to the groin where, having looped around the genitals, it rises to the central abdomen to loop around the liver, gall bladder and stomach. From here a deep channel rises via the back of the throat to the nasal cavities and eye, and thence to the top of the head, with a secondary channel circling around the mouth and lips.

It is worthwhile spelling out this pathway at length because the state of the Official's residence can tell us much about the Official himself. Not only that, the energy in this channel feeds the Official, and when acupuncturists work on the meridian they are communicating directly with the Official himself. If this energy is full and free flowing then all the areas which the meridian feeds and supplies will flourish. It is equally true, however, that whatever blocks the flow in the channels will harm the Official himself. This is a point which we must always bear in mind in diagnosis.

The health of the Official is also visible in parts of the body with which it has a special relationship but which are not necessarily connected either with the organ or the meridian. The connection with the eyes and sight is one which we have already looked at in relation to the Wood Element, as has the relationship with the ligaments and tendons. These are very much to do with the **functions** of the Liver Official. The ability to see and have vision, and the capacity to move flexibly and with purpose are the physical aspects of the broader functions which the Liver Official has. When the Official is healthy this is reflected in clear eyes and vision, and supple tendons.

The eyes are often a key sign of sickness in the Liver Official. Dry or red eyes, myopia and other distortions of the lens, 'floaters' in the eye which impinge on someone's vision, photophobia, puffiness and inflammation, and blurring of vision are a very clear sign that the Liver is out of balance. Weakness in the eyes can arise from a failure of function or a lack of energy in the Liver meridian itself. This is important to recognise, not only for the relationships which unfold as we see more deeply into the economy of the body, mind and spirit but also because it demonstrates just how observant we have to be in looking for signs of imbalance.

The tendons and ligaments may also lose their suppleness when the Liver Official is sick. They become rigid and tense, and not only does the person move in a way which reflects this but the tendons themselves tear and snap easily. Angular and rigid movements, or injury and pains in the tendons, especially at the joints of the elbow, knee and ankle are quite common. People become like rigid trees that cannot bend with the wind, and stiffness and cracking are the result of losing the flexibility that comes with good health. With tendons as taut and rigid as these it is no surprise to find that there are often cases of chronic spasms and cramps alongside the more acute problems.

The Liver Official has a special relationship with the nails. If we want to get clear, first-hand evidence of the health of this Official we need look no further. Strong, clear nails without blemishes and spots are usually an indication that all is well with the Official. When it is sick, however, these are often the first place where we can see the manifestations of imbalance. The nails become brittle, pitted and ridged, the toe nails usually being affected first and the finger nails later on.

We need to bear in mind the pathway of the meridian when we look at symptoms which may arise from sickness in the Official. The meridian, for example, passes through the genital area, and it is not uncommon for energy disturbances in the Liver to cause swollen genitals, spasms and cramps in the penis or vagina, and poor sexual function. Similarly the meridian flows through the abdomen and its weakness or disturbance can cause poor digestion, distension of the abdomen, wind, ulcers, and the acid reflux which we naturally associate with the sour taste which comes from the Wood element. The deep channel which rises to the top of the head often brings with it the headaches which are characteristic of the upward rising energy of the Wood element going out of control.

We need to be observant, however, because these problems which arise along the meridian's flow could equally well be functional problems. The Wood element gives us the power to see on all levels, the power to reproduce and regenerate, and the power to organize. Once the Wood element in us is disturbed it is natural that the physical functions of the Liver Official should show signs of distress. This need not necessarily manifest in channel problems, however. It is perfectly possible for the Liver meridian to be free flowing and for there still to be problems with the eyes and genitals which arise from a different level of disturbance within the person.

While we look at the physical disease which may arise from a Liver imbalance it is perhaps worth mentioning some of the problems in the body's rhythms which depend on the Planner's abilities. The menstrual cycle, for example, is often very badly affected by Liver disorders. Infrequent or over-frequent periods, mid-cycle bleeding, too much or too little blood may all arise from the breakdown of the plan. Digestion, too, may be disrupted as food arrives in the wrong place at the wrong time; nagging gastric pains and abdominal distension are often the result. Everything which should flow with ordered ease may become unstable as the plans cease working. This translates even into the movements of the body which we can see in a serious disturbance of the Liver Official. Instead of flexibility and grace there is stumbling and awkwardness, even dizziness and vertigo, as the body loses all sense of its simple plans for movement.

There really is not enough space in a book of this nature to run through all of the physical problems which can arise from sickness in the Liver Official. I have not, for instance, mentioned itching and rashes, both of which are fairly common, especially in people weaning themselves off drugs and whose Liver Official is struggling to regain control. Details like this are fascinating, but disease strikes us on all levels, and there is more disease arising from the mind and spirit in these days than from physical causes alone. If we concentrate on the body we may not learn to recognise the signs of sickness of the Liver

Official in mind and spirit, where its true cause may lie.

When the Liver Official fails to function at the mental level we may find that someone literally cannot make plans. Their life is a muddle because they have no idea where they are going or what they are doing. Someone who has this kind of problem has no choice but to be vague, wandering around and blowing with the wind, because they have no real idea of a future which they can achieve other than by sitting around and waiting to see what happens. Too much planning can be just as damaging: new projects here, there and everywhere, and none anywhere near completion. The plan is all, the result is nothing. Others may make plans that have no room for contingencies or alternatives. They stick rigidly to what they see, inflexible and brittle to the last, their lives structured and organized to the last detail in a way that closes down all other options.

The effects of a sick Planner may not only be a problem for the person with the imbalance but also for people around them. Some people cannot resist telling others what to do, organizing their lives and giving advice whether it is wanted or not. More often than not they cannot plan anything for themselves but think nothing of jumping straight in with both feet to put someone else straight. There are others to whom we give simple tasks and yet they cannot organize themselves at all, and end up wandering around feeling lost and aimless. When we think of the frustration and anger which are associated with the Wood element we can easily see how any or all of these situations would give rise to the utmost irritation on both sides.

When we do the Traditional Diagnosis, however, we have many opportunities to observe this Official at work in the way that patients present their information to us and show us how their minds' function. If we keep in our mind's eye the picture of the Official in good health we will immediately be struck by the signs of his distress. The Diagnosis may be a total muddle, or we may find ourselves seated next to someone who runs through a list which they have prepared and from which they are not going to depart. 'Firstly', they will say, and after rambling around for ten minutes we hear them say, 'Secondly', and on it goes.

At first sight examples like these may seem more confusing than helpful, but as I have said, this is not an exhaustive list, and nor could it be. Each of us is different, and a Liver imbalance will manifest in a unique way in each of us. If we are aware of the extremes of mental disturbance which can occur, we can get a sense of the health of the Official by asking ourselves whether there is a

The Relationships of the Elements

tendency towards any of these problems. If nothing presents itself we can ask about future plans, aims and aspirations in order to get a sense of whether the Liver official is healthy.

When the problem is at the level of the spirit, we may not need to apply our minds in quite the same way. We have only to observe the patient and listen to their words to hear this Official's cry for help. Someone with no plans or purpose for their whole life will be as despondent and despairing as we can ever imagine. What greater feeling of depression can there be than a life with no sense of future and growth? Some of the most terrible depressions arise from sickness of the Liver Official at this level. From our spiritual goals we often derive the feeling that our lives are worthwhile. When someone cannot see any future they may feel that they might just as well give up. That is often how they present themselves to us, resigned and slumped.

Having a spiritual goal is not enough in itself, however, to guarantee a full and happy life. Having just the one rigid plan to adhere to whatever happens can sometimes be just as bad. This is a recipe for a life of missed opportunities because the person cannot unbend enough to grasp the choices which enrich our lives so very much. Worse still, a person can become very inflexible and even intolerant if anyone else does not share what that person sees as their future.

Our language never really does justice to this level of function within the Elements and Officials. It is far easier to describe the problems which arise from a sick spirit or a sick mind than it is to present a picture of how the mind and spirit thrive when each Element and each Official functions as Nature ordained. Rather than talking at levels of abstraction which might obscure the wisdom and beauty of the Official we can do no worse than turn to the acupuncture points on the meridian in order to see the true essence of the Official.

Very often we find here that the names of points on the meridian of each Official capture the essence of their function and their meaning. One point which perhaps more than any other embodies the essence of the Liver Official is the fourteenth point of the meridian, 'Qi Men'. This is translated as 'Gate of Hope', and in this simple image is the profound wisdom of the Official. When this official is in good health we can see a way out of the darkness and into a better future, and with it we have the capacity to plan our way towards and through the door which leads to our goals. If we find a sick and diseased Planner in a patient there is no point better for reaching the spirit of the Liver Official and

Classical Five-Element Acupuncture

helping this official to regain strength in order to lead the patient into a bright, new future.

Before moving on, however, I want to add one more picture which will help to emphasize the importance of this Official to the function of all the others. Most people are familiar with assembly lines, and the intricacy with which all the parts fit together and the workers all combine. If we imagine the Officials as the twelve workers in a line and then the Planner goes off sick we may begin to picture the utter chaos which results. For a while everything struggles on according to its given plans, but as soon as problems occur or the task in hand is finished there is no-one to establish contingency plans or new plans, and no-one to stand in the planner's place. Without planning and organization bickering and argument are bound to start, and anger and frustration will build up as people no longer know precisely what to do.

This one Official, with a role exactly equivalent to the General who excels in planning, has the capacity to hold everything together and, when sick, to allow everything to fall apart. When we use this picture to illuminate our understanding of the Officials it should make clear what this system of medicine always emphasizes, that symptoms of this distress can come from anywhere when this happens. When the planning fails any one of the eleven other Officials can be the one where distress leads to disease in body, mind and spirit.

THE OFFICIAL OF DECISION MAKING AND JUDGMENT - THE GALL BLADDER

It is all very well to have good plans, but these are of no value unless they are translated into something concrete. The Official who excels in decision-making and judgment, the Gall Bladder, is the member of the team whose work fulfills the planner's hopes and dreams, and at the same time feeds back decisions to the planner as the basis for future blueprints. In Chinese medicine the Gall Bladder is said to be the only Official who works with pure essence; all of the others either store or come into contact with polluted or dirty energy. By contrast the Gall Bladder only handles bile, a pure secretion of the body.

This purity is vitally important for the making of sound decisions, and this in turn is so critical because we are making decisions for every second of every hour of our lives. The planner and the decision-maker never rest, and it is not for nothing that their peak time of energy, what we call the 'horary time' according to the Chinese Clock, is between 11.00pm and 3.00 am. While we sleep these two are busy working out their schedules for the body, mind and spirit, and ensuring that we start each day with a new optimism and new plans for our lives. We know this by instinct when we talk about needing to sleep on our important decisions. We are leaving this work for our Officials to do when they are at their best.

People may object that "We don't make that many decisions" in a day, and if they do we can take them through a little pantomime about eating their breakfast - "Shall I have coffee or tea, one piece of toast or two? Shall I put the kettle on first or get the toast on? Shall I spread the butter while the tea is brewing? Shall I pick up the post and the paper now, or shall I wait?", and so on. The process is so automatic that we just get on with it, and yet every day we make thousands of small decisions which get us out of bed, take us to our work, bring us home, and choose what to do with our leisure time.

The word 'choice' is very important when we look at this Official's work. There are choices in everything we do, and it is through this Official that we are able to choose. When we looked at the Liver Official we touched on the hormone systems and the blood clotting process, the wonderful plans and emergency routines which the Planner creates. Each second of the day there are decisions even at this level in the body which must be made for the plans to work. Someone has to decide when to activate the blood-clotting process, to release hormones, and to secrete digestive bile. Every single plan and system which we find in the body works only by virtue of the power which this Official gives to us to carry out the Liver Official's work.

The Gall Bladder's work is not limited to this level of function within the body. Most of our daily life involves planning where to be and where to go, and making sure that we move in such a way as to get there. Every physical movement of our body is a collection of split-second decisions which keep us in balance and put our arms, legs and body weight in the right place. When our Decision Maker is healthy we are a triumph of co-ordination. Some of this is outside our control, for just as we have a whole series of automatic functions within us, so we have unconscious reflex responses in our whole bodies which govern our movement. When we touch a hot plate our hands and arms recoil without us having to decide consciously to do anything. We also, however, have the dexterity and balance to move where we choose, and getting to the right place at the right time is an ability which comes from the Gall Bladder.

The real expertise of the Gall Bladder lies in our mental abilities. All of the words we associate with this Official - deciding, judging, evaluating, co-ordinating - are faculties which we use in almost all of our mental processes. When we have before us the plan which we take from the Liver Official, we are all the time making decisions about how to carry it out and comparing where we are with where we should be, or would like to be. Everything which we say and which we think is a response to some form of stimulus either from inside ourselves or from other people, and at every moment we are making decisions about what to say and making judgments about what things mean. The better the health of our Gall Bladder the clearer out thoughts and thought processes will be.

The fact that our minds are where the Gall Bladder most obviously excels in its work should not overshadow how important is the ability to judge and to evaluate the more profound goals which we draw from our Planner. It is no good to be told that we need to search for this truth or that truth without being able to judge and decide whether it is a goal worthy of being pursued. No plan is without fault and not every aim is worth valuing. The Gall Bladder alone is able to bring a wonderful power of judgment to the body, mind and spirit to evaluate the worth of the goals which we set ourselves.

This ability is something which we should treasure in these modern times. There are so many people trying to convince us of the value of their codes of belief and their teachings for the spirit, that we need a healthy Official of Judgment to guide us to the truth. The purity of this Official's work is our only guarantee that we can see to the heart of the ideas and beliefs around us and can see the rights and wrongs that lie within.

Even more so than with the Liver Official the comparison between this Official and the physical organ makes nonsense of a literal equivalence between the two. The gall bladder in western physiology has the simple function of storing bile which has been secreted by the liver. Even this function is not indispensable, for when the gall bladder is diseased and seriously interferes with the release of bile or the work of the liver it is removed without greatly affecting the patient's overall health.

When we look at the physical problems which arise within the body from sickness and disease in the Gall Bladder Official, these arise less from the physical organ than from the Official's functions as they are reflected in the physical body. That is not to say that cases of cholecystitis and jaundice never arise from a Gall Bladder deficiency or excess; there are times when the physical organ does bear the brunt of disease from the imbalance. The broader role, however, is reflected in many of the organizational aspects of bodily function. Because many of these involve the release and movement of fluids and the organization of all the body systems, an imbalance here can create symptoms anywhere. The more obvious ones tend to occur when repair systems for the body do not work: blood fails to clot and cuts and bruises heal slowly. In essence, any body system in which all the components are present but the work does not get carried out may show the possibility of a Gall Bladder problem.

A more obvious range of physical problems arise from the Gall Bladder's task of maintaining balance and co-ordination. When the Official is distressed we may find that someone becomes very clumsy, their movements indefinite and imprecise. The Official's indecision is represented literally in the tentative nature of what the person does. Equally possible, however, is the other extreme, an almost robotic precision with every movement betraying a rigid and inflexible order. The overall balance within the body may also be affected. The co-ordination of left and right, above and below, and inside and outside belong to this Official's function. On many occasions a patient will present with all left-sided symptoms, or with many symptoms in the lower half of the body alone, and these can both be a sign that the Decision Maker is sick. A classic symptom of Gall-Bladder distress, for example, is a one-sided headache.

Imbalances rarely produce symptoms on one level alone, however, and the most striking problems arising from this Official often come from the mental functions. Some people lose the ability to decide, even in the simplest matters. A person whose Gall Bladder is weak may all the time use words like, "Don't know" and "I can't make my mind up", and constantly defer decision-making to others. The dithering and procrastination are as clear a sign of illness in this Official as a gall-stone.

When we come across this weakness it teaches us to be extremely careful how we observe the predominant emotions which are reflected in someone's behavior. We may see panic and immediately think of the Water element or the Fire element, when what we are really seeing is the panic of indecision,

Classical Five-Element Acupuncture

scanning the options but thinking: "Oh God, I don't know what to do next, I can't decide". We see someone who has awfully complicated relationships and we might automatically think of Fire and the need for love and warmth without thinking, "Here is someone who can't choose, who is stuck because they can't decide how to clear things up".

Imbalances can run to either extreme and someone can decide too much. More often than not this spills over into deciding things for everyone else. When decisions take on this amount of weight, they begin to have a kind of fixity which becomes rigid and inflexible. People talk about "my decision" and "the decision", as though it could never be changed and was never something decided by an ordinary human being. Out of the window go compassion and the other person's point of view. Like the rigid and unyielding nature of diseased plants they give way to no-one and seem to be ready to crack at any moment.

The faculty of judgment may also be affected by this rigidity. Making decisions for people will involve making judgments for and about them, and a Gall Bladder Official in distress can often lead to the person becoming extremely judgmental. People "should do this" or "shouldn't do that", and the overall effect is reminiscent of a silly placard that people sometimes put on their office walls, "Be reasonable: do it my way". They have decided what should be done, the rules which have to be followed for every situation, and there is no room for discussion.

Poor judgment and indecision wreak the greatest havoc in the life of the spirit. There are many paths to the Dao, and many people who offer themselves as guides and as holders of the true values which will lead people to their true path. We have to be able to make judgments of value here more than anywhere. When this faculty goes awry we are open to all manner of temptation and poor judgment. We chose the wrong things, flit between paths because we cannot decide to travel in one simple direction, and cannot choose between right and wrong. The distress which affects the spirit, the unrest, the feeling of uncertainty, and the sense of floating about without direction, is without equal in the spirit. It is small wonder that there are many cases of madness and insanity, and even suicidal behavior arising from imbalances here.

The Official's residence, the meridian, is as extensive as that of the Liver. From its first point by the side of the eye the superficial pathway traverses the head several times before descending to the back of the neck and to the shoulder.

The Relationships of the Elements

From here it travels down the lateral side of the body to the hip, and from here down the lateral side of the leg to the ankle and onto the foot to finish by the nail of the fourth toe. The deep pathway connects directly with the physical organ and other deep pathways.

Even this cursory description of the meridian reveals a connection with some of the more familiar symptoms of this Official's distress. Problems with eysight, headaches, tense and stiff shoulders and neck, abdominal distension, hip pains which are sometimes called arthritis and rheumatism, sciatica, muscle cramps, sore and itching shins, rigid ankle joints, and tendon problems in the lower leg - all of these can and do arise from malfunctions in this Official's pathway.

As with the Liver Official, however, we have to be careful not to get too carried away with seeing symptoms like these arising from the meridian alone. If someone cannot make decisions and will go to any lengths to avoid doing so we are just as likely to find functional disturbances arising from this Official. Someone may literally not be able to see, or to hear, or to talk as the Gall Bladder withdraws from contributing to these faculties. A headache, nausea, vomiting and diarrhea all effectively remove someone from the responsibility of deciding and acting, and this Official is important enough to the functioning of all the other Officials to have these direct effects.

When we look at the Officials at work in the person we always have to keep in mind its function rather than look immediately to the physical signs. If someone cannot see we have to ask ourselves why this is rather than concluding straight away that the Liver or the Gall Bladder is sick because the eyes are closely associated with both. Disease rarely occurs on one level alone, and it is only when we look at the whole person and see a total inability to plan or to decide on all levels that we can then begin to make associations with the presenting symptoms.

The spirit of the Gall Bladder Official is revealed in some of the points on its meridian. Two points in particular which capture the essence of the Official are VII.37, 'Bright and Clear', the junction point, and VII.24, 'Sun and Moon'. Clarity, above all, is what we get from this Official when it is operating at its best. A clear mind, clear sight, clear judgments and clear decisions are what characterize someone who really knows where they are going and can see how to get there. 'Sun and Moon' reminds us of the balance which we should see between the different parts of the body, mind and spirit. The sun and the moon share the day between them, each having their greater and lesser share as the days and year pass, and giving way graciously to each other. When there are unequal divisions in the person between right and left or above and below, and between body and mind or mind and spirit, arising from an imbalance in the Gall Bladder, this point can draw on the essence of the Official to re-establish the harmony which it brings when it is at its best.

The two Officials of the Wood Element, therefore, are united in their task of bringing a sense of growth, purpose and hope to the body, mind and spirit. We shall see in later chapters how they can do this not only for the person as a whole but for each of the other Officials. What should already have emerged clearly, however, is that the functions of both permeate everything that we do, and that if we cultivate our powers to observe, we shall be able to ask at all levels in our patients how these Officials are faring and recognise their response.

CHAPTER ELEVEN

THE OFFICIALS OF THE FIRE ELEMENT

1 - HEART PROTECTOR AND THREE HEATER

The control and distribution of the warmth of the Fire Element in the body, mind and spirit is entrusted to four Officials: the Heart Official, known as the Supreme Controller; the Small Intestine Official, the Official who Separates Pure from Impure; the Circulation/Sex Official which is known as the Heart Protector; and the Three Heater Official, the Official in charge of the Three Burning Spaces.

What immediately springs to attention is there is no physical organ which corresponds to either the Heart Protector or the Three Heater. These Officials are in a real sense pure functionaries. The Heart Protector is loosely associated with the pericardium, a fibrous muscle sheet which encloses the heart and is in a very literal sense a layer of heart protector, but this is not a function in western physiology which raises the pericardium to much prominence. There have also been in recent years attempts to link the Three Heater with a part of the hypothalamus which seems to regulate body temperature, but neither of these two rough equivalences is of great importance in understanding what each Official does. They are perhaps the clearest example of the importance of function over structure in the concept of the Officials, and to understand them we have rather to look to the essence of the Fire Element in body, mind and spirit than to the medical textbooks.

CIRCULATION/SEX OFFICIAL - THE HEART PROTECTOR

The name given to this Official really sums up the essence of its work. It protects the Heart Official, the Supreme Controller, from insult and injury; it is responsible for all the arterial and venous circulation; and it is responsible for all internal and external sexual secretions. Some readers may think, "Well, that seems fairly clear; on to the next one!" I only mention this kind of response because it is one which we sometimes hear from people who do not know the breadth of the concept of an Official, and even sometimes from acupuncturists who want to be technicians, working on the body rather than touching the spirit of the person. The labels give only the smallest hint of the real meaning of these tasks.

The Supreme Controller, the Heart Official, is responsible for maintaining order in the whole system, for setting limits and boundaries for the other Officials. This task is of such enormous importance and involves such effort and energy that the Supreme Controller does not have the power within to be self protecting from the blows which come its way or from the ingratitude and harm which are sometimes aimed in its direction. The Official could not dispense wisdom freely if it was necessary all the time to worry about its own safety and well-being, and the other Fire Officials all play their part in protecting the Supreme Controller who can then conduct the affairs of the 'inner state' without fear and without limit.

Of the other three Fire Officials the Heart Protector is the one whose work is most directly linked to this task in the role of the imperial bodyguard and who, on a physical level, wards off the physical traumas and shocks which assail the physical heart. All the stresses and strains of our modern life place a terrible load on the heart and it is the Heart Protector which selflessly shoulders the burden for the Supreme Controller. When we suffer from physical shock, either from accident or trauma, from over-indulgence or over-exercise, or from harmful drugs and food, the Heart Protector stands in the way of the Heart and takes the blows.

This has enormous significance for us when we look at distress and illness in the Fire Element. If this Official is working well, it is here that we find the evidence of strain and illness rather than in the Heart itself. About eighty five percent of what we describe in the West as heart disease affects this Official, and not the heart itself, for that is the Heart Protector's role, to take the knocks and sustain the damage instead of the Heart.

Just as important as this physical protection, however, is the protection which the Heart Protector offers from the mental and emotional injury that is probably more commonplace in modern life. Although people tend to think of the heart more as a simple pump these days our language still underlines our intuitive understanding of the heart's importance. "We are heartbroken", we say; "My heart stood still". Emotional upsets are, "A blow to the heart", and when we are nervous or anxious, "Our hearts are in our mouths". If this were truly the case we would not last five minutes. So important is the Supreme Controller to our well-being in giving leadership and wise command with compassion to every other Official that we cannot afford to have serious upsets daily which weaken or distress this Official. The Heart Protector is that part of us given by Nature to ensure that we are safe, for by taking the emotional knocks, both the accidental injuries and the deliberate insults, this Official protects the very center of our being. The way of this protection is through giving love, compassion and kindness, for this is the greatest protection of all.

Since it is easy to recognize right away the importance of this protection for our bodies, minds and spirits it takes no great leap of imagination to see how the Heart Protector's protection of the spirit of the Heart Official must be the most important task. The spirit of the love which comes from the Fire Element is our connection to the universal spirit in Nature, and no more important a connection can exist in man and woman. Nothing can be allowed to threaten this, and the Heart Protector alone carries the responsibility for providing all the good and wonderful connections of the spirit to flow from the person.

The Heart Protector's role should not come as a surprise to us since there are many parallels in Nature around us of the same function. The bees protect their queen with millions of workers so that she can be allowed to do her work without fear of invasion and attack. Herds gather themselves around their leader, and fend off threatening attacks. This is a pattern which we have copied throughout our own history. There have always been imperial bodyguards since the days when our ancestors realized that the wisest leaders were not necessarily the strongest, and chose to protect their wisdom by asking others to devote their lives to the task of being their strength.

It would be wrong to think of the Heart Protector as a little person with a shield, however, standing guard and letting nothing pass. By virtue of this Official's closeness to the Supreme Controller the Heart Protector is as much an ambassador as a guard, and in whose other functions, as controller of arterial and venous circulation and of internal and external sexual secretions, lies the evidence of how this Official helps to distribute and dispense the warmth.

In looking at the control of circulation we have to go beyond our western ideas about blood in order to grasp how important the Heart Protector's function is. Blood in Chinese medicine goes hand in hand with Qi energy. Qi energy is said to be the commander of the blood, while blood is seen as the mother of Qi energy. By maintaining the flow of blood in the arteries and veins this Official is helping to provide the flow of energy to every cell in the body.

What this gives us is not only the physical warmth and nourishment, but the mental and spiritual warmth. For above all what the blood provides in its flow to every cell of the body is contact and communication. All of the qualities of the Fire Element which make our lives so rich, the generosity, the compassion, the understanding and the forgiveness, the inner warmth which flows from the Fire Element, are spread to every corner of the body, mind and spirit by virtue of this Official's work.

The association with the control of internal and external sexual secretions also relates directly to the spreading of warmth and love. This comes both from the control of blood which sustains the fluids themselves and from the function which the fluids perform. They make possible the expression of physical love between man and woman, and even in saying this it is obvious that when this function is at its best 'physical' is a very poor way to describe what such a union means. It is an exchange of mind and above all spirit that embodies the essence of the Fire Element in the contact between two people, an expression of pure love and joy which has few equals in our experience.

With such important functions under its control, any illness or disease which affects this Official is bound to have profound effects. On a physical level many of the symptoms which we associate with the heart itself arise from the Heart Protector, especially ones like heart pains, angina and palpitations. This runs counter to what most people think. These pains are usually attributed to the heart itself without question, and most treatment is aimed at the heart. This is a mistake, for in many ways these pains are a sign that the Protector is doing its job well and taking the strain which would otherwise fall on the heart.

This has important implications for any treatment aimed at dealing with such pains. The Heart must be treated with respect, and any intervention, in either Western or Oriental medicine, should be kept to a minimum (Japanese acupuncturists, for example, rarely treat the Heart or Heart channel directly). Occasionally, however, a shock can be so great that it breaks through the Heart Protector's guard and goes straight to the Heart itself, but the circumstances of this are likely to be so obvious that there will be no difficulty in recognizing this as a special case and giving help and support directly to the Heart Official. This does not mean that we can always ignore the Heart except when cases such as these arise. This would be very foolish: after many years battering even the most dedicated Heart Protector will give way and any further shocks will go straight to the Heart. What we must do, however, is set aside an automatic assumption that a pain in the heart results from an imbalance in the Heart itself. We are most likely to see the results of weakness in the Heart Protector in the kinds of problems which people have in their relationships. We especially need to have our protection in affairs of the heart because the heart is by itself very vulnerable. When this Official is sick we may often find that people either become incredibly over-protected or so open that they have no barriers at all to hurt and upsets.

When the barriers are locked solid there is no way that the love from fire can get out and precious little chance of it receiving anything from outside. When this happens a person has no communion with anyone else on this level. Their own warmth is trapped inside and none is allowed in. People like this, and there are many of them, sometimes seem really cold and unloving while inside their hearts may be wilting for want of warmth and love or have turned hard and cold. Once the protector has taken a great many knocks it seems to say, "That's enough of that", and lets nothing pass in or out.

The opposite is just as common. After years of battering, the Protector just gives up and leaves the Heart Official vulnerable to all sorts of emotional battering. This gives rise to people who wear their hearts on their sleeves. They have absolutely no defences, and are wide open to one emotional beating after another. In both of these imbalances the person's history of relationships is likely to be anything but easy, for without strength here there is no stability in all of the things that matter most in relationships: the sharing, the compassion and the love. Many people with these kinds of imbalance in fact tend frequently to fold their arms across to protect their chests and to cover their exposed center, and sometimes even go so far as to hug themselves unconsciously for the warmth they cannot find anywhere else and are unable or unwilling to provide.

When the Protector is weak this Official's other two functions, the blood circulation and the sexual secretions, can equally be a source of problems. Without proper circulation there is no inner warmth and this often results in the symptoms which we usually ascribe to poor circulation, such as cold hands and feet and pale, blotchy skin. There are often problems with the arteries and veins themselves such as varicose veins, hemorrhoids, arterio-sclerosis and the terribly aggravating conditions like Raynaud's Disease.

Blood is more than just a physical substance, however; it is the medium by which the warmth of the spirit is passed to all parts of the body, mind and spirit. When the blood flow is affected then there cannot be a proper flow of the warmth which makes compassion and understanding possible, and the simple pleasure of sharing with other people is often that much more difficult. When this happens someone can become intolerant and hard, full of hatred and hostility for want of the love which would lighten their spirit.

The Fire Element is just as much about joy and fun as about warmth; the ideas flow together as naturally as the qualities of energy with which they are associated. When this energy does not circulate freely none of the Officials can go about their tasks with any sense of enjoyment. People whose Heart Protector has become sick are often among the most joyless of people, flat and uninspired, miserable and grudging to an extreme. There is no inner warmth that we can reach within them any more than they can reach it inside themselves. This often leads to one of the most characteristic signs of an imbalance in the Fire element. People whose lives lack this inner fire may do their utmost to induce joy in us so that they can feed off our joy in a desperate attempt to warm their very core. This is where the inappropriate laughter and joy find their root and source.

The name given to this meridian, Circulation/Sex, should also remind us that this Official controls the sexual secretions. When these secretions do not flow we commonly find conditions of frigidity and impotence, although these labels are not in themselves very helpful. What does frigidity mean other than 'coldness', an absence of the warmth that comes from the blood and helps fluids to flow? On occasion the opposite can be the case, and we may find that some people's sexual energy may be excessive because their flow of secretions is running unchecked and may even lead to someone being drawn to perverted sexual expression.

The pathway of the meridian, the residence of the Heart Protector in the body, shows how this Official can have such profound effects. A deep channel starts in the thorax in the pericardium, emerges in the center of the chest and from here one branch travels down the body to connect with the Three Heater Official in each of the Three Jiao. The other branch travels laterally just beyond the nipple where it emerges as the superficial channel to arch over the axilla and down the center of the anterior surface of the arm. Crossing the center of the wrist it runs down to the palm of the hand and terminates at the nail point of the middle finger, with another branch running from the palm to the ring finger to meet the

Three Heater meridian.

Many of the symptoms of distress and imbalance in this Official lie along this channel, especially the retro-sternal pains which we commonly ascribe to the heart itself. As we saw with the Liver and Gall Bladder meridians there is a great deal of overlap between the parts of the body which involve the functions of the Officials and the parts traversed by the channels of the meridians themselves. When the Official is sick we might see conditions like cold hands, aches and pains along the arm and into the lower shoulder, and problems in the elbow joints arising from a failure of function or from a failure in the flow of energy in the channel. The pains of angina pectoris, which often follow the pathway of this meridian as well as along the Heart meridian itself, can equally well arise from problems with flow or with function.

In the previous chapter we looked at one or two points which helped to reveal the nature of the Officials. The nine points which can be needled on this meridian all more or less reflect the Heart Protector's role. From Heavenly Pond and Heavenly Spring (V.1 and V.2) to Gate of Qi Reserve (V.4), The Intermediary (V.5) and Inner Frontier Gate (V.6), and to the fire point of the meridian Palace of Weariness (V.8): each represents an aspect of the Heart Protector's work in controlling access to the inner core of the Heart and at the same time bringing this Official's warmth to the other Officials.

Of these, however, it is the Palace of Weariness which embodies best the protection and warmth which comes from the Heart Protector. Palaces had very powerful connotations for the ancient Chinese. These were places where resources were stored and where the gods' representative on earth lived. For a tired and weary soul a palace would be the ultimate sanctuary, a place of warmth and comfort, of nourishment and support, the heart of the region. Within it is the Emperor, cocooned and protected by its walls, and its stores feed and sustain the people both within and outside its barriers. When we use points like this on patients whose Fire is ailing we connect then to the spirit of the Fire Element in all its power and depth.

THE THREE HEATER OFFICIAL -
THE OFFICIAL IN CHARGE OF THE THREE BURNING SPACES

The Official 'paired' with the Heart Protector, its blood sibling, is the Official in charge of the Three Burning Spaces, sometimes described in the Chinese classics as the Official with 'a name but no form'. For all that, the ThreeHeater Official's work is no less important than every other Official in the body.

The Three Heater is so called because the Official looks after the Three Jiao, the three 'burning spaces', areas into which the trunk is divided. Each contains the organs with which the other Officials are associated. The Upper Jiao, which 'contains' the Lungs, Heart and Heart Protector, lies above the level of the nipples and is very much to do with receiving Qi energy. The Middle Jiao lies below this as far as the umbilicus, and 'contains' the Spleen, Stomach, Liver and Gall Bladder. This Jiao is responsible for rotting, ripening and transforming the Qi energy. The Lower Jiao, which lies in the area beneath the navel, 'contains' the Small and Large Intestine, the Bladder and the Kidneys. The Officials in this Jiao are most concerned with separating the pure from the impure energy and expelling wastes.

The Chinese often likened the three Jiao to fluids in various states: the Upper Jiao is a mist; the Middle Jiao is a muddy pool; and the Lower Jiao is a drainage ditch. This connection with flow is worth remembering because this Official is often described as the Official responsible for the circulation of Qi, Blood and Fluids, and for the harmonizing of the digestion of liquid and solid food. In the Five-Element tradition of acupuncture, however, the functions of harmonizing and regulation are as much concerned with the warmth and heat of the Fire element in which the Official resides.

The Three Heater is responsible for maintaining an even balance of heat between the Three Jiao and, just as importantly, between the whole body and its surrounding, and whose work is one of service to the general good. Without an even temperature between the Three Jiao and within each individual Jiao the other Officials could not work at all. There is a parallel to this in the modern western medical concept of homeostasis, the idea of a balanced working environment for the internal organs maintained by small and continuous adjustments to internal temperature and climate in response to changes in internal and external conditions. Although the parallel is not exact there are some similarities in the work which the Three Heater Official does.

Through its functions in the body we have often given this Official the nickname of the 'Heating Engineer', because this gives us the most graphic picture of the Three Heater's work. In an office block, for example, there are

The Relationships of the Elements

many floors of people busy managing, accounting, typing, designing and occasionally sleeping, and all need to have a comfortable environment for any work to get done. If the heating engineer does his sums wrong and sets the heating too high, very soon there are raised voices and lost tempers, people sitting around feeling lethargic, and even more people sleeping. If the engineer misjudges in the other direction, the temperature drops, and the bodies and minds of all the staff start to freeze up as well. Work stops as people restrict their movement, and look forward to their warm tea at eleven or the log fire in the pub at lunch time.

Someone entrusted with this job has to make sure that all of the building is evenly heated, so that no floor is hampered and falls out of step with everyone else. The person also has the even more vital job of keeping an eye on the weather outside to make sure that this internal balance does not rise too high or fall too low as the outside conditions change. Such a task calls for very delicate and precise skills. What this picture describes is exactly the same function which the Three Heater Official has within the body, mind and spirit. Every time we lower ourselves into a bath ten degrees hotter than we are, this Official acts to maintain the internal temperature at 98.4 Fahrenheit. Every time that we upset our internal balance by breathing really cold air, drinking scalding hot liquids, or creating heat by digesting hot food, this Official shares out the heat or disperses the excess safely. Without the Three Heater's work life would be at best uncomfortable and at worst unlivable.

We must not let this picture make us become over-attached to the physical level of this Official's work, however. The Three Heater belongs to the Fire element and the warmth which this particular Official balances and distributes is just as much warmth for the mind and spirit as it is physical heat. All of the Officials need to feel the warmth and love of the spirit of Fire as much as body heat. There could be nothing more divisive than to have some Officials sharing in this wonderful warmth on all levels while others are provided for physically but cold in their spirit. The quality of disharmony arising from this is far worse than being physically cold.

Equally important is the balance between the inside and the outside. This Official is all the while adapting and regulating the internal warmth as conditions change, and does exactly the same function for our minds, emotions and spirit. We need to be in balance with the levels of warmth and love around us, not only for our own protection but also for the way that it enriches our relationships and social ties. Just as the Heart Protector gives us the security to venture outwards into relationships the Three Heater enables us to reach an appropriate balance with the emotional and spiritual temperature outside, and to change and flow just as it does.

This Official is working away for twenty four hours a day, doing a job that would be impossible for us to do consciously and yet without which we cannot function. When the Three Heater falls sick it is immediately obvious from the Official's function that its illness will affect every other Official. It is always important to ask, however, whether an imbalance in this Official's work arises within the Three Heater or within another Official. For just as its work affects all of them, so their sickness affects it. If someone on the third floor lights a fire during the high summer or opens all the windows on a cold day the heating engineers may try their best to compensate but will eventually fail. They may ultimately be so tired from their efforts that they can no longer do their job properly, but the initial cause lies elsewhere. For this reason we often find that imbalances in other Officials which cause one of the Three Jiao to become very hot or very cold will have an effect on the Three Heater and we may often find ourselves treating this Official as well as the main imbalance in order to restore harmony to the whole system.

When the Three Heater is sick, on a physical level there are often the kind of symptoms which we would expect when a heating system fails. There may be hot and cold flushes, cold extremities, a red face and neck, and all the other signs which are associated with heat in the system. This can equally manifest in all the signs which appear when there is not enough heat: stiffness, stabbing pains, pallid flesh and lips, blue nails, and the like. Not every sign of an imbalance in hot and cold traces back to the Three Heater, but it would be unusual for this Official to be in distress without some indication of heat or lack of heat. Indeed, one problem which does arise quite often from this Official's imbalance is of an inability to maintain a stable temperature with the result that the person suffers from alternating chills and fevers.

With this Official, more than any other, an imbalance is going to have massive effects on the whole system. If the whole body is running at the wrong temperature, be it too hot or too cold, then all of the Officials are going to be in extreme discomfort. The range of symptoms, therefore, that can arise from an imbalance here is enormous, each reflecting the way that every function is affected.

The Relationships of the Elements

The uncertainty which arises in the mind and the emotions when the Three Heater operates erratically is captured by some of our natural language. People are sometimes said to, "Blow hot and cold", and no better or simpler expression could be found to describe some of the emotional and mental problems which arise from this imbalance. When someone loses the ability to tune themselves in to their surroundings, the power to regulate and harmonize their actions and words with others is affected. There are going to be times when they seem far too enthusiastic or emotionally overpowering, and just when people are used to this behaviour the balance may tip the other way and they can suddenly appear indifferent. A frequent manifestation of this is for someone to have a temper like a volcano, all fire and brimstone, and then ten minutes later to be totally unconcerned, as though nothing had happened.

Someone with an imbalance in the Three Heater Official may often have a history of uncertain and unsatisfactory relationships, not least because this Official provides the heat which fuels and creates our feelings of warmth. Without this we would not even want to draw close to anyone else. When we are close to our partners or our friends, however, we are constantly adjusting to each other, altering our emotional and social thermostats to keep in step with each other. If someone lacks this ability it will begin to create the kinds of difficulties and mood swings which drive friends and lovers to desperation. Expressions like, "give and take", and words like "sharing", only have any meaning when we are able to balance and regulate our lives and our social ties with those around us. Just as devastating is the imbalance which fixes our inner temperature far too hot or far too cold for our social surroundings. When we looked at the Fire element we touched on people who are stuck in excess joy or stuck in utter joylessness. We can begin to see from the work of this Official how this can happen, and how any failure in the Official's work can lead to someone having only the one highly inappropriate response to all situations.

The problem of being stuck or blowing hot and cold has just as profound an effect on the spirit. Nowhere else is the harmony and ability to be in tune with the flow so important. The best that we can hope to achieve in following the Dao is to do and to say what is appropriate; the whole concept of balance and harmony in this system of medicine is the ability to meet each situation with an effective and appropriate response. If someone cannot help oscillating between over-enthusiasm and indifference, between excitement and boredom, it will be difficult to maintain anything like an appropriate balance with the spirit of Nature within and around us.

When someone cannot regulate their inner heat to share in the warmth of the spirit in Nature it may well cause the greatest distress. The names which we might give to this distress are only labels and not very precise ones at that. If we try to imagine, however, what the feeling must be like, the inability to fall in step with something so wonderful, we might be able to get a sense of the agitation, the anxiety, the depression, and the other mental and spiritual turmoils which more often than not lead people to psychotherapy and counseling.

There is a danger in portraying types, for as I have already said, many practitioners begin to believe that it is possible to work backwards and deduce the imbalance from the behavior; it is not, for the imbalance can only be diagnosed based on one color, sound, odor and emotion which is out of balance. However, when the Three Heater is out of balance we sometimes find that someone takes on new paths, new ideas, and new relationships with incredible excitement and intensity, and then two weeks later it is as though they had never existed. The person has not rejected it or cast it aside; it has simply ceased to interest them and as quickly as it is taken up it is let go. This uneven response and sudden change is what characterizes this Official's sickness. This should not surprise us when we remember that the Three Heater belongs to Fire, and that fires have the capacity to flare up and die unpredictably when they are disturbed.

It is not difficult to imagine the disturbances which daily try the Three Heater's strength. All of the stresses and changes of a fast-moving day have to be absorbed and handled by this Official, and when it falters this meridian often shows the niggling signs of oncoming disease. The meridian starts at the tip of the ring finger, travels up the posterior surface of the forearm between the radius and ulna, and thence to the shoulder. From here a deep channel crosses the shoulder and travels down to each of the Three Jiao, connecting at CV.17 with the Heart Protector. The main superficial channel rises up the lateral surface of the neck and orbits the ear before ending just lateral to the eyebrow. Another deep channel connects with several points on the Gall Bladder and Bladder meridians on the face.

As with all of the meridians on the arm there are often pains along the course of the channel and especially in the elbow, shoulder joints, neck, face and ears which arise from weaknesses in the energy flow to and from the Official. Another set of problems concern the deep channel which connects the Three Jiao. I have not covered at any length the inter-relationship of the Jiao, but it

The Relationships of the Elements

should be fairly obvious that the circulation of heat and the control of the movement of fluids and Qi between the Three Jiao, always described as a part of the Official's function, are in essence very similar and draw their strength from the downward energy of the Official's pathway. When this is weakened or blocked, Qi and fluids may become stuck in whichever Jiao is affected. This may lead to abdominal distension and indigestion in the Middle Jiao, asthma and congestion in the Upper Jiao, and constipation and thick discharges from the Lower Jiao.

Many of the points on this meridian are given names which involve the control of water flow. The command points, the first ten points of the meridian which lie between the finger tip and elbow illustrate this perfectly. There are gates - Rushing the Frontier Gate, Fluid Secretion Gate, and Outer Frontier Gate; sources of supply - Yang Pond and Heavenly Well; and all the intricate networks which an irrigation system demands - Branch Ditch, Three Yang Crossing, and Fourth Gutter. Each of these lends itself to establishing flow and harmony, to allowing heat and energy to flow in a controlled and measured way to all parts of the body and especially to the trunk.

The Three Heater and Heart Protector are perfectly matched in their work of bringing the essence of the Fire element at all levels into our lives. Where one gives the power of self-protection the other gives the power of regulation and harmonizing . The two junction points, Inner Frontier Gate on the Heart Protector and Outer Frontier Gate on the Three Heater, capture the essence of this. One guards the access to our inner self and the other allows us to balance the inner and the outer conditions and allow a flow inside and outside.

CHAPTER TWELVE

THE OFFICIALS OF THE FIRE ELEMENT

2 - HEART AND SMALL INTESTINE

These two Officials embody the spirit of the Fire Element as much as the Heart Protector and Three Heater. The importance of the Heart Official as the Supreme Controller is such that it is often regarded as the root of life itself, and because of this needs the two Officials which we have already looked at to preserve its defense and maintain the balance of its kingdom both within its borders and in relation to the world outside. We shall now see in the work of the Small Intestine Official a further layer of protection given to the Heart to enable it to carry out its vital functions.

When we look at the other Officials of the Fire element, however, we must not assume that the three Fire Officials are subordinate to the Heart Official or in any way less vital. The Small Intestine is paired with the Heart; they are blood brothers in the same way that the Liver and Gall Bladder are joined. One can no more exist without the other than the body can without the head, or the mind without the spirit. The ruler of a kingdom is only as powerful as the love and respect which his rule commands, and he must work as hard for this as his protectors work hard in his defense. The Small Intestine, therefore, is every bit as important, and makes its own contribution to the economy of the body, mind, and spirit.

SMALL INTESTINE OFFICIAL -
THE OFFICIAL WHO SEPARATES PURE FROM IMPURE

On a superficial level there is some similarity between what we understand by the physical organ in the West and the function of this Official. In Western physiology the small intestine consists of three parts, the duodenum, the jejunum and the ileum. Although the gut is a relatively narrow tube, its length of twenty feet or more means that the part-digested food from the stomach takes a long time to pass through, allowing most of the nutrients and vital substances to be absorbed through the gut wall. In Classical medicine the Small Intestine has much the same physical function. The Stomach Official passes the rotted

Classical Five-Element Acupuncture

and ripened food to the Small Intestine Official to extract the pure Qi energy and pass the remainder on to the Colon Official. For this function the Small Intestine is said to be the 'transformer of Qi', because in its hands the raw Qi energy of food is separated into pure Qi for the body, mind and spirit, and into 'dirty Qi' which is sent to the Colon. 'The Separator', as we often call it, has the ability to identify and retain only the clean and pure energy which we need for our bodies, minds and spirits. In this lies its connection with the essence of Fire, for by using the heat of the fire to transform Qi energy in this way and keeping nothing but the clean and the pure and discarding the impure, there is maximum joy in our lives. The warmth and love of which we are capable is not tainted by corruption or wickedness.

The importance of the Separator's work in our body, mind and spirit is obvious when we look at its physical function alone. Our food has never been so polluted with additives and chemicals, and our dietary habits have never been so poor. Yet for all that most of us manage to take enough pure Qi energy from our nourishment, however poor its quality, to live reasonably full and healthy lives. This is a testament to the work of this Official who will, even on a diet mainly of burgers, fries and cola, carry on extracting every ounce of goodness from it and throwing out the impurities. As long as this Official remains healthy we can usually eat whatever we like in moderation and still get by.

This does not mean that we can disregard the Separator's needs and gamble on eating rubbish any time. Like any of the Officials this Official demands respect, and if not accorded any will eventually give up and leave us stranded. What we choose to eat, however, will only be of value as long as the Separator is healthy. There is absolutely no point in changing someone's diet and adding supplements and tonics if this Official is sick and unable to retain their goodness. This is something which we have to bear in mind when someone comes to us whose food does not appear to nourish them. We should ask ourselves first of all how the Separator is faring, for if this Official is sick, a change in diet will benefit the person very little. They will be as likely to retain the rubbish as the quality nutrient.

We can get some idea of the Separator's health from the way that this official manifests in mind and in spirit. Just as our food is more often than not contaminated, so is the food which we take into our minds and thoughts. It is not being too judgmental to say that there is more filth and garbage around us to foul our eyes, our ears and our thoughts than ever before. This seems to me

The Relationships of the Elements

a sad but inescapable fact. There seems to be no end to the perversions and tasteless habits which pervade the media and the streets where we live. Somewhere in amongst all this rubbish lie the simple values and simple information we need for our lives, and even here we are now faced with more information than we can handle in a single lifetime. It is only by virtue of the Separator's function that we can extract what we need from this untidy mess.

We have no need to be judgmental about this. Nature itself has its share of rot and rubbish amongst which the pure essence is found. Each of us has in this Official, however, the power to separate the pure from the impure, to keep what we recognize to be good and to throw out the rubbish and pollutants. When we are in good health and this Official is doing his work we can find the goodness even amidst the nastiest surroundings, and ignore the worst excesses which the sickness of others has wrought. We can find out what we need to know for our present purposes and set aside all the trivia and rubbish which would divert our attention. The Separator helps us to extract sense from the general confusion.

We should all be familiar with the Separator's work within ourselves because it is the part of us which knows the right and proper path to take whatever the temptations which come our way. When we come across conflicts and differences which we need to resolve it is this part of ourselves where we find our sense of natural justice. We appeal to this often, and even though it has no written basis we all tend to share the same views of what is right and what is wrong, what is good and what is evil. This is the gift of our Separator whose work is the foundation of our most precious moral codes.

It is not only for how the Separator guides our choices that we should respect this Official. Words do not do justice to the path of the spirit which we have to follow, but here more than anywhere else we need to be able to recognize and take in the pure essence from amongst all of the other things which fill our lives. Within our everyday existence and our simple relationships with each other exists the essence of the Dao itself. If we are balanced, strong and healthy in our spirit, we may be able to perceive it by the grace of the work of this Official.

We also give the nickname 'The Sorter' to this Official. The way in which I have described the Separator's work may make the Official sound like a glorified filter, but while it may appear like this from the outside this does not do full justice. If we re-consider the Separator's part in the digestive process we can see how active this role is. The food which comes to the small intestine is just a jumbled mass, and in order to take in the pure Qi the Small Intestine Official must first sort it out into some kind of order before taking his pick. This task also depends on the the Official of Decision-Making and Judgments, but if the Small Intestine itself is weak, nothing can be sorted out from which a decision can be made, and with no distinction made between good and bad any decision is purely random.

The separating and sifting which this Official does fulfills the role which the private secretary or deputy takes on in making sure that only the most important and vital matters are presented to their minister or chief. It is the Separator who sifts through and sets out everything for inspection before passing on the most pressing issues worthy of consideration and leaving aside the rubbish. That way the minister can deal with matters of the greatest weight and moment rather than the trivia which would waste precious time or the impure matter which might poison his spirit. In this way The Separator affords another layer of protection for the Supreme Controller.

All the while, therefore, The Separator is working away, sifting through and sorting out our ideas, our thoughts and every aspect of what we take in, leaving aside that which is evil or dirty and retaining the pure. Since this Official has such an important function, the problems which arise from the Separator's sickness are bound to be immense. On a straightforward physical level the body becomes full of impurity and rubbish. It becomes literally gummed up with rubbish. Words like 'thick', 'coagulated' and 'dirty' begin to apply literally to the flow of energy. On a physical level we are going to see adhesions, swellings and lumps. Toxins may gather in the skin as spots, acne and eczema. The heat of the Fire element, within which the Official resides, will often result in painful inflammations like boils, carbuncles and ulcers, and the skin may look red and poisoned.

Every joint in the body which depends on pure fluids for its movement will be threatened by growths and deposits, and what we in the West call arthritis, rheumatism, or gout often arise from the impurities which the Separator leaves in the system. The western names which we give to these conditions are by and large irrelevant, however. When all the joint fluids are gummed up it is obvious that this will result in cases of people being unable to articulate freely and comfortably.

When the cleanliness of the blood and Qi is affected the flow will coagulate as surely as if we had mud in our veins. Small wonder that people get cold hands and feet, all manner of period problems with clotted blood and pain, and digestive disorders. The blood and Qi is so fouled that it cannot flow to the places where it is needed. When this happens all of the other Officials suffer just as badly, and every other function of the body, mind and spirit suffers. Deprived of their pure food they run on dirty fuel and find poisons beginning to ruin their own delicate balance.

If the sickness of this Official can create a polluted, evil and stinking body it is just as capable of creating a polluted, evil and stinking mind. Impure thoughts of every description find free rein because the mind no longer has the ability to distinguish between good and evil. People with imbalances here often take delight and revel in things which are depraved and disgusting, things which if they were healthy they would cast aside because they represent the worst and most evil of which we are capable. All manner of crude jokes, bad language, and foul behavior may have their root in a sick Separator. If our mind is full of poison then all our senses will be poisoned, and our perceptions and observations will be warped.

The sickness of the poisoned spirit is the saddest. At one level we may see the same inability to distinguish between good and evil, and the following of spiritual and occult practices which are anything but healthy and good. Where the spirit suffers worst, however, is in the veil which this pollution places between it and what it holds most dear. Veiled in impurity there is no way that we can improve ourselves. The realization of this can create some of the deepest depressions and anxieties which we shall ever come across. For just as the poisoned body cannot move as it gums up with impurities, so the spirit also loses its power to flourish, and is deprived of the essence of the Fire element which allows us to reach out and communicate with the spirit in Nature and in people around us.

The sickness of this Official often manifests in patterns of behavior. When someone cannot sort out what they take in there is bound to be a great deal of confusion in their minds. The Separator is quite closely related to the ears and the faculty of hearing, and imbalances here often leave people unable to concentrate if there is minimal distractions. When anyone tries to explain fairly simple ideas to them they may look blankly back, unable to sort out the sense in what is being said. They may even range their eyes backwards and forwards, left and right, in a state of confusion as they try desperately to pick out the sense from your words.

Everywhere on the mental level there is likely to be confusion and instability. This may even go as far as some of the more strange and bizarre behavior which borders on insanity, and this is no surprise when we remember that this Official is a part of the Fire element and responsible with the others for disseminating the heat of fire evenly throughout the body, mind and spirit. When the flow is blocked anywhere in the system from impurity and rubbish, the fire within it will start to concentrate and overheat, causing pain and damage wherever it is lodged. If this lies within someone's mind and spirit we may see hysteria and manic behavior which come from the uncontrolled blaze inside him or her.

The pathway of the Official lies in the upper half of the body. From its starting point by the side of the nail on the little finger the superficial channel travels along the edge of the hand and, with the hand flat against the body, along the posterior 'edge' of the arm to the shoulder blade. Here it traverses the scapula and rises onto the base of the neck before crossing over to the supraclavicular fossa. One branch travels deep down through the heart and on to the small intestine itself, while the superficial pathway continues up the neck and onto the cheek. Here one branch joins the bladder meridian in the medial canthus of the eye, while the other turns laterally to end in front of the tragus of the ear at the nineteenth point of the meridian, called appropriately Listening Palace.

I mentioned earlier the inability to freely move joints. The fact is that joint problems like a frozen shoulder resulting from the toxins and rubbish that clog up the system are more likely to happen along the meridian of the Official itself, the Official's residence within the body. If the Small Intestine Official cannot maintain purity for others it is unlikely to be able to maintain its own purity. Problems in the arm, the elbow, the shoulder, and also the neck are very common when this Official is out of balance, and many symptomatic treatments use points on the Small Intestine meridian to try to unblock the flow.

There is an important point to be made here, though, which helps to show the dangers of purely symptomatic treatment. Even if the imbalance which causes the symptom does lie within this Official or meridian, the most likely effect of using these points will be to make things far worse. The problem may arise because of a blockage formed by impurities in the energy in the ear, or the shoulder, or the elbow, like silt in a river. A muddy river is already bad enough, but if we are careful we can still draw some water when the mud settles. If we stir the flow with a stick, we cannot even do this; we make the water dirty and spread a large cloud of poison to everywhere else. This is exactly the effect of using one of these points locally without regard to the state of the Official, and the reason why we can never condone the use of local doctor or symptomatic points that do not form part of a Traditional Diagnosis and treatment plan. The role of the Separator shows us graphically the futility of this approach to treatment.

THE HEART OFFICIAL - THE SUPREME CONTROLLER

By reviewing the role that three of the four Officials of Fire have in supporting the Heart Official it should already be clear that this Official's role in the body, mind and spirit is so important that nothing can be allowed to cause it harm. We should also bear in mind that the Chinese were not accustomed to use words like 'supreme' and 'great' lightly. By referring to the Heart Official as the Supreme Controller they were emphasizing just how special this Official is.

Each of the Officials is like a minister of court with their own allotted tasks. Someone, however, has to take the responsibility for order amongst this group, to decide who should do what, and to reconcile all the different aspects of the tasks which they are performing. Amongst the Officials this is the role of the Supreme Controller who is like an emperor who both delegates tasks to ministers for them to do and at the same time depends on them for every aspect of his own life. The emperor controls and co-ordinates, but his commands can only succeed as long as they accord with the wishes and desires of his people.

The breadth of the Supreme Controller's role is not that difficult for us to understand even in our Western culture and tradition. The physiological function of the heart is still given a great deal of respect, but many more people now hold a view which better reflects the truth of the matter. At this level the heart is only a very efficient pump. We do indeed depend on it, but we depend on the liver and the lungs just as much, and with the wonders of modern surgery and technology we sometimes depend on the heart less than either of these. The heart has always been seen, however, as the seat of our feelings and as the ruler of our lives. Our language is full of expressions which place it in the center of our internal stage. Our heart is where we feel that our passions, our deepest love, and most profound feelings develop, and when we want to emphasize the extent of our connections at the level of emotion or at the level of the spirit itself we describe it as coming from the heart.

The Chinese recognized this same quality in describing the Heart as the residence of Sheng, the spirit. I have already mentioned the connection between the Heart and the complexion, and the way that a Chinese doctor will judge the strength of the Sheng from this. The same applies to the eyes, for when someone's Sheng is strong and their heart is in what they do, the same joyous brightness and sparkle lies there too. When the Heart is strong and the Sheng is strong it affects not only the whole of the physical appearance but the very presence which a person has, their spirit as even we in the West understand it.

On a physical level the Heart is involved with the Heart Protector in circulating blood to all parts of the body. The role of the Heart is more to do with the production of the blood itself and the force and power with which it dispatches it to the extremes of the body through the network of arteries and veins. In the Chinese classics the Heart is said to govern the blood, and when the flow is strong and plentiful nourishment can reach every corner of our physical being.

Important as this role is at a physical level, however, it is overshadowed by its place in the Supreme Controller's function in mind and spirit. The blood is the medium of communication to all the Officials through which the Heart Official is able to carry out tasks. Like any ruler who creates order, this Offical sets out limits and boundaries within which everyone must work, and determines the priorities which apply to their tasks. Whenever people work within boundaries there are always disputes and confrontations, and the wise ruler is the one who arbitrates and mediates between the rivals without taking sides. Without this impartial role the Official would never be able to command the respect of the court and in order to carry out this role must be in touch with all of them all of the time, telling them what to do and hearing what they have to say. The blood as the medium of the Heart Official's communication is absolutely vital.

What makes the other Officials welcome these judgments and the Heart's control is the greater gift which they get in return, the warmth and the unconditional love which come from the Fire Element in the form of the Heart Official. There is nothing conditional or reserved about this gift; it is as open and generous as we can imagine. For this reason alone the Heart needs layers of protection, for no barriers within this Official can be allowed to interfere with the flow. When the Heart Official is healthy everyone is filled with a sense of

The Relationships of the Elements

enthusiasm and joy, and their work becomes a source of pleasure. The goals and purposes which they all pursue are a source of fun, no matter how hard their tasks are. When the king is happy the whole of the kingdom cannot fail to be happy too.

The difficulty of describing the Officials one at a time and in isolation from each other is never more great than when looking at this Official. Nowhere else is interdependence and ultimate unity so manifest. The Heart is a bringer of joy, a giver of love, and a home for the spirit, and yet has to control this kingdom with only these resources. The Heart depends completely on the other Officials for the power to plan and the power to decide, the power to balance and regulate and the power to sort and separate. Without the other Officials the Heart is nothing, and yet without this Official their work has no focus and significance. Like the leader of a harmonious kingdom the only evidence of the Heart's presence is the joy and love which abounds between and among this Official's subjects.

When the Supreme Controller is sick, however, everything goes to pieces. When there is no-one to guide and to lead the consequences are: tremendous fear, apprehension, panic and even hysteria. There are no orders and no commands, and all the carefully drawn boundaries and limits disintegrate. When someone's Supreme Controller is out of balance their whole life may become dominated by this terrible fear and disruption on all levels. This manifests in people's behavior, especially the extreme nervousness and panic attacks which arise from the chaos within. This can be as much a problem in body as in mind and spirit. What are palpitations, insomnia, vivid dreams, sweating and cardiac arrhythmia but the physical manifestation of extreme nerves? No wonder someone cannot sleep when the Heart is sick. Every Official has reason to worry, and each in turn will cry out for attention and for order when their daily time arises, none daring to rest until everything is resolved.

It is not just the order and control which has gone. Without the Supreme Controller there is no love and warmth in the whole of the body, mind and spirit, and no light at the end of the tunnel. Many are the cases of depression and utter joylessness which come from an imbalance here. People may try to go routinely about their business but there is no spark and life in what they do, merely the mechanical rhythms of a pointless treadmill punctuated by the panic attacks and agitation which arise from this Official's distress.

Listing the possible symptoms for an imbalance in this Official in isolation from the others is not always helpful. We have to add to the ones emanating from the Heart itself all of the conditions which arise when the other Officials try to do their jobs without warmth and without limits. There are bound to be Liver problems, Gall Bladder problems, for who is to set a limit to the plans and decisions, and the tasks of the Spleen Official become almost impossible. The other Fire Officials which depend on his warmth to transform and move Qi energy, or whose task it is to spread warmth evenly, cannot possibly do their work. Everywhere there will be signs of the chaos which ensues from the Supreme Controller's sickness.

We must not forget, either, that the distressed Official may not be listless and idle. The same panic which afflicts others can afflict the Supreme Controller. When a monarch fears for his kingdom's safety he may start to interfere in everyone else's job and take on all the responsibilities. What better way to ensure control than to try to assume all of it oneself? This may be reflected in the behavior of people whose Heart Official is sick. They may become the kind of people whom it is difficult to be around, who are forever controlling us and everyone else around them and setting us limits which they have no right to do. Many people associate this kind of bossy behavior with imbalances in the Liver and Gall Bladder Officials, but this is not just a case of planning and deciding for others. When we are on the receiving end of this kind of behavior it is like being given an imperial command.

This interference is just as damaging to the other Officials as no order at all. When someone else interferes with what we do we may tolerate it for a while, but in the end we are going to give up and let them get on with it. We become resentful and petulant: "OK, if you can do it better, you can damn well take all of it." One by one they all leave their functions to the Heart who gradually collapses under the weight of responsibility and perpetual fear of not being able to handle greater and more complex tasks. The ultimate effect on someone's physical health, a 'cardiac arrest', sums this up perfectly: the person just comes to a dead halt.

The pathway of the Heart meridian shows us how the physical problems which relate to this Official's functions also have their basis in the flow of energy. The meridian begins in the deep tissue of the heart itself. One deep pathway flows down to the small intestine to connect with his brother Official, and another rises up to the mouth and then to the optic foramen. The main pathway rises with the aorta and travels to the armpit, from which the superficial channel travels down the medial border of the arm and across the palm of the hand to terminate at the ulnar nail point of the little finger. When this Official is sick all of the pains which we associate with heart disease can arise along this channel, either in the heart itself or along the arm as in angina pectoris.

The points which lie on this meridian also demonstrate the importance and power of this Official. The first point which is available to needles bears the name Utmost Source. When we use this point, the entry point of the Heart meridian, we are drawing from the deepest well, the Official's connection to the spirit of the Fire Element. Then we have Blue-Green Spirit, Spirit Path and Spirit Gate, all of which connect with the Heart but reach right to the spirit of the person. The Official's Fire point, the Fire point of a Fire meridian, is Lesser Palace, and as I have said already about the point Palace of Weariness, a palace is a haven and source of riches for those who arrive here. The junction point of the meridian is called Penetrating Inside, and when we needle here we are like visitors seeking an audience, asking for our treatment to be taken to the very heart of the patient.

This last point should, indeed, also remind us of the tremendous respect which we owe to this Official even as we treat the person. The names of the points, their very spirit, tells us that they are powerful and affect our whole being, and for that reason we most often approach the Heart Official through the Official's ambassadors and protectors. When we treat the Heart Protector, the Three Heater and the Small Intestine, we are communicating with the Heart in a way which allows ministers to veto what we offer, and only when this route fails do we go to the Heart Official. We have to be this careful; some of the points, like Blue Green Spirit, which is absolutely forbidden to use, are so powerful that 90% of our patients will faint if this is needled, causing terrible and unnecessary chaos.

This Official, therefore, and the Official's three ministers within the element Fire are the means by which the light and warmth of the spirit are kept alive in us. Like the two Officials of Wood which we have already looked at, each seems in turn to be the most important, the one without which we could not hope to live any kind of meaningful and happy life. This pattern will continue as we look at element after element, and if nothing else, should help us to develop a respect for the many functions which we may take for granted in our daily lives.

CHAPTER THIRTEEN

THE OFFICIALS OF THE EARTH ELEMENT SPLEEN AND STOMACH

The Element Earth is our connection with mother Earth herself. From her we receive our physical nourishment which, along with the air from the heavens, is the only way that we can replenish and revitalize the Qi energy with which we are born. We also receive from her the mental and spiritual nourishment which gives us the feeling of stability and security, the center and equilibrium on which our whole lives are founded. The Officials of the Earth Element, therefore, are vitally important to the whole economy of the body, mind and spirit.

Between them the Stomach and Spleen Officials digest and transform our physical nourishment and transport it to every cell in our body. Without them nothing could live or move, and through them every other Official receives the nourishment which it needs to carry out its own function. Here we mean not just the physical nourishment but also the mental and spiritual nourishment. As we have seen with the other Officials they are interdependent; for the Earth Element to flourish within us these two have to work together in harmony.

THE STOMACH OFFICIAL - THE OFFICIAL OF ROTTING AND RIPENING FOOD AND DRINK

For all its importance nowhere are we more disrespectful to an Official than to the Stomach. We tend to think of it as a kind of loose sack into which we pour food and drink and from which, with the addition of a few digestive juices, the mixture make its journey down to our gut for absorption. We have really no idea of how far-reaching its work is. Whenever students are taught about this Official, the first thing I do before we even look at the function of the Official is to guide them through its pathway in order to show them the extent of its influence within the body, mind and spirit.

The superficial channel of the Stomach meridian starts just under the eye, and from there travels down the side of the face to the lips. From here one branch

Classical Five-Element Acupuncture

goes up towards the ear and high into the temple to meet the Governor Vessel in the center line of the head, while the other branch descends via the throat to the supra-clavicular fossa. It then descends on the nipple line through the nipple and down over the lower abdomen, from which it travels down the antero-lateral part of the thigh and lower leg, and thence onto the foot to terminate by the nail of the second toe.

This is the far-reaching extent of the superficial meridian without even touching on the deep pathway which joins the channel to the stomach and also to the spleen. Nor have I mentioned the fact that several of the points, and Stomach 12 in particular, are major meeting points with the other meridians. The reason for looking at the meridian straight away is to dash at once any illusion that the Stomach Official is just the stomach, and that any disorder or imbalance in this Official is going to manifest in stomach ache, vomiting, or abdominal distension. The Stomach Official's home is throughout the whole body. It is the body's connection with the nourishment of Mother Earth and builds up and tends stores of energy for all the Officials.

When the imbalance of this Official brings sickness to the body, therefore, it can turn up anywhere within the body. There may be eye problems, ear problems, headaches, throat diseases like laryngitis, pharyngitis, and all the other '-itis' problems of the throat. The pathway runs onto the chest and here we may find pains and arrhythmias so bad that a person may think he is having a heart attack. Lower in the abdomen there may be bowel disorders and problems with fertility. As the pathway extends to the limbs there may be leg pains, weakness of the muscles and foot disorders. We can cast aside immediately, therefore, any notion that the Stomach Official is limited to the organ that bears its name. We may often find, in fact, that what we in the West call 'stomach disorders' have as much to do with the Gall Bladder and Small Intestine as the Stomach Official.

The Stomach's physical task is not dissimilar to our modern understanding of the work of the stomach. In the Nei Jing it is given the name of the Official responsible for rotting and ripening because that is what it does to the food which we send down to it. This may not seem very different from how we understand it now, except that we tend to think of it as a passive process. Most people would probably find that a kind of internal concrete mixer fitted their picture of the Stomach's job. If that were the case we would do well to consider exactly what a concrete mixer does. Our food is like the cement and sand, our drink and digestive juices the water which is put in to mix it up. If someone makes a mortar with too much water, it will never set and the bricks laid with it will simply fall over. The same applies if it is too dry; it will crumble away to nothing. The ingredients are exactly the same as for a good mortar, but the mix is totally wrong. It has to have exactly the right consistency for the job which it has to do and if the consistency is wrong the mortar is useless.

To use an analogy closer to most people's homes we could take eggs, flour, milk, water, butter and fruit and make a mouth-watering cake. With the same ingredients, however, we could get the blend wrong and end up with a lumpy or crumbly cake so disgusting that no-one would dream of eating it. The point which needs to be stressed over and over again is that the Rotter and Ripener does more than break the food down into the sort of stew from which the nutrients can be absorbed. This Official has to make a blend that is palatable and appetizing to the body, to the mind and to the spirit.

When we look at this Official we can see, just as we did with the Small Intestine, that if someone is malnourished a change of diet may do no good at all. If the Official is sick and no nourishment is getting through, it may well not be the ingredients which are to blame. When sick, not even the best ingredients can be blended into something which we can stomach. Changing the diet, in fact, may not only do no good but may even do a great deal of harm. A common response to long-term stomach upsets and disorders is to put someone on a diet of the purest food of the highest quality and make the job of the Stomach Official as easy as possible. All that this does is to make it lazy and unable to cope with the variety which is normally sent down. When a normal diet is eventually restored, the Official may no longer have a clue what to do with it. I am not suggesting that we should toughen up our stomachs by sending down the worst imaginable garbage that forces the Stomach Official to work overtime, or huge mouthfuls of undigested food which take hours to break down. A balance, however, of good and bad is what would normally be expected, and that is what we should provide.

This kind of preamble is worth spending time on because this Official is the one which provides all of the other Officials with their nourishment. The Stomach Official is the direct link between them and the Earth, and what is prepared for the other Officials has to be palatable and appetizing. We constantly need to replenish our Qi energy for every activity which our Officials undertake, and when the other Officials can depend on this Official to do this without fail it is

13.3

a source of tremendous comfort and security. It is like having an anchor, a point which grounds us to the Earth and guarantees us the same sense of connection which we had when we were babes in arms and depended entirely on our physical mothers.

This same anchor is just as important in our mental and spiritual lives. The Stomach is just as involved in taking in our mental and spiritual food. Our whole language is full of expressions which make it clear that we have understood this function without having to be taught about it. We talk about "digesting" information, "chewing" over problems, and "swallowing" dictionaries. In a thousand other ways we contrive to take in a huge bulk of words and information which we break down in order to extract what we need. If we did not do this our mental and spiritual food would be as useless as undigested physical food. Our Separator would have no chance of picking out the pure, the good and the valuable from this great block of matter.

Taking in food for our mind and spirit is every bit as powerful an anchor for us as the physical food which we eat. The direction which we associate with the Stomach is downwards, for that is the pathway that Qi energy follows in the digestive process. Just as this grounds us to the physical Earth, the work of the Stomach grounds us to the mind and the spirit of the Earth. Taking in food and assimilating it on these levels gives us the same sense of peace and security which we get from our natural mother. When this Official is strong, there is no greater sense of balance and equilibrium to be found anywhere.

It is not surprising, therefore, that sickness in the Stomach Official is devastating to the whole person. What happens, for instance, if food is not properly digested when we send it down? The first result on a physical level will be that no Official can use the mixture sent to feed them. It is unappetizing and unusable. Some of it will be left standing, and here we see the cause of so many of the niggling physical problems which arise from sickness in this Official, the mucus and the phlegm which are the lumpy residue of badly prepared Qi energy blocking up the channels. If we think of the pathway of the Official we can see the headaches, neuralgias, eye problems, tinnitus and deafness, asthma, and all the other blockages which this poor quality food will cause.

When this lumpy rubbish is the only food the Officials have there is little pure Qi to be had. Without it there is bound to be extreme weakness, tiredness, fainting and exhaustion, especially in the muscles of the limbs which are the

The Relationships of the Elements

special responsibility of the Earth Element. Some of the Officials are going to reject this food outright and send it back, and that is where we see the abdominal pains, the distension, the retention of food in the stomach which causes acid regurgitation, and finally the vomiting which sends the food up and not down.

Not all of these problems arise from a Stomach balance, and it is dangerous to use signs and symptoms without considering the functions of the Official, what these are trying to do for the body, mind and spirit. We need to look at the whole person for evidence of this. It is rare for there to be only physical symptoms, and if this Official is sick there will be signs from the mind and spirit which show us clearly that the Official is the one who needs help. When our mental food is indigestible it can no more go in and stay in than the physical food. Someone affected in this way may not be able to take in information of any kind, because they have no faculty for digesting it and for blending it into a mixture which they can absorb.

It is sometimes said that people with Stomach imbalances have a tendency to look blank when given detailed information, and to have no memory of being told what to do even though something was said to them only a minute ago. Their mental food never gets in unless we cut it up into small lumps to make it easier for them, or give them plenty of time to digest each single piece. If we do not do this we may often find a sense of real confusion and instability which comes of not really being able to take in what is going on around them.

The word instability is really important in understanding sickness in this Official. If the mind is confused and the person does not know what is happening, that can be a terrifying situation to be in. It is like a small child losing touch with its mother. There is tremendous apprehension, anxiety and worry until he finds her again. When we are cut off from the mental food we need we should not be surprised to be feeling something very similar.

Without proper nourishment for the mind, and especially the spirit, there is no connection with the mother to anchor and ground the person. Here we may find some of the more unusual instabilities where people seem to go off on the kind of spiritual and mental trips that leave them literally off balance and up in the air. The mind and the spirit lack the stability to hold them in harmony with the body, and they seem to leap off at tangents with the least prompting. We even describe people who behave like this as having their feet off the ground and needing to be brought down to earth, as though we had literally seen the imbalance for exactly what it was.

Underneath all of these manifestations, however, will be the one single problem which overrides everything else. When the Stomach is sick no-one else can have any nourishment, and that is what we often see in the person. Every part of them which can make itself heard will be screaming out for food, and from this arises the excessive need for sympathy, the search for the mother's love, the cravings for sweet-tasting food which goes directly to the Earth Element within us, and all of the ways in which children cry out for their mothers when they are hungry, tired and lonely. After a while may come the other extreme, the bitter rejection by the child that no longer trusts its mother. Everything that is offered which comes from the mother is cast aside: sympathy, nourishment, sweetness, and so on. We must never forget this root of the Official in the Element when we are making a diagnosis.

Many of the points which lie on the Stomach meridian reflect its role as the storehouse and supplier of the other Officials. Points like Earth Granary on the face, Qi Cottage, Qi Door, Storehouse, Receiving Fullness, and Lubrication Food Gate all relate directly to this. Other points such as Great Oneness and Heavenly Pivot, placed as it is in the center of the abdomen and almost in the dead center of the meridian, tie up with the sense of equilibrium and balance which come from the Earth Element.

The two points which above all others embody the essence of this Official are Stomach 40, Abundant Splendour, and Stomach 9, the Window point People Welcome. The very image which Abundant Splendour conjures up is of the end of harvest time when all the gifts of Nature have been gathered and stored for the coming year, and we have before us all the riches of the harvest from which to choose and on which to feed. When the Stomach Official is sick there is no better point for reuniting the Stomach Official with this essence and through it to feed all the other Officials in body, mind and spirit.

People Welcome, by contrast, speaks more of the loneliness and isolation which afflicts people when they have lost the love of the mother. The child that has been cast aside by the mother has been cut off from love and warmth, and far from accepting the sympathy which others offer to make up for this terrible loss, fends them off and closes them out, such is the distrust and hurt which the loss creates. In the chapter on the Earth Element I mention the rejection of sympathy being as sure a sign of an Earth imbalance as the exaggerated need for sympathy. With this point we are able to show people the sharing and compassion that belong to the Earth Element, and can begin to reunite them with the Earth in Nature and especially in other people.

The Stomach Official, however, is only one half of the team. The rotting and ripening of food for the Officials is only of value if that food can be sent to every corner of the body, mind and spirit. Even the best ingredients properly mixed are only of value if we can get our hands on them. This task, equally as important as the Stomach's, falls to the Spleen Official, who ensures that we are always provided with the nourishment, day and night, for every day of our lives.

THE SPLEEN OFFICIAL -
THE OFFICIAL OF TRANSPORTATION AND DISTRIBUTION

The task of getting the Qi energy to where it is needed falls to the Spleen Official. This Official is also involved in the process of transformation of Qi energy when it enters the body, but it is the transportation of Qi which is the most vital. The spleen Official's role in the body is similar to that of a transport manager, the head of a distribution network with carriers on the road twenty four hours a day and every day of the year, carrying vital Qi energy to every corner of the body, mind and spirit.

Some readers may think that the image of a road haulage system does not do justice to the wisdom and beauty of this system of medicine, but in truth there is no better example from our daily lives than this. When the food has been harvested, stored, or brought to market, it has to be taken to where it is needed as soon as possible or it will rot. Exactly the same applies within the body, mind and spirit. Someone may be eating an exemplary diet and have a very efficient Stomach Official, and yet the food is never reaching the other Officials because the transport system is defective. Not only does this leave the body, mind and spirit under-nourished but the food begins to rot where it lies in the stomach and generates a great many symptoms there through no fault of the Stomach itself.

It does no harm to dwell a moment on the analogy of a road haulage fleet. Very few people live any longer by the crops which they have tended and harvested for themselves. Even farmers more often than not send all their crops to market and buy their daily food from the supermarket. We all depend on someone laboring through the night and traveling vast distances from country to country just to provide the basic necessities of our lives, and we rarely give a thought to this massive operation.

The Spleen does just the same job within us with the same dependability and reliability, and with just as little recognition as we usually extend to the transporters of our physical food. Without the work of this Official there would be the same panic in the Officials as would follow if we ourselves could not get our daily bread and vegetables, our staple foods and our drink. We would see the same desperation and anxiety as we encounter in famine relief operations where the food is flown to massive warehouses and yet the starving people cannot get their hands on it for want of the transport to get it to their doors. The Spleen Official is not just in charge of the transportation of Qi energy, however; its task also covers the movement of all the other substances throughout the body. Everything which needs to be transported comes under this Official's jurisdiction: blood, urine, lymph, faeces, and all the other substances which move in the body. All of these are just as vital to our health and well-being as the food which we eat.

The responsibility for movement extends to the mind and the spirit as well. The mind cannot function without movement. We recognise this well enough; we even talk about our minds being stuck and we are happy when things start to flow again. This power to move and to flow comes from the Spleen Official. Through its function thoughts are transmitted to the furthest corners of the mind, and are also brought back from our inner 'filing system'. We will find, therefore, that there is often a very close connection between a healthy Spleen Official and the ability to remember and the ability to study and to concentrate.

The ability to dispatch energy to every corner also gives us the security and stability of the Earth Element in every aspect of our being. As I have already said in the preceding pages, we must never forget the connection between the Officials and their Elements. The Spleen's ability to transport and distribute the nourishment from the Stomach Official is our only means of receiving the warmth and love of Mother Earth in every part of our spirit. Between them they are our only means of replenishing and revitalizing the whole of the body, mind and spirit from the moment we are born to the moment we die.

When the Spleen Official is weak, it behaves like any other driver who is tired and cannot be bothered to finish his rounds. The stops near the end are ignored and he may well turn round early and head for home. Small wonder, therefore, that a sick and weak Spleen Official often leaves a person with cold hands or cold feet. There is no energy in the extremities, and precious little delivered elsewhere. It is very common to find weakness and lethargy throughout the whole body when this Official malfunctions.

Besides the symptoms of lack of nourishment there are going to be problems of movement within the body, both movement of substances and movement in general. The distinction is somewhat artificial because the one leads to the other. When there is no movement of energy and fluids there is no fuel for the muscles and what little there is tends to coagulate and thicken because the flow is too poor. With the Spleen Official as well as the Stomach Official we tend to see mucus and phlegm-related conditions like asthma and bronchitis, and sometimes even more solid lumps like fibroids and stones, where the movement is so sluggish that the thickening becomes extreme. With this kind of deprivation and coagulation going on we may well find that movement as a whole stops and some forms of paralysis of the limbs may well set in.

The Spleen Official also helps to move the blood, and when it is sick the weakness of the flow may well create the perfect conditions of stagnation for the onset of varicose veins and hemorrhoids. Not surprisingly there are often also menstrual difficulties from this same lack of movement; the blood needs to be carried away and transported out of the body. When this transportation is inefficient and erratic, many of the problems arise to which we give names such as amenorrhoea and dysmenorrhoea. The blood never arrives, or it is so thick and clotted it is painful to pass. Many of the points on the Spleen meridian have a direct bearing on the quality and regularity of the menstrual flow, and can do much to ease the transport of the blood.

Again, however, we have to be careful not to see the distress of an Official entirely in terms of physical problems, and remember that these examples are only used to show how imbalances in the general functions of movement and transport manifest in physical disease. The same functions are also disturbed in mind and spirit. In the mind, for example, a lack of movement may result in things like poor concentration and a sense of being stuck. When we looked at the Earth Element we noted that many people with Earth imbalances were often troubled by worry and anxiety, and with the failure of transportation in the Spleen we can see its root. Worry and anxiety are as much forms of being stuck and coagulated as catarrh and phlegm in the body. The power to study and to think problems through is also likely to be affected. Every mental activity which depends on movement, what we sometimes call mental agility, will show signs of losing the flow which comes from the Transporter.

This all follows quite naturally from the uneven distribution of nourishment. Some parts of the mind are well-nourished, and others are crying out for food where the Transporter has not managed to reach them. How can there possibly be balanced thought and mental powers? The Officials responsible for the parts which are starving are unlikely to be able to join in the team effort, and when the Officials who are being nourished swiftly become overloaded with the burden, the whole mental apparatus begins to fall apart.

In the spirit the same sort of distress arises from the lack of proper distribution of the nourishment. The Officials between them ensure our connection to the spirit of Nature and the Dao, and each has to work to full capacity in partnership with the others to achieve harmony and balance in all our affairs. If some are under-nourished because this Official cannot transport Qi energy to them there will be the same sort of rootlessness and agitation which we see in the motherless child. Lack of comfort, lack of love, and lack of compassion in some and not in others is going to lead to all of the disunity we see when some children are better cared for than others. The jealousy, spite, attention-seeking, depression and isolation shatter the harmony of the spirit, and only when a solid connection with Mother Earth is re-established will the Officials, together as a whole, be able to breathe a sigh of collective relief.

This same lack of movement is also going to affect the spirit as a whole. People sometimes find themselves too entrenched, unable to move towards the goals which they have set. We should not get carried away that everything to do with Spleen imbalances is always deserving of sympathy. There are going to be people troubled in this way who are the epitome of laziness, who can see what they need to do but cannot be bothered to move towards it. A caricature of someone with this Official out of balance is the person who solves all the problems of the world from the armchair but is not moved to do anything about it, spinning thought upon thought while achieving nothing.

The meridian of the Spleen Official, is nearly as extensive as that of the Stomach. The superficial channel begins at the medial nail point of the big toe, runs up the medial side of the foot, ankle and leg, before joining the trunk at the inguinal margin. The pathway deviates to the mid-line twice, the second and higher of these channels joining the meridian to the spleen, stomach and pancreas. The main pathway continues upwards in the nipple line and then diverges laterally until it reaches the second intercostal space from which it descends to the axillary line of the lateral surface of the trunk to the exit point Spleen 21. From here a deep pathway rises through the inner surface of the chest, up the oesophagus, and on to the base of the tongue from which it spreads all over the tongue.

Many of the physical signs of imbalance which have already been mentioned are not only related to the function of the Spleen but to the pathway of the Official. Like that of the Stomach which heads downwards and covers most of the body, the Spleen Official's upward pathway also extends nearly from bottom to top. The one aspect of its powers which I have not yet mentioned is that of being said by the ancients to be the granter of the five tastes. When the Spleen is healthy we can enjoy all the flavors which Nature provides. In the pathway we can see how the tongue is connected to the Official and enables it to have this power.

With the previous Officials I have drawn on the spirit of one or two points on the meridian to illustrate the essence of the Official. There are points such as Great Horizontal which emphasize the balance and equilibrium which come from the Element Earth, but the two points on the Spleen meridian which best reflect its functions are Spleen 21, Great Enveloping, and Spleen 4, Prince's Grandson. Spleen 21 is the junction point of all the junction points on the body. If it is needled with that intention it promotes flow in all the junction points which operate between the paired meridians. When we think about the Spleen encouraging and promoting movement in the body, mind and spirit there could be no better example of its function embodied in a single point.

The other particularly special and beautiful point is also a junction point, Spleen 4, Prince's Grandson. It is perhaps not without reason that Abundant Splendor, the Stomach point mentioned earlier, is also a junction point, as if to emphasize the importance of the relationship between these two Officials and the wealth which they bring and share. The connection between Chinese royalty and Heaven has already been mentioned, but to appreciate fully the importance of this point we have to remember that the descendants of the royal line were always favored and special, and that the role for which they were being prepared was that of landowner and ruler. For the Chinese, the Prince's Grandson would have represented continuity and wealth, the guarantee of a movement towards the future and the security of the succession. Above all the title would speak of the riches of the earth, and the inheritance which it represented for all the people living off it. Here we see, both in this point and in the Junction Point of the Stomach meridian, all of the nourishment and resources, the harvest and the security which comes from the Earth Element through its two Officials. Whenever we look at their tasks we must always remember how their work not only feeds and sustains the other Officials but keeps them grounded and safely in contact with the spirit of the Mother.

CHAPTER FOURTEEN

THE OFFICIALS OF THE METAL ELEMENT
LUNG AND COLON

The functions of the Officials of the Metal Element are in many ways the easiest to follow; they share a great many similarities with the physical functions of their equivalent organs in Western physiology. The lung and the colon are unlike the liver or the spleen, whose functions and even location are in the main poorly understood. People are usually very aware of their lungs and their respiration, and equally aware of their bowels and defecation; these are difficult processes to ignore.

Their connection with the Metal Element is equally plain to see. There is no need to go over the essence of Metal again. The interdependence of the officials in metal, the letting go and the taking in, characterizes to perfection the underlying nature of the Element. We need to throw out the rubbish to take in the new breath of pure and life-giving Qi energy, and we need to take in fresh energy before we are willing to let go of the rubbish. With the Officials of the Metal Element, therefore, if one does not function the other has to fail. For this reason the problems which arise from imbalance more often appear in both Officials. We should be very careful to remember this in our Traditional Diagnosis and not be hoodwinked by the apparently 'obvious' site of any disturbance or symptom.

THE COLON OFFICIAL - THE OFFICIAL OF DRAINAGE AND DREGS

I have already described the work of this Official in Chapter Five, and as far as its basic functions are concerned there is no reason to repeat this here. The Colon is the Official charged with the responsibility of removing all the rubbish. It is found in the Lower Jiao, usually referred to as the drainage ditch, and it is here that it maintains the health of the body, mind and spirit by the elimination of all the waste matter.

For this function we sometimes refer to it in a British context as "The dustman", or as "The refuse or garbage collector", in an American context, which gives a graphic illustration in helping to grasp the essence of this Official's work. This image is most compelling when we remember that the body, mind and spirit are nothing more and nothing less than all the Officials working together. When the Colon does its work well it is cleaning away the rubbish from the home of each of the Officials, just as the garbage man empties the bins from house after house.

This description takes us closer to the reality of what it feels like to have an inefficient Colon. As far as the whole body is concerned there is always going to be the normal amount of waste product left over from the digestive process itself. After the Stomach and Small Intestine Officials have done their work on the food passing along the alimentary canal, the Colon removes the water and throws away the rest. When it is off balance and sick we may well experience the constipation or the diarrhea, and the distress in mind and spirit which accompany them.

Thinking of waste products in this way, however, ties us too closely only to the digestive process itself, and what we must remember at all times is the function of the Official, not the Western organ and how it is seen to work. The Official of Drainage and Dregs, the body's garbage collector, takes away waste from all the Officials. When it is sick it is like the street where the dustman has not been for a week. Every house has overflowing bins, there is a smell of rotting rubbish in the air, and there is a danger to health. The people in the houses may not have been sick themselves before this started, but with the smell, the germs and the potential disease, life will become very unpleasant and hazardous.

Looking at the Colon in this way takes us beyond a superficial picture, and to the heart of the reality which we face when this Official falls ill. When the Colon is sick, everyone suffers directly as a consequence. The same could be said about the Stomach Official, and how sickness within this official ends up with starvation all around. While we accord the Stomach Official great respect, however, for this very reason the Colon rarely gets any, and that is to underestimate its true worth.

Imagine the other Officials about their business, casting aside their waste for collection and having it thrown back at them and it piling up because the dustman is out of sorts. This is the effect of a sick Colon. Everything becomes

The Relationships of the Elements

polluted and stinking because there is nowhere for the waste to go. Every Official, the Supreme Controller included, is affected individually by this waste, choked and poisoned by the build-up of their own rubbish. When the Colon is sick, there is rubbish everywhere, not just in the large intestine itself. The odour associated with an imbalance in the Metal Element is, in fact, close to the self-same smell that starts to fill the streets when rubbish stands uncollected.

The physical problems which may arise from this are as diverse as the Officials themselves, because each one will to a degree be unable to perform their function as Nature ordained. What the problems will share, however, is the involvement of toxins and wastes. These may affect both an Official's function and the meridian and organ which form that Official's residence within the body. Rubbish in our food will make us sick. Rubbish in the blood may make us cold, or lead to swellings and boils, thromboses and sclerosis. Rubbish in any of the Officials will choke its physical function, and create pollution where there should be purity.

This problem afflicts the mind and the spirit just as badly. We are surrounded in our modern society by all kinds of sordid and unpleasant material, some of which we cannot avoid taking in along with what we really need. Having judged it for what it is we throw it away just as we do the unwanted part of our food. If the Colon is sick someone may end up hanging on to it because they cannot get rid of it, and they become polluted by its presence. Many people with sick Colons may literally become foul-mouthed through the disgusting things which they take in. When we come across someone whose words and whose mind are poisoned and filthy we may be in the presence of a person whose garbage is not being taken away. The bad language, dirty jokes and nasty comments about friends and colleagues all point to the garbage piling up inside.

The build-up of dirt and rubbish may even affect people in a very literal sense. The Official affects every aspect of our lives and someone who cannot let go may literally look like a total mess and, should we ever have the chance to see the home where they live, may be surrounded by total mess. Imbalances here often produce the hoarder who amidst conditions of total untidiness hangs on to possessions and oddments which no longer serve any useful purpose in that person's life. The mess around them is something they may not even be aware of because it is no different in quality from the mess within themselves.

Classical Five-Element Acupuncture

The constipation, the unwillingness or the inability to let anything go, does not only turn up in the form of rottenness through and through. The Metal Element is associated with grief, a hanging on in a different sense, wanting to let go but not being able to. Just as one person with a sick Colon may hang on to rubbish, so may another hang on to the past and to things and people which should be let go to make way for the new. In the end, however, problems will beset every level because all levels are really only One, not Many. The grief and the pain of loss are just as likely to be accompanied by the physical rubbish and filth. This is not difficult to grasp; we even talk of people letting themselves go after a bereavement and are rarely surprised when we see them lose interest in the care and cleanliness of themselves and their surroundings.

Filth and pollution in the spirit are the worst afflictions which this Official's distress can cause. There is a tendency at times to think only of the predominantly yin organs as the source of deep spiritual discontent, but this is entirely mistaken. The openness and warmth of the spirit in Nature are no match for someone whose inner pollution makes them cynical and dismissive. None of the Officials have any chance of dealing in the pure essence of the spirit when their vision and their hopes are clouded by the darkness and negativity.

This constipation of the spirit also holds people firmly in place when they need to move on and develop. When someone cannot follow the natural path of Nature by letting go in Autumn the growth that has served its purpose, we may find a person locked into beliefs and ideas that prevent one from seeing new possibilities and new inspiration. We have no choice but to grow and develop; there is never a time when we can stop and congratulate ourselves on having reached a final stage. The laws of Nature and the Dao follow their inexorable cycles and guide us in the same path. If we are denied an autumn there is no spring and no re-birth, and the remnants of last year's growth hang on, looking ever more faded and tatty the longer we stay attached to them.

The refusal to move on may be associated with behavior that is stubborn and rigid. These are both qualities which thrive in conditions where someone will not or cannot change what they are doing. They are not exclusive to the Metal Element, and may also arise in the other Elements in their own individual patterns. There is a certain stiffness and rigidity in the distressed Metal Element, however, which has almost the same quality as the solid and unyielding state of metals themselves. When someone is so blocked up that they cannot give way, working with them may feel to us like trying to bend solid metal.

14.4

The Relationships of the Elements

Problems like rigidity and blockage often afflict the pathway of the Colon Official. The superficial meridian begins at the radial nail point of the index finger, and travels down the finger to the area of the wrist called the 'anatomical snuffbox'. From here it travels along the radial border of the forearm to the lateral border of the elbow, and thence up the lateral edge of the arm to the cleft of the acromion and clavicle on top of the shoulder. It then travels to the point GV14 under the seventh cervical vertebra, and back over the shoulder to Stomach 12. One deep branch goes from here to connect first to the lungs and then to the colon itself. The other branch rises via the neck to the upper lip and crosses to the other side to the exit point Colon 20 by the base of the nose. A deep pathway joins it to the entry point of the stomach meridian under the eye and another circles through the gum and encircles the mouth.

When the Official is out of balance and clogged with rubbish this often turns up along its pathway in the 'frozen joint' problems of the wrist, elbow and especially the shoulder. More often than not there will also be spots and skin troubles along the channel as the toxins overflow into the surrounding tissue. This may apply generally to the body when it is filled with rubbish, but is bound to affect the Colon itself. The pathway on the face is often the source of aggravation too. Blocked sinuses are quite common, and in many forms of symptomatic acupuncture the point Colon 20 by the base of the nose is used to relieve sinus problems caused by the clogging up of the channels with rubbish. The point's name, Welcome Fragrance, is a wonderful testament to its powers when used in this context, the clearing of rubbish to let the power of smell function again.

The one point which above all captures the essence of this Official, however, is Colon 4, Joining of the Valleys. It is commonly known as the 'Great Eliminator', and is used not only in acupuncture but in massage and in acupressure for its powerful effects in removing blockages and encouraging the release of toxins and rubbish. The nickname for the point could just as easily stand for the whole Official, so accurately does it describe its single most important function. We must always remember, however, that the rubbish which builds up in someone when this Official is sick is not just physical but mental and spiritual. The blockages which affect the areas through which the meridian runs can just as easily be coming from the mind or spirit. We must never conclude from a normal bowel function that frozen elbows and shoulders cannot come from this Official. When it cannot let go in the mind or the spirit the body is just as likely to reflect this in the stiffness which holds everything tightly in place inside. Cases of paralysis and rigidity in the body are just as likely to arise from the cold and inert energy of a sick spirit in this Official.

Above all, though, we have to return to the Colon's main function to see the most devastating effects of imbalance and illness in this Official. The constipation which harms body, mind and spirit takes away any hope of true cleansing to make way for anything new and vital. Nothing can prosper and nothing can grow on any level while the rubbish gathers and rots where it lies. When we meet people in whom this Official suffers we shall see all the doubt and negativity, the blackness and the gloom, which makes light and positivity impossible.

THE LUNG OFFICIAL -
THE OFFICIAL WHO RECEIVES PURE QI ENERGY
FROM THE HEAVENS

On a literal level the Lung Official's title is self-explanatory, describing the act of breathing. Yet how many of us really stop to consider the importance of every breath we take? We take in food and we take in water, and are only too aware of the effects if we go on diets which force us to reduce our intake of either. But while we can last weeks without solid food as long as we have water, and days even if we do not have water, without air we are clinically dead in five minutes.

When we say that we are fed by our Father and our Mother, the Metal and the Earth Elements, it may create the impression that it is an equal partnership, that we take in the Qi energy from food and the Qi energy from air in roughly equal mix, and that our survival is thus guaranteed. We should, perhaps, instead look at our food in a qualitative way, not just in a quantitative way. For it is the oxygen in the air, the kernel of value which we extract, which unlocks most of the value of the food which we eat to fuel all of our body processes. Without this the food inside us would be as useless as petrol without a spark, or wood without tinder.

On a physical level this is clear enough. The act of breathing is usually considered in a very matter of fact way by our modern cultures, just a function which we have to protect and continue in order to keep going, like our daily bread and water. It is not for nothing, however, that many of the world's oldest and most profound religions place such an enormous importance on breathing

The Relationships of the Elements

and becoming conscious of the act of taking breath. Many of the religions of the East emphasize the act of breathing in their meditations and prayers, and recognise in their writings the value not just of the amount of air but its quality, and the appreciation of its pathways as it travels through the body. The day is not considered by many of them to be properly founded unless the believer has begun with a ritual breathing exercise to invigorate and fire up the body, mind and spirit.

The Lung Official brings in the new and the vital essence to replace the void left by the rubbish which we have thrown away. In its own way it also throws out rubbish, the carbon dioxide which fouls the body just as surely as the waste products of our food, but the act of inspiration is its most important function. In fact, using the word 'inspiration' emphasizes that it is not just an act of the physical body, but also of the mind, and of the spirit. When we think of mental inspiration, most of us have mind's-eye pictures of the specialist creators and thinkers who sit around mulling over a problem and then, suddenly, almost as if by a flash of light, see the answer to their questions. We all do the same, however, without the fate of the world or of science hanging over our heads. We have all the right ingredients in our minds to solve problems, but somehow the pieces do not fulfill our needs. The spark of inspiration is what the Lung Official brings to give them the value which they then have for us, to make the qualitative change which gives ideas life and worth.

The inspiration which this Official gives is most special and precious, however, when it feeds the spirit. The Metal Element represents the Father within us, the connection with the Heavens which gives our lives a sense of quality and higher purpose. The Receiver of Pure Qi Energy from the Heavens is the Official which establishes and maintains this connection. Words do not really exist to describe just how vital the flow is at this level. It is much easier to talk of the great chasm, the void which is left within us if we do not manage to tend and cultivate this connection, for this is exactly how it feels when the Official cannot carry out its function. We need the guidance and direction of the pure Qi energy from the heavens to inspire us and realize the potential which we have.

Examples which help us to understand the true nature of this Official's work in the spirit inevitably draw us to religious experience for illustrations. This is especially so when these experiences describe radical conversions, where an almost literal spiritual void has been filled suddenly and completely. The visions of saints, mystical experiences of the prophets of all religions, and sudden flashes of enlightenment, all speak of the profound joy which fills the person and illuminates their lives when this connection is made. For most of us nothing as world-shattering as this is likely to be the case, but we have all, I hope, from time to time felt ourselves to transcend the limits of our daily routine and to be inspired, aware of something greater and more essential in us than the mere filling of time or the completion of our mundane tasks. When this happens we are witnessing within ourselves the work of this Official in our spirits, and the depth and power of its inspiration.

The Officials work on all levels, however, and on a more prosaic level the Lung has functions which relate partly to the position of the lungs themselves in the body. They are described in the Nei Jing as acting like 'the lid of the organs'. Since they receive the pure Qi energy and send it downwards it is said that they are responsible for a downward and dispersing action as they spread their essence to all of the body. This becomes relevant when we look at some of the physical manifestations of disease in the Official.

The Lung Official is also closely connected with the skin, which itself is often described as 'the third lung'. The reason is that the skin does in fact 'breathe' and plays a part in the exchange of gases in the whole process of respiration which the Lung Official governs. The Chinese classics also point to the similarity of function of the Lung as the Official most closely in contact with the outside world and the skin as the organ most exposed to the air. Together they both act as the body's first line of defense against external injury.

These two areas of influence are important because they generate a number of physical symptoms when the Lung Official is imbalanced which point directly to its distress. Skin diseases like eczema, psoriasis and acne all point to a loss of quality in the skin and possible disease in the Official. When we look more closely at the relationship between the Officials we may even be able to see from the kind of skin eruption whether it is the heat or water within the lungs which causes specific problems to arise like the burning, the dryness, or the dampness.

Equally obvious are the various forms of lung congestion which are directly ascribed to the inability of the lungs to send energy and fluids downwards. Conditions like asthma, bronchitis, emphysema, pleurisy, and all the upper respiratory tract infections can be traced back at one level to air or bronchial fluids being stuck and not being dispersed downwards as they should. Many problems like these in the Upper Jiao stem from an imbalance within the lungs, whether this be where the original cause lies or whether the lung's balance is affected by imbalance elsewhere.

We can, however, trace the same patterns of physical disease by looking at the function which the Lung Official has. When the Official is sick we cannot take in the pure Qi energy. How better to describe the actions of the asthmatic, desperate to gulp down air but stuck and rigid, the lungs unable to let go of the air that they hold to allow the new air in, or in some cases unable to suck air in through the blocked passages. The bronchitic patient and the emphysematous patient both suffer with a depressed lung function so weak that it no longer allows them to take in a full breath. The breathless patient can pull the air in but cannot hold it long enough to extract its vital essence. All of these can be equally well understood in the functions of the Officials of the Metal Element, failures in the steady rhythm and flow of taking in and letting go.

This has to be emphasized over and over again because the Western labels for disease all place the blame in the physical function of the lung, and as I have tried to stress, the different levels are ultimately not distinct. There are going to be many people whose physical bodies manifest the outward signs and symptoms of asthma or shortness of breath but whose lungs show little or no physiological evidence of decay or damage. If we only treat the Lung Official on the basis of what we find in the body we are more than likely to be driven to seek causes elsewhere when in reality it is this Official in distress in our minds or spirits.

This is not as radical a statement as it may sound because our own day-to-day experience offers many examples of what the medical world calls psychosomatic disorders of breathing or 'hysterical' symptoms. There are many people who breathe perfectly normally until they are under terrible stress. Immediately they have an asthma attack, or breathlessness, or hyperventilation, all signs that the Lung Official is suffering acutely, and yet within minutes they are back to normal.

Having said that, we nonetheless have to remember that the Lung Official's function, as a part of the Metal Element within us, is to invest our physical energy with the quality which gives it the vitality we need. If this is missing the energy in our bodies, and especially our lungs, is likely to be of poor quality.

Here, then, we may see an indifferent blend, the rigidity of cold metal or the molten flow, the lack of balance between heat and flow, structure and support, which arises when this essential catalyst is missing. We may then find the dryness in the lungs, the watery secretions, or the solid, burning phlegm, all a result of the lack of quality in the Lung Official's energy which affects the Elemental balance within us.

The effect on the mind of a weak Lung Official can be an inability to take things in, which may remind us of the kinds of problems that sometimes arise with the sick Stomach Official and its inability to digest words and sounds. A similar problem may arise when the Lung Official is out of balance, except in this case the words and emotions never even really enter the mind at all. There is literally no way in because the person can take nothing in. It is not uncommon to find people with Lung imbalances who are to all intents and purposes cut off, looking entirely blank. There is not even a suggestion that they are trying to make sense of what they see or hear: it is like talking into a vacuum or to a blank wall.

We can use the idea of a catalyst to illustrate the effect of the restricted flow of this spark in the mind and the emotions. Without the inspiration of pure Qi energy in sufficient quantity to add the qualitative difference to our minds, our thoughts and emotions will remain lifeless and inert, dull and unexciting. Without the power of the spark which comes from contact with the Father there may well be in people with this imbalance a cold and chilling precision, the hard and brittle nature of unworked metal which manifests in calculating and emotionless logic.

This may sometimes be reflected in the behavior and surroundings which we observe in someone with an imbalance here. When a person is drawn to precision and logic inside one may well try to reproduce the same patterns on the outside. Excessive neatness and an obsession with order and cleanliness might point towards this Official in distress. It is as though the person is trying to make good the lack of purity and lack of quality inside by surrounding themself in a very fastidious way with the best quality materials to be found.

Of all the Officials the Lung is perhaps the most vital in establishing and sustaining the spirit. By taking in the pure Qi energy from the heavens it brings the guidance and authority which our lives need. When someone is unable to take this in it leads to the deepest despair. If someone has no connection with the heavens there is every reason to feel lost and cast aside, cut off from the source of everything that brings life and vigor to the spirit and therefore purpose and essential quality to life. The deep and abiding grief which characterizes an imbalance in the Metal Element arises from the void that lies within when there is nothing which can fill the spirit except a connection with the heavenly Father.

This may lead to behavior of quite an extreme kind. Instead of a still and silent grief for the void within, there are many people who desperately search for new things to take in. These are the ones who perhaps recognise the awful emptiness and who chase from religion to religion to try to find and take in the essence which will replenish them. If their internal balance is gone, however, there can never be an end to this chase. None of these beliefs or creeds can ever be properly absorbed and each will in time appear as insubstantial as the last. Here we often find amongst our patients the mystics and the searchers, the people who travel to the East in search of god or nirvana, and flit from guru to guru, belief to belief, often given over to an all-consuming zeal which is followed by bitter and total rejection as they move on elsewhere. Their eyes often betray this, focused blankly into the far distance where their search lies, and often slightly upwards and above the real, material world.

As with all the Officials, the meridian of the Lung is just as much representative of its existence as the physical organ, and imbalance will strike here as well. The deep channel begins in the stomach area, loops around the large intestine, then rises to enter both lungs. From here it ascends the trachea to the level of the larynx, from which it travels inferior to the lateral end of the clavicle where the entry point of the superficial meridian lies (IX.1 Middle Palace). It then follows the anterior and lateral surfaces of the arm and forearm, over the wrist and thenar eminence and terminates at the lateral nail point of the thumb.

Its pathway demonstrates immediately why so many of the lung, breathing and respiratory problems tie in straight away with malfunctions in the Official, not just in terms of function but in terms of energy flow as well. When there is no flow in the meridian there is little hope of a regular rhythm for the breathing, and without this all of the blockages with which we are familiar will arise. Phlegm, mucus, dryness of the throat and lungs, and coughing are frequent and commonplace. Where no energy flows neither do blood or body fluids. So too are stiff joints in the arm, rigid and brittle as the metal which carries no warmth from the Qi energy within.

The points on the meridian give a very clear indication of the depth and importance of this Official. There are two 'palaces' on the pathway, Middle Palace (IX.1) and Heavenly Palace (IX.3), both of which carry exactly the same kinds of connotations as the 'palaces' which we have already described on the channels of the Fire meridians. There are the points Greatest Hole and Very Great Abyss, both of which can be read simply as descriptions of their appearance on the body but which also characterize the depression and despair which calls for their use. There is also the point Meridian Gutter which exemplifies the essence of the Metal Element, a point which, when used, can act as a cleansing force for the whole body, mind and spirit. Not for nothing is this the seasonal point of the meridian, the very essence of the autumn within the channel of the season itself.

Each of these points, and others like Valiant White/Pure White (IX.4), all draw on different aspects of the spirit of the Metal Element: the quality and purity; the riches of the earth and heaven; and the cleansing and washing away of the past. This is something which above all we must remember. We look at the Lung Official as first and foremost the Metal Element made manifest within us, not merely the physical lung and the function of respiration. The close relationship of the Lung and its blood brother, the Colon, to their western counterparts make this an all-too-easy temptation at times and may lead us to miss the true wisdom which they reveal to us.

CHAPTER FIFTEEN

THE OFFICIALS OF THE WATER ELEMENT
THE KIDNEY AND THE BLADDER

The last pair of Officials to which we now turn are the Officials of the Water Element, the Bladder and the Kidney. Their main functions deal directly with the Element itself; the Bladder is described as the Official responsible for the Storage of Water and the Kidney as the Official who Controls the Waterways. Between them they govern the major aspects of our vital fluids.

We need to emphasize again why water is referred to as a vital fluid by reminding ourselves of a very basic fact: the body consists of about 50-60% water. Water is the primary component of our blood, the primary component of all the body cells, and the only means by which anything can flow and move in the body. Without a good supply of water none of the Officials can function at all. This whole system of medicine is based on the quality and strength of flows of energy, and without water none of the cycles and rhythms of these flows could be maintained.

Since this is the case on the physical level then the same will apply just as much to the mental and physical levels. When we look at these two Officials, therefore, we should concentrate not just on the simple associations between the physical organs which we know in the West and the similar physical functions described in the Eastern tradition, but even more on the mental and spiritual levels. All of the functions of mind and spirit which we have seen in the other Officials depend on the reserves and resources of these Officials.

THE BLADDER OFFICIAL -
THE OFFICIAL WHO CONTROLS THE STORAGE OF WATER

On a straightforward level the Bladder Official has very similar responsibilities to the physical organ. The balance of water within us depends on some means of controlling how much of the water which we drink or extract from food is stored and how much is expelled. We lose water through perspiration, breathing, defecation and urination, and generally we compensate for excessive fluid loss through the first three of these routes by adjusting the volume of urine. If we sweat a great deal or we suffer from diarrhea and vomiting, the urine in the bladder reduces in volume. On cold days when our skin contracts and reduces sweating the volume of urine increases. The only difference between the modern and classical picture of this is that we tend to regard it as an automatic process where the Chinese viewed the process as a conscious and controlled one, the work of an Official with its own definite role.

The bladder is not merely a reservoir of excess water; the urine which we pass also contains a large number of waste products, the urea and excess acids, and sometimes alkalis, which result from the filtering role of the Kidney. The Bladder Official is charged with the responsibility of disposing of this waste. In classical Five-Element medicine this again is seen not just as a passive process but one which involves choice and decision, setting aside the impurities for discharge and retaining water that is needed to maintain the reservoir.

When either of these functions fail we may see the extremes of water retention or dehydration, or the gradual tainting of body fluids. When the water is poured away too quickly and the reserves are low there will be dry skin and dry hair, and especially conditions which show the same burning of the surface which happens in Nature when the sun cracks and hardens the parched earth. If not enough water is passed away and the reservoir overflows into the surrounding lands there will be ascites, oedema, swelling, and the feeling of bloatedness which comes about from being waterlogged.

If the impurities and unwanted minerals are retained, there will be a gradual poisoning of the system. This is similar to the toxicity which arises from an imbalanced Separator, but when it lodges within the fluids through a Bladder imbalance it travels directly to every cell in the body and affects the life within them. Even in Western medicine obstructive diseases of the urinary system are treated as medical emergencies because of the backflow of potentially dangerous toxins.

This may, of course, not arise just from mechanical obstruction but from a failure of function. If the Bladder Official is sick all aspects of its overall function will fail. The Official may not be able to keep separate the clean water for retention and may not be able to contain the water within its proper boundaries. As well as oedema within we may begin to see incontinence and all the cystitis-type infections which arise from poisons within the urethra. The Bladder Official may be too diseased and weak to expel urine with any force, with urinary retention and bladder wall infections as a consequence. In short, on a physical level we shall see all of the bladder problems which we recognise in Western medicine as well as ones which relate to the Official's storage duties.

In previous chapters I have always mentioned the aspects of physical imbalance which arise from the meridian of each Official, and with the Bladder Official this is of the greatest importance. The Bladder Meridian is the longest meridian on the entire body, with the superficial channel running from the inner canthus of the eye, over the head and down the back, over the posterior surface of the buttock and leg to the lateral malleolus, and thence to the lateral edge of the little toe. The meridian divides on the back to form an inner and outer bladder line, and the deep branches leave the inner bladder line to connect with the kidney and bladder organs. The sixty seven points on the meridian are the largest number on any meridian on the body. This fact alone, together with its vital function of storing water for the whole body, should always remind us of the Bladder Official's importance.

When the Official is sick many physical problems arise along the channel. Eye problems like dimness and blurring of vision, headaches, especially running up the back of the neck to the vertex of the head or over the top of the head, lower back ache, sciatica, calf muscle strains and ankle problems: all arise frequently from bladder imbalances or weaknesses. There are many points on the bladder meridian which directly affect these conditions when used as first-aid or symptomatic points, and also empirically many points on the bladder meridian which affect the bones in the lower back and the healing of bones and fractures in general.

Once we recognise the immense importance of the reserves and fluidity this Official provides for the body it is not difficult to begin to understand its importance for our mind and our spirit. When we have fluidity of the mind and we are properly irrigated we are able to let ideas and thoughts flow, and the reserves of water which lie metaphorically within the channels allow the mind to grow and flourish. Through this the Bladder makes the movement and growth of all the other Officials possible, and by the presence of the reserves which it controls this official guarantees them their security and their future.

The same is true of the spirit. The reserve which comes from the Bladder Official is the promise and certainty of a harvest and a resource which fuels the growth of spring and protects us from the heat of the summer. Many of the words which we associate with the Water Element, such as endurance, ambition and determination, are founded on the ability to have and to maintain an inner reservoir upon which everything else we do depends. By providing this on all levels the Bladder is the source of our deepest reserves and strength.

Perhaps because we forget the pervasive nature of water within us we do not readily make the associations which arise from its imbalance within us, and yet they are by and large self-evident. When the bladder does not provide enough water the mind dries up as surely as the body. There will be people whose minds and spirits are arid and in whom there is no flow at all. If the flow is poor and tainted we may expect and will find stagnation just as we see the muddy ponds in Nature around us. There will be others who are totally awash with thoughts, whose words and ideas fall out in torrents with no real control, like the streams that burst their banks and run to every corner that they can. Water is incredibly versatile; it can take up any shape and will flow into any corner and crevice it can find, always changeable and elusive. No-one can grab hold of and contain even a handful of water, and the same can be said of minds which run free in a similar fashion. People in whom this happens can seem elusive and impossible to contain, their flow too fast and too free to pin down.

The essence of imbalance in this Official in mind and spirit, however, is the tremendous fear or lack of fear which we associate with the Water Element. When the well is dry there are no reserves for the coming year, and this is how it feels inside when the inner well runs dry. When there is a little money in the bank and we run into trouble it is always a source of comfort to withdraw our 'rainy day' funds to survive. When these are gone we face an uncertain and frightening future. When there is no well everything around us becomes a potential threat and we may imagine the worst possible outcomes all the time, never able to be secure in the knowledge that we can survive. Imagine how much worse this will be when the problem is not one of money or maintaining the physical body, but of the energy needed to support and sustain the mind and spirit.

The problems are even clearer when we are awash with water. What thoughts run through the mind of the drowning person - the terror, the utter despair of the inevitable end, the feeling of being totally beyond the help of fellow humans?

The Relationships of the Elements

We would never expect anyone in this situation to be thinking of other people; one's own self-preservation and one's own future is all that concerns the person. When the mind and spirit drown the effects will be just the same. People may become blinkered in panic, thrashing about to save themselves, caught in an inner turmoil between life and death without regard for anyone else.

A total lack of fear is no more healthy. Running our reserves low or being overrun by water are states which should provoke us into action. If we greet either with a false assurance or bland indifference we endanger ourselves just as greatly. Going past the point of no return without feeling any concern will leave us high and dry or totally submerged, beyond the reach of any help from within ourselves or from others.

When someone's problems reach this kind of pitch there is a limit to how long the person can bear them without the gradual loss of a grip on reality. The strain and the torment eventually become too much, and many are the cases where people start to manifest what we describe in modern clinical terms as insanity as their means of escape. For some even this is not enough, and problems in the Bladder Official sometimes create the potential suicide, the person whose desperation at having no reserves can become too much even to contemplate.

This may all sound a little far-fetched, but when this Official is sick the distress can really be that great. There are many people walking around today who have no reserves or whose reservoirs have overflowed within them as a result of this Official's imbalance. They are no different from Nature around them, and the panic which we see in Nature will be just the same within them: eyes fixed ahead in a blank gaze, overcome by the sheer terror of it all, or darting everywhere looking for an escape route; body and limbs still and unchanging or as frantic as the flow of the rapids or the mountain streams after a storm; voice monotonous, groaning and frozen, or babbling and uncontrolled.

It is perhaps more important to remind ourselves of Nature with these two Officials, the Kidney and the Bladder, than with any other pair. It is too easy for us to overlook their importance, especially the Bladder, in the body, mind and spirit when it is compared with the complexity of the tasks of, for example, the Liver Official or the Spleen Official. Yet when it malfunctions there really is no hope and no life anywhere. The distress which arises from its sickness can consume all of someone's attention because nothing could be more important. If we want to understand how this affects the way that someone behaves with a sick Bladder Official, we have to recognise the urge for self-preservation over-riding everything else or the extreme opposite, an escape from reality in a studied and constant denial to themselves and to others that there really is any danger of any kind at all.

THE KIDNEY OFFICIAL - THE OFFICIAL WHO CONTROLS THE WATERWAYS

The Kidney and Bladder Officials work together to maintain the water supply for the body, mind and spirit. While the Bladder disposes of the impurities and acts as a reservoir, it is the Kidney which is responsible for the cleansing action which separates out the impurities and which dispatches the water to every corner of the person.

Not surprisingly, therefore, many of the problems which are associated with the Bladder can equally well arise from a malfunction in the Kidney. A reservoir is of no value if the water cannot be taken to where it is needed. There is just as likely to be distress if the distribution network fails and there is plentiful water in one place but none in another. We may find, for example, that oedema, especially oedema in the lower part of the trunk and the lower limbs, is often due to a malfunction in the Controller of Water. The reserves are adequate, but they are poorly organized.

By the same token we may well find that a supply of stagnant and polluted water may be delivered by the Kidney when the source of the problem lies in the Bladder which cannot dispose of the impurities and taints the reserves on which the Kidney draws. Between them, therefore, we may find all of the urinary problems, the swellings, and the impure flow, but we may have to depend on other signs to be able to establish which of the two is more distressed.

It is important not to underestimate the functions of the kidney as a physical organ. Most of us are familiar with the pictures of dialysis patients and the suffering and terminal effects of kidney failure. When this physical organ cannot function we can no longer cleanse our blood and fluids, and balance the minerals and salts within us. Within a matter of days we die unless the work is done by machine for us. This physical role should remind us at the very least of the importance and respect which we should attach to this Official.

The Relationships of the Elements

The Kidney Official, however, has responsibilities which go far beyond our understanding of its role in the body and which are central to its role in classical acupuncture. In classical Chinese philosophy and medicine the Kidney is the storehouse, the ancestral energy which is passed to each person by their parents, an energetic inheritance to underpin their lives and to pass on in turn to their own children. It is the seed of life passed from one generation to the succeeding one. In many ways there could not be a more graphic illustration of the function of this Official than this essence of life which is passed from generation to generation.

All reserves need to be tended and cherished and the Kidney Official receives some of the pure Qi energy from our daily supply of food and air to revitalize and replenish its store. The bulk of the energy which we take in, however, goes straight to our Officials for their daily needs. When we need energy beyond that which we have taken in for our daily purposes it is the Kidney Official which becomes the source of supply. We literally draw on our reserves, and begin to use up the power of this concentrated essence. This explains why we sometimes appear to become more energized as we push ourselves to our limits. The Kidney's store is the richest and most concentrated energy in the body, just as one tiny seed in nature contains the possibility of a new life.

This storehouse is not just physical energy. When we talk of drawing on our reserves this may be because of some physical task for which we need extra energy, but more often than not it is a mental or emotional challenge which requires all the energy which we can muster. Beyond these there are the spiritual struggles which people undertake on the path to truth, and the immense importance of a good reserve there. When the path of the Dao is hard it is this store which is the foundation of eventual success.

This function translates on a simple physical level to the strength and stamina which sustains our lives. When we looked at Water these reserves were characteristic of the Element itself. The winter is a cold and forbidding time, and qualities like endurance and survival depend on the strength of the reserves which we have built up before the season sets in. Taking good care of these reserves in the quiet time of the year help us to last through the year and make full use of the bounty which the following seasons offer. When the Kidney Official is strong we see this reflected in the physical strength of the person.

In the same way the strength and determination of the spirit come from the tremendous reserves of this Official. There are many challenges for the spirit in modern life; if anything this is where we are most under threat and least well prepared. More than ever before we need the resources here even to take the first step on the right path. The bible, like many of the religious texts which have inspired people for thousands of years, is full of stories of the travails and temptations of saints, of holy men and women, all of whom have had to show enormous resolve and inner strength to reach their goals. This power, which comes from the Kidney Official, deserves the greatest respect and reverence. Another aspect of the Kidney Official touching on this religious theme is the practice of baptism and spiritual cleansing which water has come to represent in many religions. Through it we can be assured of the purity in mind and spirit which grounds our search for deeper truths.

Aside from its deeper functions the Kidney Official has a special relationship with particular aspects of the body and physical functions. It is said to be the creator of bone and bone marrow, and is particularly associated with the lumbar and sacral spine which it governs and sustains. Bone marrow is a fairly broad category; the brain itself was regarded as a sea of marrow. The brain is not frequently mentioned in the ancient classics; it is only in recent times with the identification of thought and mind with brain that it has taken on its modern significance. In classical acupuncture, however, one aspect of what we regard as a function of the brain, long-term memory, is seen as the direct gift from the Kidney Official.

There are also very strong connections between the Kidney and specific parts of the body. In the Su Wen it is said that when the Kidney is strong and full it opens the ears and sounds can be heard with great clarity. It also has a tremendous effect on the reproductive organs. This arises partly from the pathway of the meridian which traverses the genital area, but is also a functional relationship. The inheritance of the seed of life from generation to generation is accomplished by the sexual act, and it is therefore no surprise that the Kidneys, as the storers of this inherited energy, must function as Nature intended. Both the sexual organs and the vital sexual substances fall under this official's control. It is the sperm of the father and egg of the mother which unite to carry the inherited ancestral energy to the child and create its reserve for the future.

The Kidney also has very strong connections with the anus. This again rests partly on the pathways, and also on the area of the body within which the anus lies. The connection between urination, the anus, and the Kidney Official is demonstrated best by what happens in absolute terror, the fear which we associate most with the Water Element. In the Classics the natural effect of fear is said to be to move energy downwards. When people are utterly terrified the bowels and bladder run loose. There is also the drying of the mouth and the sweat which pours off us when we panic. All of these are signs of the balance of water within us being disturbed and of the Kidney Official being under severe threat.

In the Su Wen it is also said that when this Official is strong and full, his physical energy is great and the mind is strong. Elsewhere in the same book the Kidney is described as the Official who does energetic work and excels by his ability and cleverness. This reflects the characteristic of the physical Element Water which has the capacity to find its way into every nook and cranny and to find a way around any barrier. The cleverness of which the Su Wen speaks is this same streak of what we might call animal cunning, an innate ability to find a way round the day to day problems which beset us.

When this Official is diseased the effects can be wide ranging. On a physical level, as I have already said, there are the same kinds of urinary problems which we find from Bladder malfunction. This may involve inability to hold urine, frequent and urgent urination, or urinary retention. The impurities which gather in the liquid can cause infections both in the kidneys and bladder themselves or diseases in the urinary passages like cystitis and thrush. Sometimes the impurities are of a long-standing nature and the excess salts crystallize into the more solid material of kidney stones.

Equally possible are the water distribution problems like oedema and water retention, or the dryness of skin and body tissue. Earlier we looked at constipation and diarrhea as problems which arise from the Colon, but the excess or absence of water in the body can just as easily bring these problems on from a Kidney imbalance. If there is no water in the body the stools are bound to be hard as the Colon tries to extract and save every last drop of this precious substance. As the Chinese saying goes: "when there is no water the boat cannot sail". Problems with defecation can also arise from the Kidney's control of the anus and anal area. Deficiency of the Kidney can cause hemorrhoids and anal fistula, and it is not uncommon for the discomfort which attends these conditions to generate constipation because of the pain of bowel movements.

The Kidney is also responsible for some aspects of the sexual act, especially the quality and quantity of the sperm and the egg and the release of both to pass on the energy to the baby. When the Kidney is imbalanced there may be problems of infertility, an inability to perform the sexual act, or at the other extreme an excessive sex drive. Men may find that they do not have enough sperm, or that the sperm is not particularly active, and in some cases conditions like premature ejaculation and nocturnal emission can be caused by a Kidney weakness. The Kidney also controls the process of sexual maturation, and imbalance sometimes shows in men and women whose sexual development is slow or incomplete, or abnormally and excessively developed.

The two parts of the body which have already been mentioned, the ears and the bones, tend to degenerate when the energy of this Official is low. There may often be a gradual loss of hearing, possibly with low-pitched tinnitus, and eventually total deafness. Bone and joint problems are common and the lower back area in particular is a frequent site of pain, both along the spine itself which is closely related to the Kidney, and in the area near and beneath the physical organ. The problems may be more general, however, and can be anything from poor healing of fractures to more general osteo-arthritis throughout the body.

Detail like this can be helpful as long as it is not used to deduce the primary source of imbalance. One common feature of a great many of these conditions which is readily apparent is that we associate them with old age. This association takes us to the heart of the Official, because many of the degenerative conditions are a natural sign of the aging process. The reserves which we inherit are finite; if we were meant to live forever we would be able to produce ancestral energy from our daily food and air, and we cannot. Our inheritance is one which will last us for a good lifetime if we nourish and respect body, mind and spirit, but as the reserves run low many of the functions which also rely on the source of those reserves show similar signs of weakness. Old age usually brings some deafness and arthritis, urinary problems, and loss of sexual potency. It also brings about a general loss of energy, and when the Kidney Official is weak we may well begin to see the same aging process and the same weakness in young people. When the ancestral energy is low or when it has been used up by intemperate living, there can be tremendous weakness and debility. Young people may be lethargic and dull, old before their time, and there will be such a lack of energy that they may act as though they are ready for the grave in their twenties and thirties. The same thing happens when there is long-term sickness. We use up reserves to repair ourselves and in doing so find that our

The Relationships of the Elements

recovery, far from leaving us better, has made us weak and tired.

The majority of induced weaknesses in this Official, however, come from bad habits and from long-term drug taking, be it prescribed or not. The Chinese classics are full of dire warnings about burning the candle at both ends, and always talk of the damage that is done to this Official. In modern times we see the same disregard for our long term health. People can, when they are young, stay up late or miss a night's sleep on occasion, but if it becomes a habit they are digging deep into reserves which cannot be replenished.

Similarly the use of drugs over a long period of time is particularly harmful to the Liver, which detoxifies the system, and to the Kidney, which filters them out. These Officials need their rest as much as any others. If they are driven hard they are as likely as not to run out of steam before their time. It is very common to find in long-term disease, where there has been an extended course of therapeutic drugs, that the Liver and Kidney Officials are both damaged and very low in energy.

One important point to note is that it is very rare to find an excess condition in this Official. By this I mean real excess rather than just apparent excess. The pulse and functions may on occasions appear excessive, but this is more often than not the cry of distress, not the underlying state. Since we are depleting this Official naturally from the cradle to the grave, we are never going to come across a truly full Official, only one whose strength and reserve is appropriate for the age we have reached if we have tended our reserve well.

If the physical effects of a Kidney imbalance are so drastic it does not take much imagination to realize that the effect on the mind and spirit is little short of disastrous. If the reserves are so low that the person knows that they cannot survive, what possible reactions can they have? Fear is one, a constant and terrifying apprehension about tomorrow, what it will bring and whether they can survive it. Lack of fear is another, a refusal to acknowledge any signs of trouble. Total resignation is yet another; when the reserves of the spirit are gone the physical body may survive but there is no life and vitality within.

We sometimes see this sad condition in old people whose bodies endure, whose hearts beat and lungs breathe, but in whom the mind is dull and lethargic, the power of memory begins to fade, and the spirit is all but extinguished. Even more sad today is that we see much younger people, even young adults in their thirties and forties, who are beginning to show the same emptiness when their reserves are low from illness or from youthful excesses.

When we look at the spirit of the person, therefore, we should always be asking ourselves how well this Official is functioning. If the person before us is listless and empty, resigned and despairing, we may be seeing someone in whom the vital reserve is gone and who has neither the strength nor the will to survive. The Chinese called ancestral energy, spirit and Qi the 'Three Treasures', and the Kidney Official's humble functions as a physical organ should never deceive us into overlooking its role as the root of the life.

The superficial pathway of this Official starts on the sole of the foot, rises over the instep to the medial malleolus, and after circling the ankle rises up the medial surface of the leg to the tip of the coccyx at the base of the spine. From here deep pathways run up the spine to terminate in the mouth, and from them connect with the bladder and the kidney organs. The superficial pathway emerges again from the bladder onto the lower abdomen, from which the meridian travels up the abdomen and chest slightly lateral to the midline, terminating just under the clavicle.

The proximity of the channel to the genital area and the reproductive organs in the lower Jiao emphasizes the connection with the reproductive functions, but the most profound connections are with the Governor Vessel at the base of the coccyx, and with several of what are called the 'Eight Extraordinary Meridians' either in the Kidney itself or at points on the meridian. These meridians are like seas and oceans in comparison to the rivers and streams of the superficial pathways, and have enormous powers over and effects on the body, mind and spirit as a whole. Their use can bring about profound changes, if the context and circumstances are appropriate.

The importance of their connection with the Kidney is that it emphasizes the root and reserve which the Official represents. They draw their power from the essence which this Official carries, and for this reason alone we should encourage practitioners to have the deepest respect. There is no such thing as 'just treating the source points' of Kidney. Touching this meridian and this Official here is to contact the deepest reserves in the person, and this should make us both grateful and wary once we know the power of the spirit which we are contacting.

The Relationships of the Elements

The points on the Kidney meridian reflect its function and status in a wonderful way. The first five points capture the process by which this resource enters the system. From the entry point, Bubbling Spring, the energy is heated in Blazing Valley, gathers momentum as Greater Mountain Stream, is collected in the Great Bell or Great Cup, and then becomes a Yang Stream. Pictures like this offer a profound insight into the flow of energy.

The meridian has many points which characterize the qualities of reserves and storage, but by far the most representative points are what we tend to call the 'Kidney Chest Points', a series of points on the upper thorax which are named Spirit Seal, Spirit Burial Ground, Spirit Storehouse, Amidst Elegance, and Storehouse. Each of these reaches into the very heart of the spirit, draws on the vital reserves within the person, and re-establishes their connection with the inner strength which they need when the spirit is low and the suffering has been long. It would take far more than a short paragraph here both to describe the beauty of these points and to give examples of how their use has transformed the lives of people who were slipping gradually away. Used at the right time and with the right intention, however, we are blessed through this Official with the means to resuscitate people at a level far beyond simple physical existence of the body.

When we look at Officials in this way what emerges time and time again, however, is the interdependence of all the Officials, not just each pair which embody each Element. That is why each seems so important, because by itself it can have such a profound effect, both in balance and in imbalance, on the spirit and functions of the others. As with the Elements, however, we need to go beyond any simple reduction of one function to one Official. In order to perform any single function each Official depends on the functions of every other. This will help us to avoid the trap of using the information in diagnosis in a mechanistic and unthinking way: "Lower back pain means a Kidney imbalance; therefore I must treat the Kidney", or "Cold hands and feet, ah yes, obviously a Spleen deficiency". The Officials work together and depend on each other. Just as with the Elements, where one is sick all suffer, and where the symptom lies may not be the cause of the problem.

We need, therefore, to look more closely at these inter-relationships to begin to understand more deeply the complexity and beauty of their internal organization.

CHAPTER SIXTEEN

THE RELATIONSHIPS OF THE OFFICIALS

Looking at the Officials one at a time is at best like being introduced to twelve members of a family at a party. We might remember the names if we are lucky, and perhaps even put a face to them the next day, but we could hardly claim to know them even a little until we had seen the family at work and at play together. We need to apply the same simple wisdom and common sense to learning about the Officials. The preceding chapters have been a bare introduction, the names and faces. In this chapter I hope to begin to show something of their relationships and patterns as a whole, and to remind the reader that families never stay exactly the same; they are dynamic, changing, exciting, and fractious. The Officials are no different.

THE SHENG, KE AND WEI CYCLES

The Officials are manifestations of the Elements as they are made real and alive in us. Every relationship between the Elements described in Chapter Seven, therefore, is going to be manifested in a similar way by the Officials.

THE SHENG CYCLE

The cycle of nourishment and generation connecting the Elements is both simple and fundamental; Wood generates and feeds Fire, Fire generates and feeds Earth, and so on. When we represent this in diagrams, however, the circle which we draw to link the Elements is always shown bisecting each circle representing an Element to produce an inner and an outer half. When the Officials are placed within each Element the predominantly yin Official is shown as the 'inner half' and the predominantly yang Official as the 'outer half'. In the Element Wood, for example, the Liver is shown as the 'inner' Official, the Gall Bladder as the 'outer' Official. In the Water Element, the Kidney is 'inner' and the Bladder 'outer'.

Classical Five-Element Acupuncture

The distinction of predominantly yin and predominantly yang Officials is an interesting concept. The Chinese recognized a difference between the solid organs and the hollow organs, what they called the **zang** and the **fu**. The zang, the predominantly solid yin organs, are deeper within the body and are principally concerned with the production, transformation and regulation of the Qi energy which the body uses. The fu, the predominantly yang hollow organs, are considered to be more concerned with the storage and excretion of the raw materials and waste of the body's processes. Hence they are called the 'hollow' organs, because at various times they are without any contents, whereas the same could never be said of the predominantly yin organs.

By virtue of this distinction the relationship between the Elements embodied in the Officials is one which links an inner cycle of predominantly yin Officials and an outer cycle of predominantly yang Officials. Although in overall terms the Stomach and Spleen as the Officials of the Earth Element generate and nourish the Large Intestine and Lung Officials of the Metal Element, it is the Stomach which generates and feeds the Large Intestine, and the Spleen which does the same for the Lungs.

This is a critical difference to understand when we use our knowledge in diagnosis and treatment. The Law of Mother/Child, for example, applies just as much to the Officials as it does to the whole Element. If the Lung Official is the main source of imbalance, it may well be the Spleen as the Mother of the Lung or the Kidney as the Child of the Lung which shows the main distress. The same applies to the predominantly yang Officials. A Large Intestine imbalance may cause the Stomach or the Bladder to be distressed because of the Mother/Child relationship, and the symptoms of that imbalance may manifest in either of these Officials as well as in the Colon itself.

Understanding this distinction is important for our power both to diagnose sickness and imbalance and to help Nature to restore the balance. When symptoms appear in the Lung Official, like asthma or shortness of breath or in the skin which it controls and affects, we may need to look to the Spleen and the Kidney as much as to the Lung itself, for by the same process which we looked at earlier the place where distress and disease manifests is not necessarily its cause. The Law of Mother/Child describing the relationship between Officials in this way can lead us elsewhere on the Sheng Cycle to the main source of imbalance.

The Relationships of the Elements

Each of the elements has a mother and each official has a specific official within the preceeding element that is its mother official. This is of even greater importance as a principle to guide our treatments. If we wanted to re-establish harmony between a major imbalance in the Lung Official of the Metal Element and its mother Element Earth, the relationship of the Lung to the Earth Element is principally with the Spleen. The mother of the Colon is the Stomach.

There is a tendency in some fields of Oriental medicine to play down the importance of the predominantly yang Officials. Terms used to describe them such as 'hollow' and 'outer' are sometimes taken to indicate that they occupy a place away from the center of the stage. This is not the case, and this must be emphasized again and again. No family has any member who is not important. Father may be the breadwinner and mother the keeper of the home but if the youngest baby is sick everyone worries. In a close family every single person is loved, cherished and important, and if they become ill, then the whole balance of the family is affected. This is precisely the case with the Officials, whether they are predominantly yin or predominantly yang Officials.

THE KE CYCLE

One reason, perhaps, for the fact the predominantly yin Officials are sometimes accorded more respect than the predominantly yang Officials is because of the Ke Cycle relationship. This cycle of control between the Elements, described in Chapter Seven, is the means by which they hold each other in check as their physical manifestations do in Nature. Earth, for example, contains and checks Water; Water contains and checks Fire, and so on.

On first sight it might be assumed that just as with the Sheng Cycle the two Officials of the Element should each affect their counterparts in the 'controlled' Element, that Liver should control the Spleen and the Gall Bladder control the Stomach. In practice, however, this is not the case. Only the predominantly yin Official of the pair exercises control over the predominantly yin Official of the Element across the Ke Cycle. Thus the Liver is said to control the Spleen, the Heart and Heart Protector control the Lungs, the Spleen controls the Kidney, the Lungs control the Liver, and the Kidney controls the Heart and Heart Protector.

This is an important relationship to bear in mind when looking at the balance

Classical Five-Element Acupuncture

of the Officials within the person. Some branches of Chinese medicine place very great emphasis on these relationships and use them as primary diagnostic categories. Their derivation lies in the ancient classics and many of the passages cited as an authority use very strong and poetic imagery to describe what is happening: "Liver invading the Spleen", "Metal insulting Fire", and "Kidney and Heart not Harmonized", are just some of the groups of syndromes whose physical signs and symptoms are described in both ancient and modern texts.

This kind of insight and understanding is very rich and evocative, but can also sometimes become a little too much like a formula and lead us to use our heads instead of our senses to make our diagnosis. If the Liver is too strong and dominant not only will it exert too much control over the Spleen, but it will probably put a great deal of strain on its child, the Heart and Heart Protector, and an equal strain on the Official which in turn feeds it, the Kidney. If it is too strong it will also be a major burden for the Lungs whose task it is to keep the Liver in check. If one Official is badly out of balance, therefore, it will inevitably affect all of the Officials.

In the midst of this overall chaos it is rarely going to be possible to see one simple condition, and even when we do we have to be very careful not to jump to conclusions. If the Heart Protector is sick, the Liver Official as its mother on the Sheng Cycle may well be in great distress and become hyperactive. This, in turn, may cause the Liver Official to bear down on the Spleen Official which is itself already suffering because its mother, the Heart Protector, is weak. The symptoms may show 'Liver invading Spleen' but the cause may very well lie elsewhere, in this case in the Heart Protector.

The Ke Cycle relationship, then, is another aspect of the complex processes affecting the whole of the body, mind and spirit, important as a part of the overall picture but only one pattern among many in the natural balance within body, mind and spirit.

THE WEI CYCLE

The Wei cycle of energy is one which has not yet been mentioned in this Volume. It is a flow of energy on a relatively superficial level within the body, mind and spirit which follows the Officials in their numerical order - Heart I, Small Intestine II, Bladder III, Kidney IV, and so on. The Wei Level of energy is principally a protective layer at the superficial level concerned with our defense against harmful factors in the environment and the potential onset of disease. As such the energy which it carries has a great deal of work to do in our modern polluted world in addition to warding off the external causes of disease which have always existed and will always exist: Heat, Fire, Cold, Damp, Dryness, Humidity and Wind.

The major problems which afflict this cycle are blockages where pollution and disease either weaken an Official or physically impair the flow at this level in such a way that the energy can no longer flow freely. This was described in some detail as an exit/entry or entry/exit block in the previous Volume, and a short description of this condition can be found in the Glossary.

Although the Wei Cycle is relatively superficial it is by no means something which we should take lightly. It is better to regard 'superficial' as meaning 'nearer the surface', rather than 'less important'. The meridian which becomes blocked up, deprived of its flow either by a blockage between it and the preceding meridian or choked up and bursting because of a blockage within it or in the following meridian, is the selfsame meridian which we have described as the residence of the Official within the body, mind and spirit. If the Official's residence is polluted or under serious strain, whatever the level, it cannot function as Nature intended. However superficial the blockage it can potentially disrupt the whole of the flow. Any Official which is deprived of energy at this level may react in a way similar to being deprived of the nourishment which it takes from its predecessor on the Sheng Cycle. The upset and distress can be just as severe. Indeed, one branch of Japanese acupuncture places such enormous importance on the flow in the meridians at this level that its major diagnostic and treatment procedures center on this aspect alone.

THE OFFICIALS WORKING TOGETHER

The relationships which I have described are important in any understanding of the patterns of disease in every unique individual. They all separate and divide the whole in order to narrow our focus down. From them we can find some comfort in the thought that with all the difficulties there is at least something fixed and tangible which we can grasp. For practitioners coming to terms with this wonderful and complex system of medicine this is a source of tremendous relief.

Classical Five-Element Acupuncture

I have no doubt that many readers were beginning to think about the Elements in the same way until they were introduced to the concept of the 'Element within', and then the 'Element within the Element within'. The idea that each Element draws on the powers of the other Elements in order to fulfill its own part of the cycle of energy, and that each of these powers depends in turn on the same powers within itself reflects the true richness and complexity of Nature. Not surprisingly the same thing applies to the Officials as a manifestation of the Elements. Beneath the apparent simplicity of their own functions lies a web of interdependent relationships where each draws on the powers of all the others to be able to perform its own tasks. Thus all the parts are joined together to make one entity.

The great importance and value of the concept of the Officials lies in two simple statements: no Official can do the job of any other, and every single Official depends on the functions of the others in order to carry out its own tasks. This takes us beyond knowing in which order the Officials are arranged, or which Official is the mother, child, or controller of any other. Each team member depends on all of the others all of the time, not just to do the work which each in its own way does for the whole body, mind and spirit, but for the very ability to do its own work.

This is far easier to understand by examples, and some have already appeared in previous chapters. The Liver Official, for example, is the Planner, the Official who takes responsibility for providing all of the other Officials with the blueprints towards which they are working. These plans are what holds the internal assembly line together, and what ensures that each separate and apparently unconnected operation combines to create the final product, the goal and target of all the joint efforts. Not only do the Officials need plans to make sense of what they do together, but they also need plans for their own individual tasks. If the Planner's role was isolated and separate from the others they might be able to carry on in its absence and struggle on in body, mind and spirit. Without a Planner, however, they cannot even accomplish their own tasks.

The Stomach needs to have a plan in order to be able to go about rotting and ripening in the right way. If we can liken the Stomach to a concrete mixer there has to be someone who plans what the perfect blend should be. The Spleen needs to have a plan to make sure that food gets distributed to all the places that need it. The Colon needs a plan to extract water and pass waste on for excretion. The Lung Official needs a plan to co-ordinate the act of breathing and to retain

The Relationships of the Elements

a correct intake and balance of gasses within the body and pure Qi energy within body, mind and spirit. We can go right through all of the Officials using this sort of illustration, looking at the way in which the work of every single Official is set out according to a blueprint which lays down its best and most efficient way of working. This plan not only sets out what to do in perfect circumstances but has all of the contingency plans built into it for the kinds of variations which we find in our lives.

Many people reading this will be familiar with the idea of flowcharts which show a whole series of pathways to take account of a large number of variable factors. When the Liver Official is in good health all of the Officials can adapt themselves to whatever changes and variations they come across by virtue of the overall plan. When the Liver Official is sick, however, not only does the body, mind and spirit as a whole lose its sense of direction and purpose, but each one of the other Officials as a part of the whole becomes lost without a healthy plan. The Stomach Official may rot and ripen food in a way which is useless to the body. The blend is badly organized, the release of digestive juices is erratic and unco-ordinated, and in the worst possible case the direction in which the food has to travel is affected. When someone vomits their food it may be because the Stomach Official without a proper plan has no idea what to do with the food and merely expels it out of desperation.

The Spleen Official which I likened earlier to a transport manager needs an efficient plan. We have only to look at the massive haulage fleets in action day after day to realize just how critical is the need for a strategy which ensures that everything arrives in the right place at the right time. There is no room for late arrivals, double orders, or trips too long to be completed in the time allotted. The proper distribution of food has to have the precision and co-ordination of a military operation. When the 'general who excels in his military planning' goes astray, the whole system begins to collapse.

There are dozens of examples like this in each Official's tasks of what happens when a blueprint is missing, of strategy and organization falling apart with disastrous consequences. What emerges very clearly is that the kinds of problems which arise in the body, mind and spirit are no different from those which we have already described as problems within each individual Official. The discomfort which derives from the retention of food, the weakness arising from a poor distribution of Qi, the asthma coming from a badly organized Lung Official, the diarrhea which happens when the Colon forgets to plan the

16.7

Classical Five-Element Acupuncture

removal of vital water from the faeces, the oedema when the Bladder cannot plan its storage function properly: all of these physical symptoms and more can come either from an imbalance within the Officials or from a failure of the Liver to provide suitable plans for all the Officials.

It should be clear, therefore, that there is no single and simple way that we can look at a symptom and conclude that this Official or that Official is the cause of the overall imbalance. What we must look at in each failure of function is the individual character of that failure, the kind of problems that are emerging. In order to do this we as practitioners have to work to know the Officials and to understand the individual character of each. It is always the colour, sound, odor and emotion that expresses the exact cause of the overall imbalance.

If the Liver Official is seriously out of balance, there should be signs of the failure to co-ordinate and plan in every Official, not just in one or two. The character of each Official will be stamped as clear as day across all of the signs and symptoms which appear in body, mind and spirit. To offer another example, the Spleen is responsible, as we have seen, for distributing energy to all parts of the body, mind and spirit. If it cannot do its job properly then all of the Officials are going to be undernourished or overwhelmed, perhaps some more than others, depending on their relationships. In the end all of them become imbalanced as a result of the only source of nourishment being so out of balance.

The 'obviousness' of a symptom, therefore, is anything but obvious when looked at it in this way. When the Large Intestine cannot process waste there may be constipation, but we then have to look at all the functions which go towards making its job possible. Without a plan it cannot work out what to do. Without the power to decide there is no motivation to do the job. Without food there is no strength to do the job, and then we have to know whether it is because there is no food at all or because none is reaching the Official. Without heat from the Three Heater the Large Intestine may be rigid, cold and immobile. Perhaps the circulation granted by the Heart Protector is poor, and there is no pathway for nourishment and heat to arrive. It may be that the Lungs are not taking in anything and there is no incentive to throw out rubbish. The Small Intestine may be leaving so much impurity in the system that it has become poisoned and weak. The Supreme Controller may be sick and no longer in command. The Kidney and Bladder Officials may be so desperate for secretions that they have grabbed the very last bit from the Large Intestine and left nothing to allow the easy passage of the remaining waste.

It may seem a little excessive to list one by one the effects of the Officials in this way, but it is, however, important to look at all of the possibilities like this to show the elusiveness of depending on a symptom for a diagnosis. Students of Classical Five-Element Acupuncture are, in fact, set an exercise with the twelve Officials. They take a physical symptom and explain how an imbalance in any one official may be the cause of the problem. This is a reminder of the functions of each official and how each function can affect everything that we do.

In the examples above I have stayed with physical problems for the sake of simplicity. Any mental, emotional, or spiritual problem derives from an imbalance in any one of the Officials. If the Separator cannot sort pure from impure, valuable from trivial, the mental poison passes around the whole system. This impure information becomes the basis for the plans and decisions of the Wood Officials, the setting of boundaries, regulation and communication of the Fire Officials, the mental flow and memory of the Earth Officials, the casting away of old ideas and inspiration of the Metal Officials, and the resourcefulness and determination of the Water Officials. When the other officials are fed with poisoned and useless information, with the impurity and irrelevance which comes from a sick Separator, there is little chance that the efforts of these other Officials will be carried out with the purity and clarity on which we depend.

This interdependence can be most challenging to unravel when we are confronted by problems of the spirit. Our language is inadequate to express problems of the spirit. There may be a temptation to find an easy solution to help us to understand. Adding this layer of uncertainty can be a very trying experience to many practitioners. Yet it has to be done in order to properly serve patients. When someone comes to us who says that they feel desperate and that their life has no future we cannot assume that their Wood Element, and their Liver Official in particular, are the cause of their spirit's pain. We have to ask ourselves whether the Liver Official is sick, or whether the person cannot see a future because one of the other Officials is the cause of the overall disturbances. The lack of vision regarding a future is merely a symptom. The colour, sound, odor and emotion will express the actual cause of distress.

If, for example, the Separator is casting aside the pure and leaving the impure how could we expect the Liver Official, looking to the future, to find any hope? If there is no protection and warmth from the Heart Protector and Three Heater, and no love from the Heart, why should a lonely and abandoned Liver Official feel hopeful for growth and future prosperity? If the Stomach and Spleen Officials are not making the connection with the Mother Earth which grounds and nourishes the spirit, where is the seed of hope to be planted? A rootless and off-balance Official cannot settle enough to fix long term objectives. When the Lung and Colon Officials cannot provide the connection with the Heavenly Father there is no guidance and no quality, and the void which this leaves can sap the spirit of the Liver Official as if the sickness were its own. And what of the reserves and will which come from the Kidney and Bladder? When these are weak and the Liver Official cannot draw on their resolve to see things through there is no hope, let alone the hope which the Planner, the Liver Official, can bring to all of the Officials.

Some may object that characterizations like this are carrying things a little too far. In answer to that all I can say is that there is nothing here which I have not seen in patients over the last fifty-one years and nothing which cannot be seen by anyone reading this book, who is prepared to use their senses and **observe** before rushing into intellectual conclusions about this or that imbalance. The Officials as a concept are a way of describing every aspect of us, and reminding us that we are One, not an aggregation of parts. If one part is sick then all parts must be affected, each one in a unique way because of the relationships which they all have with one another. Characterizations like these remind us of the complexity of these interactions.

In practice, of course, these levels of apparent complexity and ambiguity are not complicated at all. The patterns which emerge from disturbances in the Elements and the Officials are very simple once a diagnosis is made. The colour, sound odor and emotional balance are obvious and as clear as day once a practitioner is willing to focus all attention on this feedback. It is the classical way to encourage practitioners to rely on their senses rather than their heads. Relying on intellectual formulas is a form of laziness at the expense of seeing, hearing, smelling and feeling. These senses have to be regained by the practitioner. We are all born with these abilities and, unfortunately, the ways of the modern western world have been to lead us into our heads and to abandon our senses. Common sense does, however, play a great part in classical medicine of any variety, and classical acupuncture is no different. There are natural patterns of movement in the body which we have to take into account

The Relationships of the Elements

whenever we look at the Officials during diagnosis.

Imbalances in the Stomach Official are a good illustration of this. Most of us know the main pathway of food through the body and the main stages by which it is physically absorbed. If the Stomach cannot perform its function properly the result will be improperly digested food passing down into the gut. We need not go to the lengths of considering the effects of this on a functional level to realize that the first consequence will be half-prepared food in the Small Intestine. What is the Small Intestine to do? Its program says, "Prepare for nourishing broth", and what it gets instead is a lumpy and undigested mess. Small wonder it passes the mess on without further effort because it cannot even recognise what it is. The resulting mess then finds its way into the bowel where the Colon Official doesn't really know where to start. If it is not given what it expects to find it cannot really do its job either, and is as likely as not to pass it on untouched. The undigested food then carries on through until it is passed as a particularly unpleasant form of loose stool. The actual cause of this process can only be ascertained through a diagnosis of the imbalanced color, sound, odor and emotion.

There are several pathways in Western medicine and in Chinese physiology for the production of blood, the circulation of body fluids, the excretion of waste, and the regulation of body temperature and metabolism. If one of the Officials in a pathway falls sick then it will be true that all the Officials will suffer to a greater or lesser extent but the more closely related in terms of function may show the signs a little more quickly or obviously.

This is an important aspect to bear in mind because we shall not always see the Officials as a whole in a state of decline through the weakness of one or two Officials. Disease is a process, a gradual loss of the balance of energy in body, mind and spirit. Eventually all of the Officials are going to be screaming out for food, or water, or purity, or warmth, but to begin with the ones to show the first signs of distress may be those which are most closely dependent in function.

A special case of this which has already been mentioned several times is the relationship between the pair of Officials within an Element. This is, if anywhere, the place that the signs of weakness and illness will appear, since it really is as an imbalance in the whole Element which arises with the imbalance of one official within.

The point of running through all these possibilities is to remind readers again that for us, as practitioners of this wonderful system of medicine, the main aim should be not to know more, but to know better. There is no way at all that we can go through the permutations of Officials acting on Officials, Elements acting on Elements, and produce a template of symptoms which can be dropped over a patient like a grid and used to check the match. It is only by developing the use of our senses that we can begin to apply what we learn, and even then our main aim has to be to observe, to see, hear and feel, before we rush in with the book learning and the mind-work.

Each patient that comes to us, each person that we meet in our daily lives, is a unique combination of Elements and a unique combination of Officials. We would never dream, and should never dare, to walk in on a group of people we are meeting for the first time and make snap judgments. Our first impressions are quite often wrong. The tremendous excitement in this system of medicine comes, when we see the way that the effects of imbalances echo throughout the whole of the body, mind and spirit, and then treatment also echoes throughout the wholeness of the person, the body, mind, spirit as One.

GLOSSARY

AGGRESSIVE ENERGY (AE). This is a condition in which the flow of Qi energy in the body, mind and spirit becomes polluted. This tainted energy destroys the creative work of the elements and officials. It begins with contamination to one of the predominantly Yin officials, such as severe shock or repeated battering to an official and spreads through the system across the Ke Cycle.

AKABANI TEST. This is a short test used in the physical examination to determine the relative levels of energy in the two channels of each bilateral meridian. Any major discrepancy between the amounts of energy in the two channels is referred to as an Akabani imbalance and may be corrected by simple treatments early in the course of treatment.

APPROPRIATE. This is a key word for this system of medicine and for the wider Chinese philosophy of Daoism with which it shares many concepts. All of the pictures of harmony and balance within the tradition contain patterns of elements and phases which should follow and complement each other as a part of the ceaseless flow of Nature. The elements also create and contribute all of the faculties and attributes which human beings have. If the flow of energy is good and the elements are in balance one will be able to meet all the situations with an appropriate response. When there is danger one will be afraid. When there is loss one will grieve. When the flow is poor and the elements are out of balance, one cannot make appropriate responses and may act inappropriately by laughing off loss, being angry when offered warmth and so on.

ASSOCIATED EFFECT POINTS (AEP'S). These are points on the Bladder meridian on the back which are directly linked to the organs and officials. Any of the points can be used to bring direct and powerful assistance to an official. The Associated Effect Points of the predominantly Yin officials are also used in the test for Aggressive Energy.

BODY, MIND AND SPIRIT. These three words are used together nearly all of the time in classical Five-Element acupuncture when we wish to discuss the patient's symptoms, the treatment which we give and the changes which we see. They remind us that there is no such thing as 'a body' or 'a mind' or 'a spirit' separate from the whole. There is one flow of energy which moves through all three levels. Using these words together reminds us that the flow can be interrupted

Classical Five-Element Acupuncture

anywhere and have effects across the whole person. Hence a problem of the mind or spirit can just as easily emerge as a physical problem, or a physical problem may be caused by a problem of the mind or spirit.

CAUSATIVE FACTOR (CF). This is one of the central natural laws of Five-Element acupuncture. The Causative Factor is the name given to the one Element whose weakness, whether congenital or caused early in childhood, is the key to all the patterns of disharmony within the body, mind and spirit. Diagnosing the Causative Factor is the aim of the Classical Five-Element Diagnosis and is revealed by the Color, Sound, Odor and Emotion. Treatment is geared to restoring balance within the Causative Factor and therefore encouraging the whole system to return to balance.

CAUSES OF DISEASE. The ancient Chinese had relatively few concepts of disease as a result of bacterial or viral infection. If disease arose it was assumed to be either the result of extremes of climate or prolonged exposure to one climate, the so-called 'external causes' or extremes of emotion and the prolonged effects of a single emotion, the so-called 'internal causes'. In practice, matters were never quite that simple and the ability of the body to resist an external factor would depend also on the internal constitutional strength. Although the internal causes are often more relevant to modern clinical practice, the external causes do still feature in many case histories.

CHINESE CLOCK. The Chinese Clock is the name for the cycle of energy expressed in the Law of Midday/Midnight (q.v.).

COLOR. This specifically refers to the color which appears on the face when one of the elements is out of balance. It is seen predominantly on the temples and also, but not as reliably, around the mouth, under the eyes and on the cheeks.

CONCEPTION VESSEL. This pathway runs mainly along the anterior mid-line of the trunk. This, and the Governor Vessel, are rather like seas in comparison to the rivers of the twelve meridians associated with the officials. Points on these two meridians can have a profound and powerful effect on the patient.

CURE, LAW OF. This is one of the Laws of the Five-Elements. It is most simply expressed by saying that as the body, mind and spirit return to balance, symptoms tend to re-appear in reverse chronological order, to disappear from above to below, and to leave the body from within to without. This arises from the idea that the disease, which travels deeper as imbalance increases, reverses its path as Nature effects a cure. Patients commonly report a short recurrence of earlier symptoms,

Glossary

sometimes even more severe than the first time, but carrying with them a sense of 'feeling better inside.'

DAO. The Chinese word 'Dao' literally means 'way' or 'pathway' and is virtually untranslatable in its philosophical context. Its general meaning is that of the pathway which all living things must follow in order to find their individual fulfillment. It cannot be precisely defined. In fact, the classical Chinese text of Daoism, the Dao De Jing, opens with the line, 'The Dao that can be told is not the eternal Dao.'

DRAGONS. This is an alternative name given to the treatment used to release a possession (q.v.) in a patient. The Chinese pictured the person as a being taken over by internal or external demons and the two sets of seven points used to deal with this imbalance were seen as internal or external dragons which were released to expel the demons.

ELEMENT. The term element, in the context of 'the Five-Elements', describes a stage in the ceaseless flow of energy in Nature and in the person. The Chinese word is sometimes translated as 'phases' to avoid any suggestion that the elements are like the ultimate building blocks of all matter, a concept that arises much later in Greek and Roman philosophy. This does not do justice to the idea, however, that an element is vital and alive at all times, not just in its 'own time'. The elements do indeed describe the way in which the different facets of the whole come to the fore in their natural rhythms, both annual and daily. The Fire element, for example, represents the phase or the cycle where things and people are in their summer stage of warmth, fullness and maturity. By association this is extended to include many of the mental, emotional and spiritual qualities of a similar type. In contrast, the Water element represents the winter stage where growth has decreased and activity is under the ground and characterized by determination, resolve, and a will to survive until the spring. The elements together represent a whole cycle of birth, growth, decay and death, and rebirth; the faculties and attributes which they control and create are with us all of the time and allow us to meet the changing circumstances of our lives appropriately.

EMOTION. This is used to denote one of the five emotions (Joy, Sympathy, Grief, Fear, Anger) associated directly with the five elements . Its most common use as a term is in the phrase 'Color, Sound, Odor, Emotion' where emotion is taken to mean the emotion which manifests most inappropriately in the person as a result of the elemental imbalances and forms a key part of the diagnostic conclusion. It is also possible to find a 'lack of' any of these emotions.

Classical Five-Element Acupuncture

GOLDEN KEY. There are occasions in a diagnosis where patients tell us something, or occasionally do something, in a way which reinforces the Causative Factor. This can be in the words themselves, especially those using the correspondences of the elements (a famous film director is reputed to have intoned in a deep groaning voice that, 'What I fear most is the deep blue sea'), or more often in turns of phrase which show us the person without the mask at all.

GOVERNOR VESSEL. This vessel runs along the posterior midline of the trunk and over the top to the head to end on the upper jaw. Points on this meridian can have a profound effect on the person (q.v. Conception Vessel).

HUSBAND/WIFE, LAW OF. This is one of the Laws of the Five Elements. This law states that when the sum total of energy in the elements represented in the pulses of the right hand side are qualitatively stronger than the sum of energy in the left hand pulses the patient is said to have a Husband/Wife imbalance. This is a serious disturbance in the energy which must be treated urgently prior to ordinary treatment.

KE CYCLE. This is one of two major relationships between the elements. Whereas the Sheng Cycle (q.v.) is a cycle of nourishment, the Ke Cycle is one of control. The element Fire is said to control Metal, Earth controls Water, Metal controls Wood, Water controls Fire and Wood controls Earth. Some Qi energy flows naturally along this cycle. Also, when Aggressive Energy spreads, it travels across the Ke cycle.

'LEGS OF A STOOL'. This is an expression stating the importance of having adequate evidence for a conclusion in a diagnosis. The four 'legs of the stool' are Color, Sound, Odor and Emotion and the expression states that one or two legs are insufficient for a conclusion and that three are only just adequate.

MIDDAY/MIDNIGHT, LAW OF. This is one of the Laws of the Five Elements known as the Chinese Clock. It states that in a twenty-four hour period each official has a two hour period of maximum energy, which is known as the 'horary time'. Treatment of the corresponding official at this time is more effective than at other times during the day. This law can also be used to advise patients on how they can most efficiently organize their days to help their natural functions, e.g. that stomach is at its peak first thing in the morning (7:00 - 9:00 am local time) and food eaten then is digested better than food eaten at any other time.

MOTHER/CHILD. This is sometimes referred to as the Law of Mother/Child and is one of the Laws of the Five Elements. The relationship of the elements on the

Glossary

Sheng Cycle is one of nourishment and care, with each one being described as the mother of the following element and as the child of the preceding element. The wisdom of this description is to direct our attention to the elements on the cycle when we see symptoms coming from a particular element. When the child is sick, the mother can be even more distressed. Treating the child will only have a short term effect because it is not addressing the real problem. The importance of the picture is to remind us of all the relationships between the officials and elements before we jump to any conclusions based upon distress signals.

NEI JING. The Nei Jing, The Yellow Emperor's Classic of Internal Medicine, is one of the earliest and most important Chinese medical texts. The form is a series of dialogues between the Yellow Emperor and his minister and teacher Qi Po which cover both the theoretical basis of classical Chinese medicine (mainly in the first half, the Su Wen) and also the practical details of acupuncture and moxibustion (in the second half, the Ling Shu). Much of what follows in all traditions of classical Chinese medicine has arisen from detailed exposition and elaboration of themes in this book.

ODOR. This is generally used in the sense of the predominant odor which is used as the basis for the diagnosis of the Causative Factor. The five odors (Scorched, Fragrant, Rotten, Putrid and Rancid) are a sign of major elemental imbalance.

OFFICIAL. The concept of an official comes from the Nei Jing. It describes a group of faculties, physical, mental and spiritual, which are seen as under the control of the official and as its domain. The picture used for the officials is that of a group of ministers of the court and great importance is attached not only to what they provide for the whole person, but also how they are vital to the functioning of each other. The concept of the official embraces both the meridian associated with it and also an organ, and yet not reducible to either.

POSSESSION. This is a condition in which there is a deep disturbance in the energy within a person which acts as an invading force. The effects of this can range from total insanity, where the person is literally beyond reach, to something barely noticeable which nonetheless is a barrier to successful treatment by any therapy.

QI, QI ENERGY. Qi Energy is the basic force of energy which pervades all living things. However, the Chinese concept is much broader than the modern Western notion in popular use and the idea of living things would extend to cover everything on the face of the planet. The Chinese would see the heaviest and thickest materials as the most dense manifestation of Qi energy and spirit as its least substantial with everything else in between. The Chinese were more concerned with understanding

Classical Five-Element Acupuncture

what the various actions of the Qi energy were within the body, mind and spirit than with trying to analyze philosophically what it was.

SEDATION. Sedation is a specific treatment procedure which encourages an excess of energy to be dispersed in a variety of different ways, depending on the overall situation.

SHENG CYCLE. The Sheng Cycle is the cycle of nourishment where the natural flow of the elements is seen as one in which each element feeds and nourishes the following one in the cycle. The cycle runs Fire, Earth, Metal, Water and Wood. The direction of the flow is important for determining how and where to move energy during treatment and for understanding how a failure of one element may produce effects elsewhere on the cycle because of the lack of nourishment.

SOUND. This is most often used in the book to describe the sound of voice which becomes apparent when there is an elemental imbalance. The five sounds are Laughing, Singing, Weeping, Groaning and Shouting and the voice of a person develops one of these as its predominant sound when the corresponding element becomes the Causative Factor.

THREE JIAO. The trunk of the body is divided in classical Chinese medicine into three areas: The upper chest from the level of the nipples upwards, the area from the nipples to the navel and the area below the navel. These were called the Three Jiao. The three 'burning spaces'. They should be roughly similar in temperature and are tested for this in the TD. If there is a marked disparity in their relative temperatures it can point to serious imbalance in the organs within the Jiao or imbalance in the Three Heater official which is responsible for maintaining an even and settled temperature within the body.

TONIFICATION. This describes the needle action used to stimulate energy, the principal feature of which is that the needle is only inserted for a very short time and stimulated to achieve the necessary effect.

WEI CYCLE, WEI LEVEL. The Wei Cycle describes a flow of energy along the meridians which follows the numerical order of the officials (I-Heart, II-Small Intestine, etc.). This is at a relatively superficial level within the body and serves as a protective layer of energy for the body. However, any blockages here, either along or between meridians, can effect the flow at the level of the Sheng Cycle and are treated seriously.

Glossary

YIN AND YANG. These two terms are fundamental to an understanding of the Chinese philosophical landscape within which classical acupuncture exists. The literal meanings of the terms are, 'The shady side of the mountain' and 'The sunny side of the mountain'. What they express is a central feature of Chinese culture and philosophy inasmuch as they reveal that the emphasis is on the relatedness of all things and the complementary unity of parts within the whole. To understand change and transformation is to look at the whole as much as at the individual parts. This is very different from the Western approach which has more of a tendency to look at discrete units and to seek individual causes without reference to the whole. The symbol of Yin and Yang is said to show the relationships between them, namely that each creates the other and that each transforms into the other.

Classical Five-Element Acupuncture

INDEX

Abdominal Distension 10.6-7,10.14,13.2.

Anger 2.3-4,2.6,7.8-9,7.12.

Angina 11.4,12.11.

Ankle 15.3.

Arthritis 10.15,12.4,15.10-11

Associations 1.1,7.12.

Autumn 1.7,1.9,1.11-12,5.1,5.4,6.5,7.4,7.6,8.8-9,14.4.

Balance 1.1,1.4.

Bladder 6.4,9.3,11.8,15.3,15.9

Bladder Official 6.3,8.11,10.2,15.1-9,16.1-2,16.8-10.

Blood 3.3,11.3-4,11.6,11.8,12.5,12.8,13.9

Blue Green Spirit 12.11

Body, Mind and Spirit 1.5,1.8,4.1,4.3-4,4.6,5.2,5.4,6.1,6.3,6.6,6.8,7.12, 8.1,8.5,9.1-9,10.1-3,10.15-16,11.1,11.4,11.6,11.9,12.2,12.6-7,12.9, 13.1,13.5,13.7-8,14.1,15.5-6,15.12,16.4-8,16.12.

Bones 8.11,15.3,15.10

Cardiac Arrest 12.10.

Cardiac Arrhythmia 12.9.

Causative Factor 2.5,7.2,7.8,7.11,9.9.

Chinese Clock 10.10.

Circulation 11.5,16.9.

Circulation/Sex 11.1,11.6.

Classical Five-Element Acupuncture

Climate 8.3-8,8.10.
Colon 9.5-6,14.1,14.5.
Colon Official 9.4-8,12.2,14.1-6,14.12,15.9,16.2-3,16.6-11.
Color 9.9.
Color/Sound/Odor/Emotion 1.12-13,11.12,16.10-11.
Complexion 3.4.
Constipated 9.5-6,14.2,14.4,15.10.
Correspondences of the Elements 1.1,2.4,7.12,8.1-3.

Dao 1.1,3.8,7.1,9.2,10.14,13.10,14.4,15.7
Decision Making 10.10-1,12.4.
Diagnose/Diagnosis 13.6.
Diarrhea 9.5-7,10.15,14.2.
Direction 8.3,8.5-10.
Disease 1.13.
Dizziness 10.7
Drugs 10.5,10.7,11.2,15.11.

Earth Element 1.4-10,4.1-9,5.2,5.8,7.1,7.4-5,7.7-8,7.11,8.1-2,8.7-8,13.1, 13.3-9,13.12,14.6,16.1-3,16.9.
Elements 2.5,4.9,7.3-4,9.2-3,9.9,10.1,10.9,13.8,15.13,16.1-3,16.6,16.11, 16.12.
Elements
    The Five Elements 1.1-2,1.4,1.6-7,1.9,1.12-13,2.1,2.6,2.8,6.8
        7.12,8.1-2,9.1,9.7-8,11.8.
    Earth 1.4-10,4.1-9,5.2,5.8,7.1,7.4-5,7.7-8,7.11,8.1-2,8.7-8,13.1,

Index

13.3-4,13.6,13.8-9,13.11,14.6,16.1-3,16.9.
Fire Element 1.5-6,3.1-9,6.3,5.8,6.8,7.3-5,7.7,11.7-9,11.12-13,
12.1,12.4-6,12.8,12.11,16.1,16.3-4,16.9.
Metal Element 1.9-10,5.1-4,7.5-7,8.1-2,8.8-10,9.4-5,9.7,14.1,14.3-7,
14.9-12,16.2-4,16.9.
Water Element 1.11-12,2.4,4.8,6.1-8,7.5-9,7.11-12,8.1-2,8.5,
8.10-11,9.7,15.1,15.4,15.7,15.9,16.1,16.3,16.9.
Wood Element 1.2-4,1.6,1.9,2.1-3,2.6-12,3.1,4.2,4.9,7.3-8,7.10,
8.1-6,9.7,10.1,10.4-7,10.16,12.11,16.1,16.9-10.
Element Within Element 7.2,7.8-11,16.6.
Emotion 1.12-13,2.4,3.4,4.5,7.11,8.2,9.9.
External Physical Manifestation 8.3,8.5,8.7-8,8.10.
Eye Disorders 2.11,5.8,8.4,10.5-6,10.14,12.8,13.4,15.3.

Faint 12.11.
Father 1.10,5.2-3,5.5,5.8-9,14.7,14.11,16.10.
Fear 2.5,6.2,6.5-6,7.8-9,7.12,15.4-5,15.11.
Feeling 3.6,9.6.
Fire Element 1.5-6,3.1-9,6.3,5.8,6.8,7.3-5,7.7,11.7-9,11.12-13,12.1,12.4-6,
12.8,12.11,16.1,16.3-4,16.9.
Fire Official 11.2,12.1,12.7,12.10.
Five Elements 1.6,1.12,2.1,2.6,6.8,7.12,8.1-2,9.1,9.7-8,11.8.
Frozen Shoulder 12.6,14.5.

Gall Bladder Official 10.1-2,10.10-15,11.7-8,12.1,12.10,16.1,16.3.
Gate of Hope 10.9.

Classical Five-Element Acupuncture

Gout 12.4
Governor Vessel 13.2,15.12.
Great Eliminator 14.5.
Grief 7.9,7.12,8.9,14.4

Harvest 1.5-9,4.2,4.5-8,6.2,7.4.
Headache 2.11,10.6,10.13-15,13.4,15.3.
Hearing 12.5,15.10.
Heart 11.1,11.4,11.7,12.11.
Heart Official 11.1-5,11.7-8,12.1,12.7-11,16.3-4,16.10.
Heart Protector Official 11.1-8,11.10,11.13,12.1,12.8,12.11,16.3-4,16.9-10.
High Blood Pressure 3.4.
Horary Time 10.10.

Imbalance 10.12.
Infertility 15.10.
Insanity 12.6.
Inspiration 5.1,14.4,14.7-8,14.10,16.9.
Itching 10.7,10.15.

Jiao, the three Jiao 11.6,11.8,11.10-13,14.1,14.9,15.12.
Joy 1.5,1.13,2.5,3.1-2,3.9,7.5,9.3,10.4,11.6,12.9,14.8.
Judgmental 10.10,10.12,10.14.

Ke Cycle 7.6-7,9.7,16.1,16.3-4.
Kidney 15.6.

Index

Kidney Official 6.3,8.11,9.3,9.7,10.2,11.8,15.1,15.6-13,16.1-4,16.9-10.

Large Intestines 5.1,5.7,11.8,16.2,16.8-9.
Late Summer 1.6-8,4.1,7.4,8.7.
Laughing 8.5.
Law- Mother/Child 7.4,16.2.
Letting Go 5.1,5.4-5,14.1,14.4,14.9.
Liver Official 9.3,9.7-9,10.1-12,10.14-15,11.7-8,12.1,12.10,15.5,15.11, 16.1,16.3-4,16.6-10.
Love 1.13,3.1-2,3.6-7,3.9,4.1,5.8,6.8,7.5,7.8-9,12.9.
Lower Intestines 9.3.
Lung Official 5.7,11.8,14.1,14.6-8,14.10-12,16.2-4,16.6-10.
Lungs 5.1,9.1,14.1,14.8-9.

Mental Instability 12.6.
Metal Element 1.9-10,5.1-4,7.5-7,8.1-2,8.8-10,9.4-5,9.7,14.1,14.3-4,14.6-7, 14.9-12,16.2-4,16.9.
Mother 1.7-8,1.10,4.1-2,4.6-7,5.2,7.4-5,13.6,13.11.
Mother/Child 7.4,16.2

Nails 8.4,10.5-6.
Nausea 10.15.
Neck 10.4,15.3.
Nei Jing 3.8,5.2,9.3,13.2,14.8.
Nose 8.9.

Classical Five-Element Acupuncture

Odor 1.12,7.11,8.2,8.6,9.9.
Officials 7.12,8.11,9.1-4,9.7-10,10.1,10.9,13.8,16.1-12.
    Bladder Official 6.3,8.11,10.2,15.1-9,16.1-2,16.8-10.
    Colon Official 9.4-8,12.2,14.1-6,14.12,15.9-10,16.2-3,16.7-11.
    Gall Bladder Official 10.1-2,10.10-15,11.7-8,12.1,12.10,16.1,16.3.
    Heart Official 11.1-5,11.7-8,12.1,12.7-11,16.3-4,16.10.
    Heart Protector Official 11.1-9,11.13,12.1,12.8,12.11,16.3-4,16.9-10.
    Kidney Official 6.3,8.11,9.3,9.7,10.2,11.8,15.1,15.6-14,16.1-4,
        16.9-10.
    Liver Official 9.3,9.7-9,10.1-12,10.14-15,11.7-8,12.1,12.10,
        15.6,15.11,16.1,16.3-4,16.6-8,16.10.
    Lung Official 5.7,11.8,14.1,14.6-8,14.10-12,16.2-4,16.7-10.
    Small Intestine Official 9.3,12.1-2,12.4,12.11,13.3,14.2,16.9,16.11.
    Spleen Official 9.2,11.8,12.10,13.1,13.7-11,15.6,15.13,16.2,
        16.4,16.7,16.10.
    Stomach Official 9.3,12.1,13.1-11,14.2,14.6,16.2-3,16.7,16.10-11.
    Three Heater Official 11.1,11.6-13,12.1,12.11,16.9-10.
Orifice 8.9

Palpitations 11.4,12.9.
Power 8.3,8.5,8.7-10.
Practitioners of Acupuncture 1.1.
Psychotherapy 11.12

Qi Energy 1.1-2,1.4-5,1.10,3.1,3.3,3.9,5.2,7.1,7.4,8.1,9.2,11.3,11.8,11.12-
    13,12.2,12.4-5,13.1,13.3-4,13.7-8,13.10,14.1,14.6,14.9-11,15.7, ...

Index

15.12,16.2,16.7.

Rashes 5.7,9.5,10.7.
Relationships 3.8,15.8.
Relationship of the Elements 7.1.
Reproductive Organs 15.8,15.12.
Reserves 1.11-13,3.3,4.2,6.6.
Rheumatism 10.15,12.4.

Sciatica 15.3.
Season 1.1-3,1.5-9,1.12.
Self-esteem 5.6.
Sense Organ 8.3,8.5,8.7-10.
Sheng Cycle 3.1,7.2-6,9.7,12.8,16.1-5.
Shoulder 10.14
Skin 5.7-8, 8.9,11.5,12.4,`4.5,14.8,15.2.
Small Intestines 11.1,11.8,12.4.
Small Intestine Official 9.3,12.1-2,12.4,12.11,13.3,14.2,16.9,16.11.
Sound 1.12-13,7.11,8.2,9.9,15.8.
Spirit 3.8-9,4.2,4.5,4.8,5.3-4,5.8,6.4,6.7,9.4,10.4,10.7-8,10.12,11.3,
    12.9,13.8,13.10,15.4,15.12,16.9-10.
Spirit of Earth Element 1.8.
Spirit of the Elements 1.1-3,1.12-13,9.7.
Spirit of Fire Element 1.5.
Spirit of the Officials 9.1,9.7,9.9.
Spirit of the Wood 1.3,2.9-10.

Classical Five-Element Acupuncture

Spleen 4.2.
Spleen Official 9.2,11.8,12.10,13.1,13.7-11,15.5,15.14,16.2-4,16.6,16.10.
Spring 1.2-7,1.9,1.11-12,2.2,2.5,2.11,7.3-4,7.10,10.2.
Stomach 4.2,9.4,11.8.
Stomach Official 9.3,12.1,13.1-12,14.2,14.6,16.2-3,16.6-7,16.10-11.
Stress 14.6.
Suicidal Behavior 15.5.
Summer 1.5-7,1.9,1.11,3.1,7.4,7.7.
Supreme Controller 11.1-3,12.1,12.4,14.3,16.9.
Su Wen 15.8-9.
Symptoms 1.13,3.4,7.5,7.7,9.10,10.6,10.10,10.13-15,11.4-5,11.7,11.10, 12.10,13.5,13.7,13.9,14.8-10,16.2,16.4,16.8,16.12.

Taste 13.11.
Tendons & Ligaments 2.7,10.6,10.15.
Three Burning Spaces 11.1.
Three Heater Official 11.1,11.6-13,12.1,12.11,16.9-10.
Three Jiao 11.6,11.8,11.10,11.12-13.
Tongue 3.5.
Traditional Diagnosis 2.4-5,2.11,3.8,7.2,7.7-8,10.8,12.7,14.1.
Transformation 1.1-2,2.1.

Urination 15.2-3,15.9,15.11.

Vertigo 10.7
Vision   2.9-10,9.8,10.4,14.7.

Index

Voice 3.5,8.6.

Vomiting 10.15

Water Element 1.11-12,2.4,4.8,6.1-8,7.5-9,7.11-12,8.1-2,8.5,8.10-11, 9.7,15.1,15.4,15.7,15.9,16.1,16.3,16.9.

Wei Cycle 16.1,16.4-5.

Whole Person 1.1.10.15,13.5.

Wind 8.4,8.6,16.5.

Winter 1.2-3,1.5,1.7,1.11-12,6.1,6.5,6.8,7.4,7.7,7.9,8.10.

Wood CF 7.7,8.2.

Wood Element 1.2-4,1.6,1.9,2.1-3,2.6-12,3.1,4.2,4.9,7.3-8,7.10,8.1-6, 9.7,10.1,10.4-7,10.16,12.11,16.1,16.9.

Yin and Yang 2.1,9.1,9.7,16.1-3.

Classical Five-Element Acupuncture

Index

Classical Five-Element Acupuncture